10

KISS HIM, NOT ME!

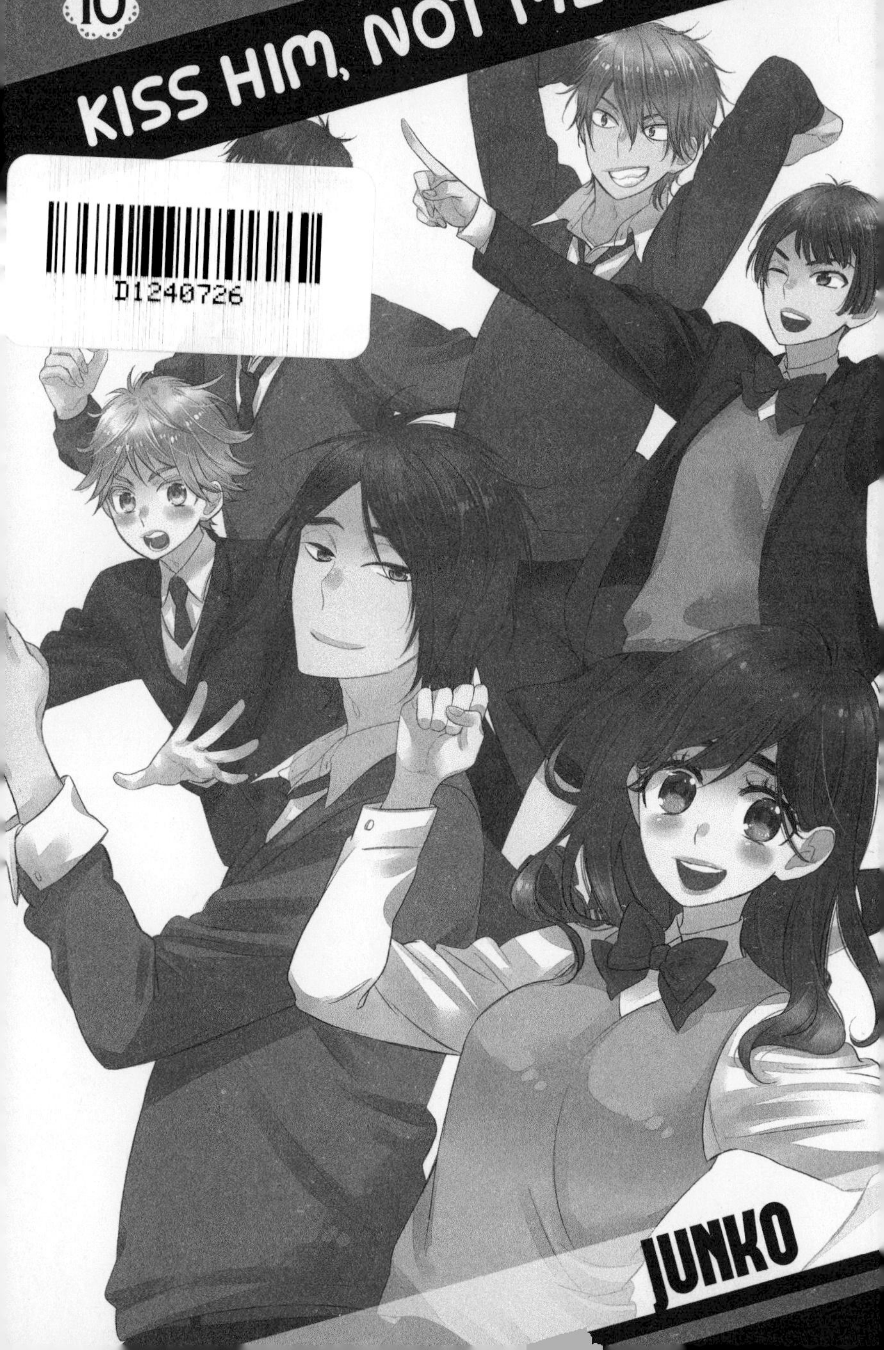

JUNKO

CONTENTS

STORY

ARCH 3RD IS **KAE'S** BIRTHDAY. THE GANG GOES ALL OUT FOR HER RTHDAY, EACH OF THEM GETTING SOMETHING READY FROM KAE'S WISH ST. BUT **IGARASHI**, WHO COULDN'T GET THE GIFT THAT **KAE** WANTED, ALLS HER OUT AND GIVES HER A NECKLACE AS HER **BIRTHDAY PRESENT!** JUST AS THINGS ARE ABOUT TO HEAT UP (?), **IGARASHI** BUMPS INTO HIS EX-GIRLFRIEND, **KOTOHA!** THE NEXT DAY, **KOTOHA** FINDS OUT THAT **IGARASHI** AND THE OTHERS HAVE CONFESSED THEIR FEELINGS TO **KAE**, AND ARE WAITING FOR HER TO RESPOND BACK. HEARING THAT, **KOTOHA** TELLS **KAE** NOT TO "LEAVE THEM HANGING FOR AN ANSWER." FEELING WORRIED, **KAE** DECLARES THAT THE PERSON WHO DEFEATS HER IN A GAME WILL BE THE ONE TO GO OUT WITH HER! **MUTSUMI** EMERGES AS THE **WINNER**, BUT HE KINDLY TELLS KAE THAT HE WILL WAIT FOR HER UNTIL SHE FEELS READY TO MAKE A DECISION, AND THE GAME IS **RESET!** EVERYONE IS RELIEVED, BUT FOR HOW LONG...?

I ♥ BL

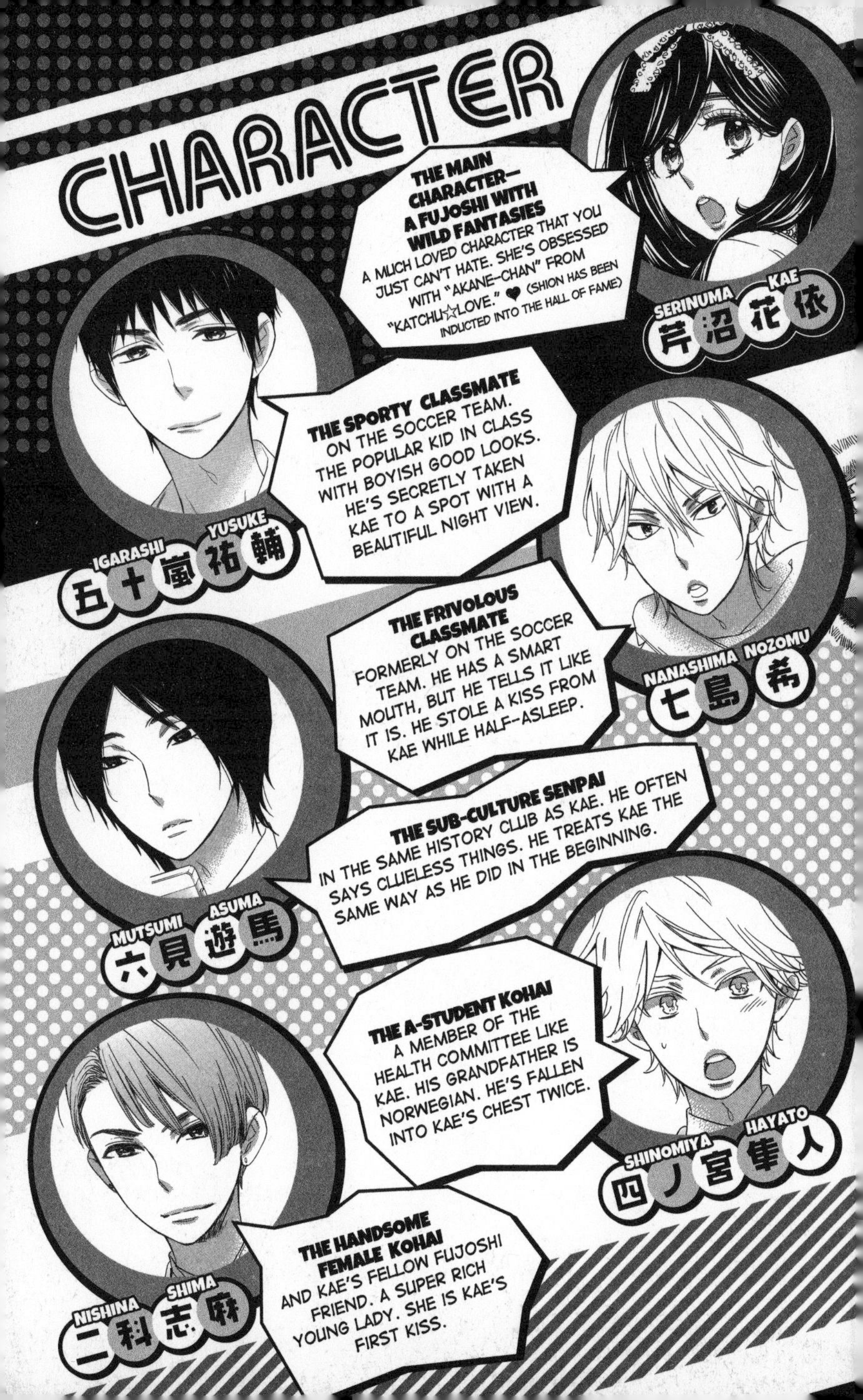
CHARACTER
THE MAIN CHARACTER— A FUJOSHI WITH WILD FANTASIES
A MUCH LOVED CHARACTER THAT YOU JUST CAN'T HATE. SHE'S OBSESSED WITH "AKANE-CHAN" FROM "KATCHU☆LOVE." ❤ (SHION HAS BEEN INDUCTED INTO THE HALL OF FAME)
SERINUMA KAE
芹沼花依
THE SPORTY CLASSMATE
ON THE SOCCER TEAM. THE POPULAR KID IN CLASS WITH BOYISH GOOD LOOKS. HE'S SECRETLY TAKEN A KAE TO A SPOT WITH A BEAUTIFUL NIGHT VIEW.
IGARASHI YUSUKE
五十嵐祐輔
THE FRIVOLOUS CLASSMATE
FORMERLY ON THE SOCCER TEAM. HE HAS A SMART MOUTH, BUT HE TELLS IT LIKE IT IS. HE STOLE A KISS FROM KAE WHILE HALF-ASLEEP.
NANASHIMA NOZOMU
七島希
THE SUB-CULTURE SENPAI
IN THE SAME HISTORY CLUB AS KAE. HE OFTEN SAYS CLUELESS THINGS. HE TREATS KAE THE SAME WAY AS HE DID IN THE BEGINNING.
MUTSUMI ASUMA
六見遊馬
THE A-STUDENT KOHAI
A MEMBER OF THE HEALTH COMMITTEE LIKE KAE. HIS GRANDFATHER IS NORWEGIAN. HE'S FALLEN INTO KAE'S CHEST TWICE.
SHINOMIYA HAYATO
四ノ宮隼人
THE HANDSOME FEMALE KOHAI
AND KAE'S FELLOW FUJOSHI FRIEND. A SUPER RICH YOUNG LADY. SHE IS KAE'S FIRST KISS.
NISHINA SHIMA
二科志麻

KiSS HiM, NOT ME!

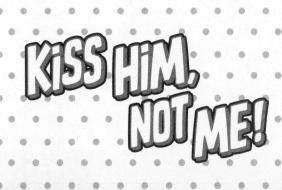

#37 REUNITING WITH AN OLD FRIEND

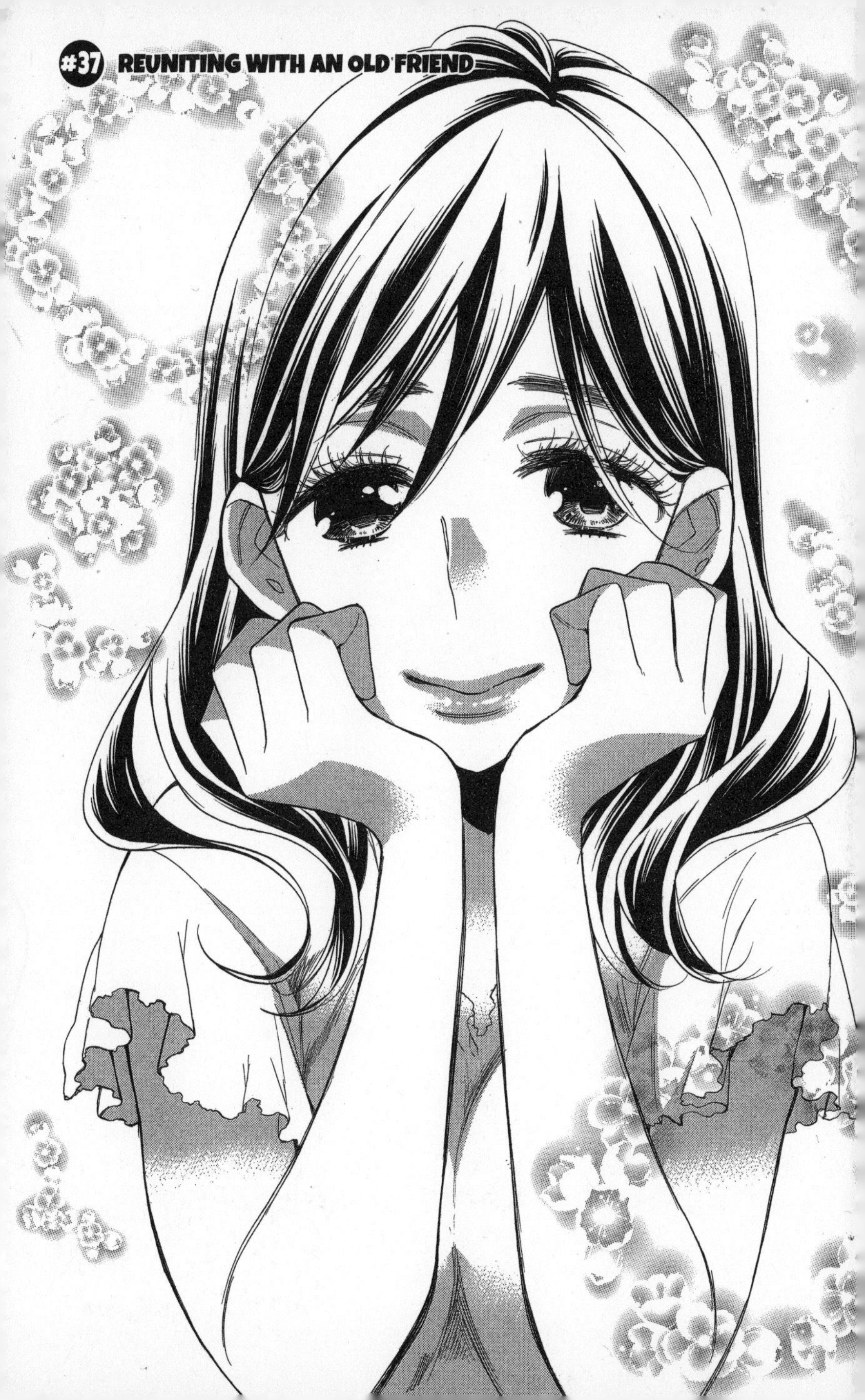

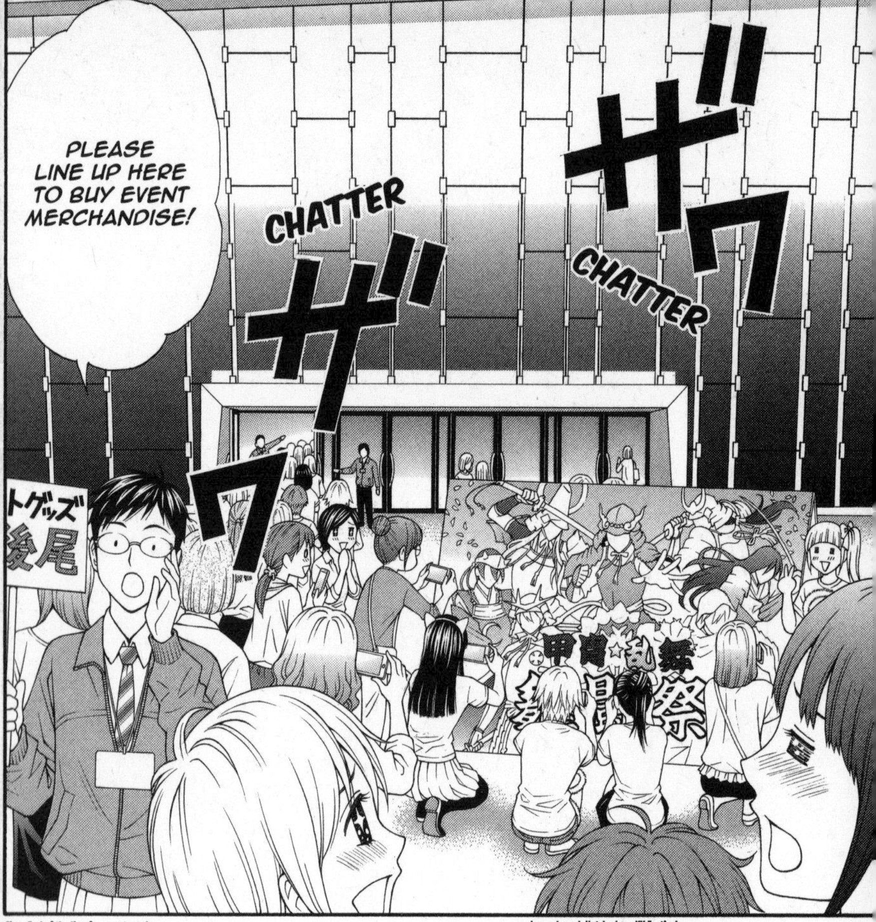
ザワ
CHATTER
CHATTER
ザワ
PLEASE LINE UP HERE TO BUY EVENT MERCHANDISE!
トグッズ
後尾

Sign: End of the line for event goods

Large board: Katchu Love XX Festival

KiSS HiM, NOT ME!

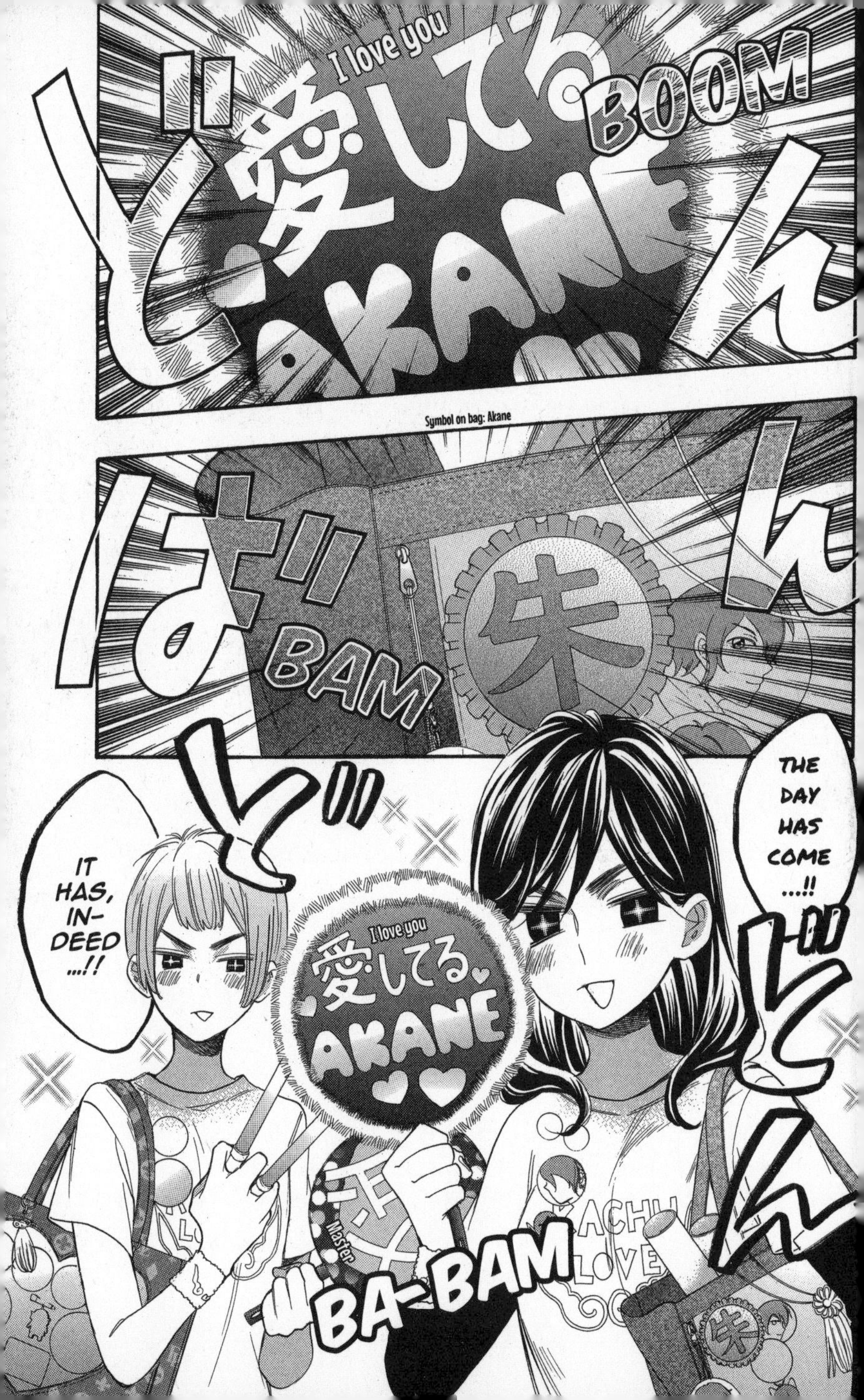

I love you
愛してる
BOOM
AKANE
Symbol on bag: Akane
BAM
THE DAY HAS COME ...!!
IT HAS, IN-DEED ...!!
I love you
愛してる
AKANE
Master
BA-BAM

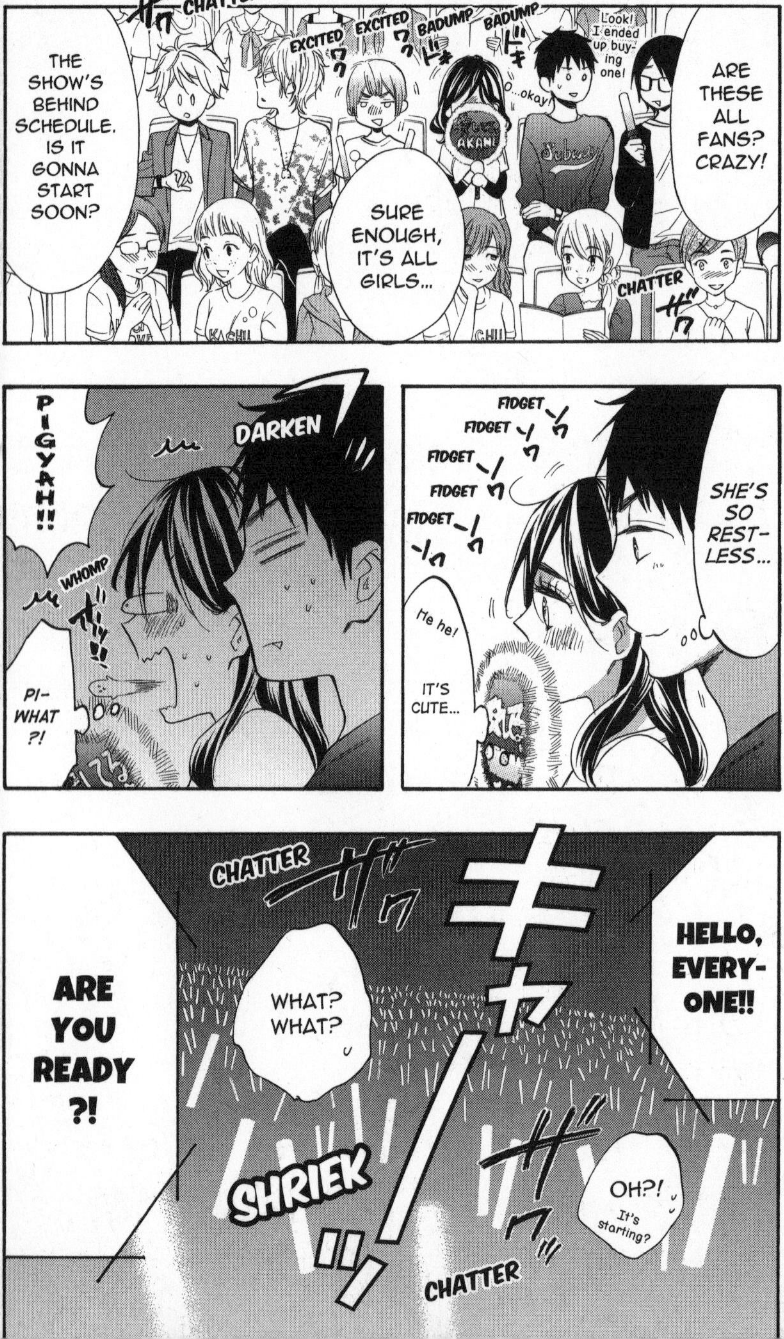
ARE THESE ALL FANS? CRAZY!
Look! I ended up buying one!
O...okay!
BADUMP
BADUMP
EXCITED
EXCITED
CHATTER
THE SHOW'S BEHIND SCHEDULE. IS IT GONNA START SOON?
SURE ENOUGH, IT'S ALL GIRLS...
CHATTER
FIDGET
FIDGET
FIDGET
FIDGET
FIDGET
SHE'S SO RESTLESS...
He he!
IT'S CUTE...
DARKEN
PIGYAH!!
WHOMP
PI-WHAT?!
HELLO, EVERYONE!!
SHRIEK
CHATTER
WHAT? WHAT?
OH?!
It's starting?
CHATTER
ARE YOU READY?!

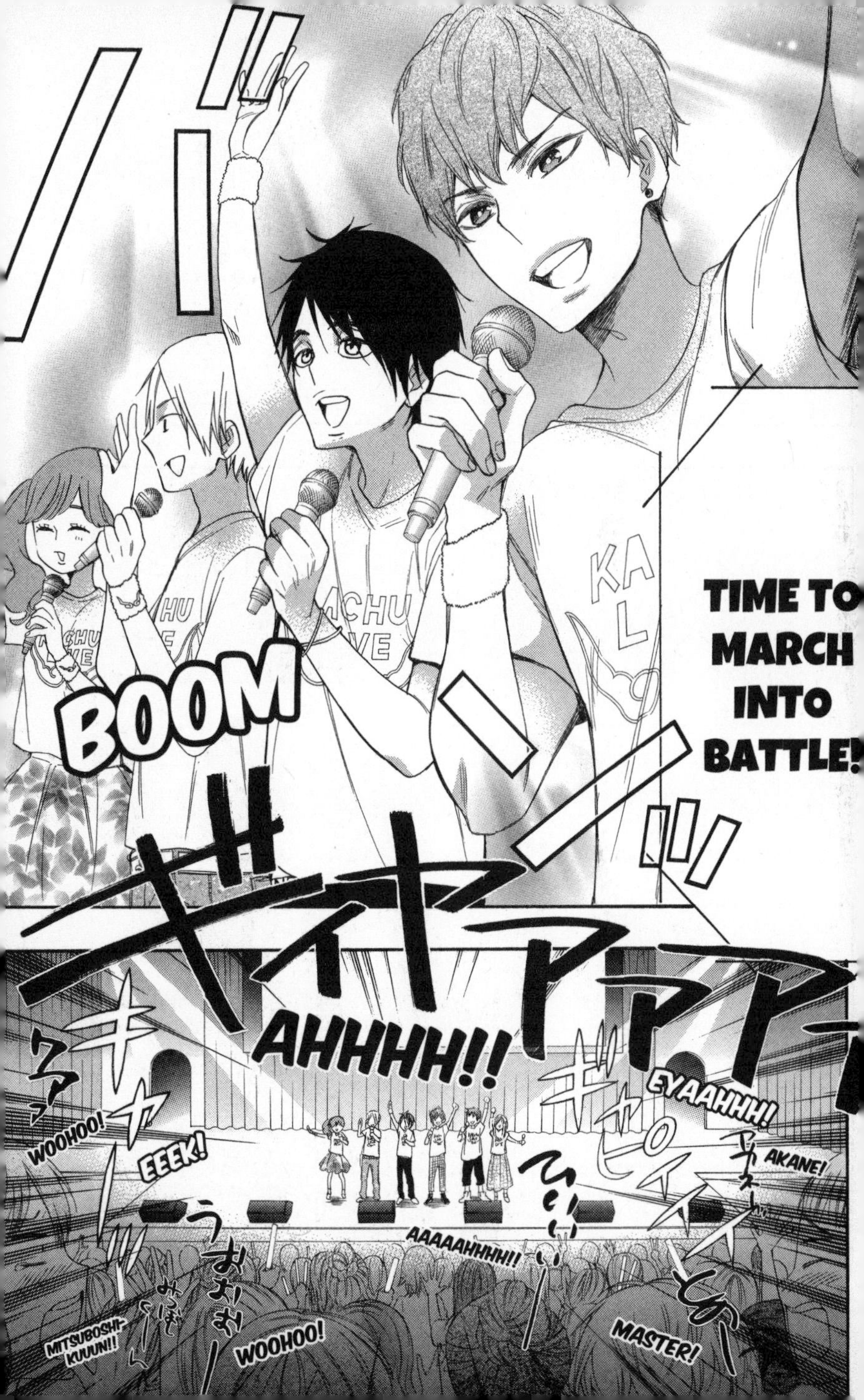
TIME TO MARCH INTO BATTLE!
BOOM
AHHHH!!
EYAAHHH!
AKANE!
WOOHOO!
EEEK!
AAAAAHHHH!!
MASTER!
WOOHOO!
MITSUBOSHI-KUUUN!!

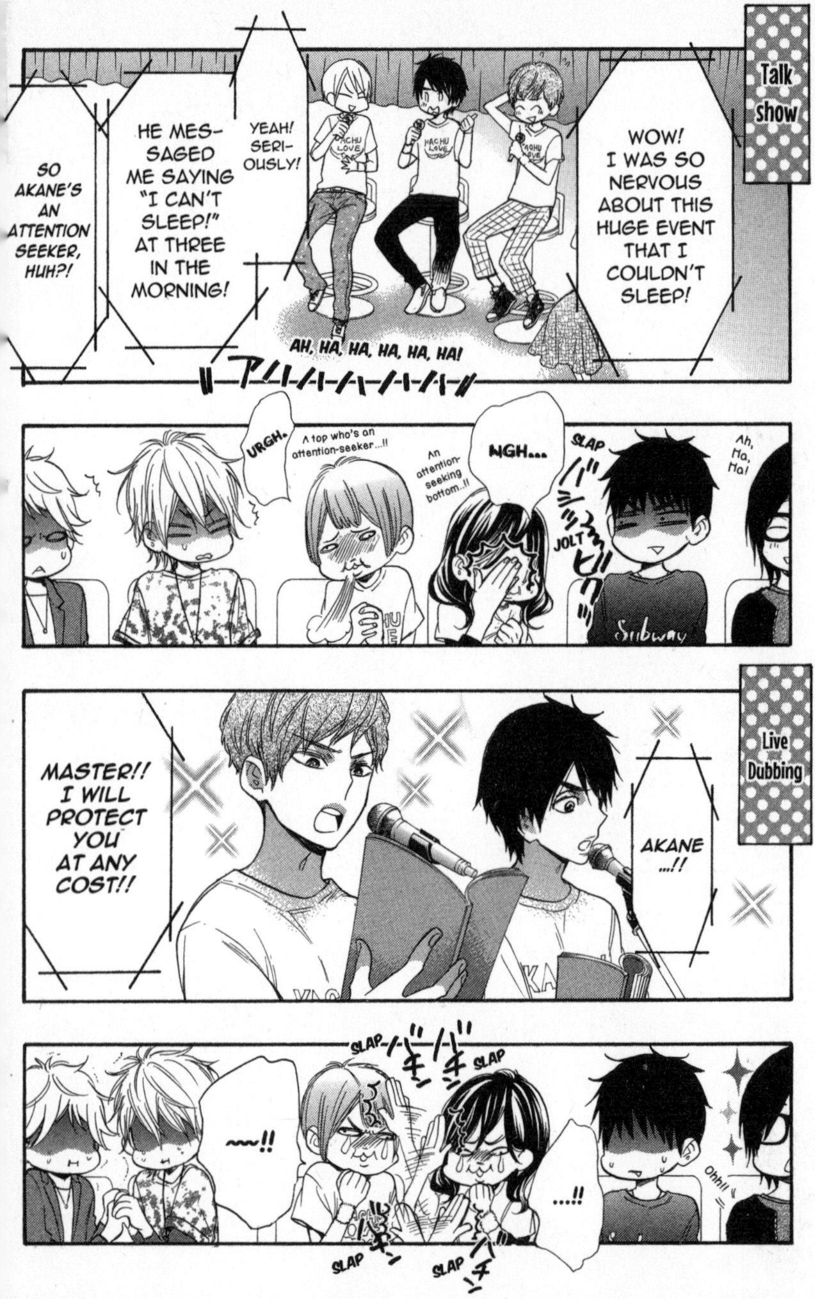
Talk show
WOW! I WAS SO NERVOUS ABOUT THIS HUGE EVENT THAT I COULDN'T SLEEP!
YEAH! SERIOUSLY!
HE MESSAGED ME SAYING "I CAN'T SLEEP!" AT THREE IN THE MORNING!
SO AKANE'S AN ATTENTION SEEKER, HUH?!
AH, HA, HA, HA, HA, HA!
Ah, Ha, Ha!
SLAP
JOLT
NGH...
An attention-seeking bottom..!!
A top who's an attention-seeker...!!
URGH.
Live Dubbing
AKANE...!!
MASTER!! I WILL PROTECT YOU AT ANY COST!!
Ohh!!
...!!
SLAP
SLAP
SLAP
SLAP
~~~!!
~~~

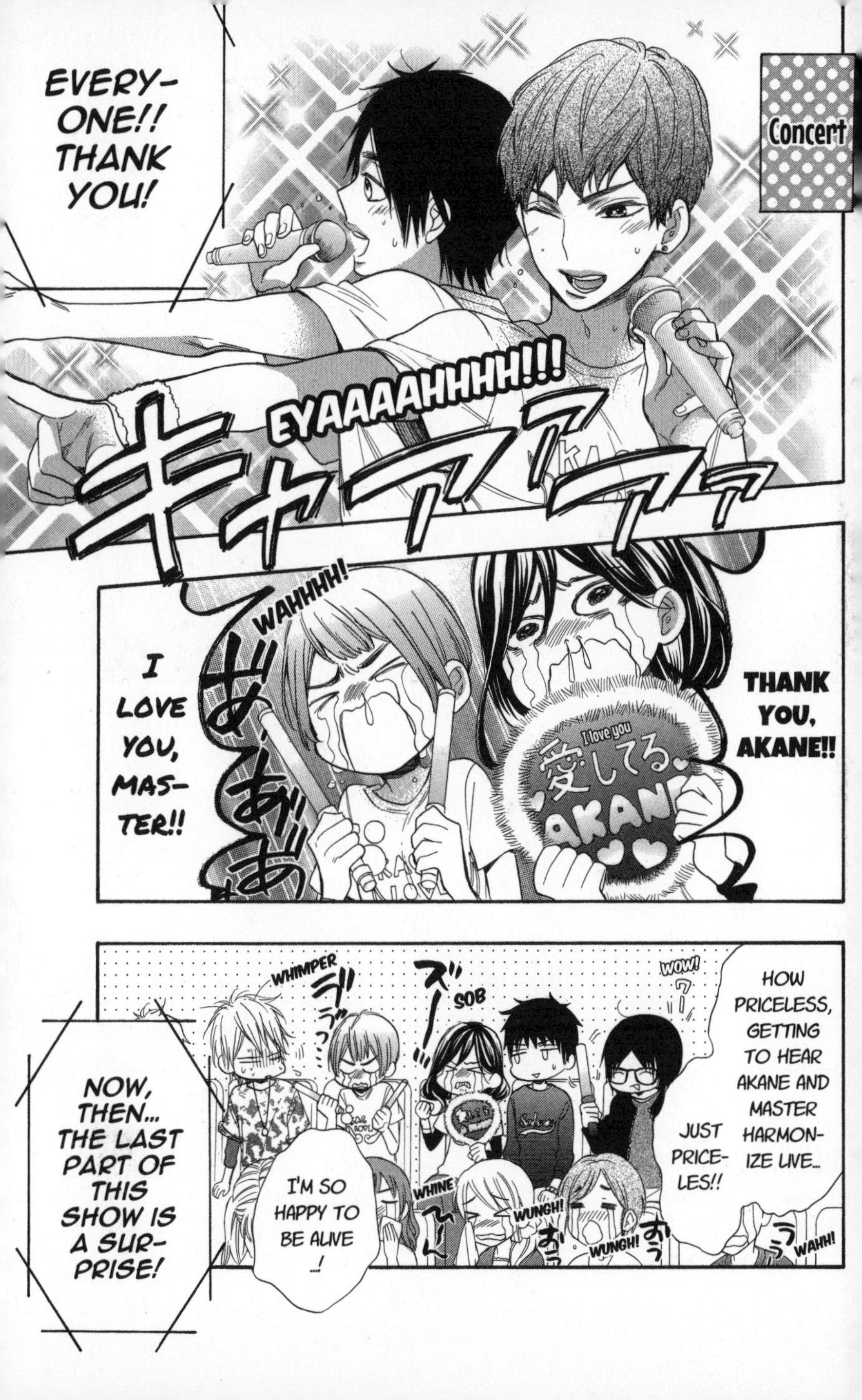
Concert
EVERY-ONE!! THANK YOU!
EYAAAAHHHH!!!
キャアアァ
THANK YOU, AKANE!!
I love you
愛してる
AKANE
WAHHHH!
I LOVE YOU, MASTER!!
HOW PRICELESS, GETTING TO HEAR AKANE AND MASTER HARMONIZE LIVE...
WOW!
JUST PRICE-LES!!
SOB
WHIMPER
WAHH!
WUNGH!
WUNGH!
WHINE
I'M SO HAPPY TO BE ALIVE...!
NOW, THEN... THE LAST PART OF THIS SHOW IS A SURPRISE!

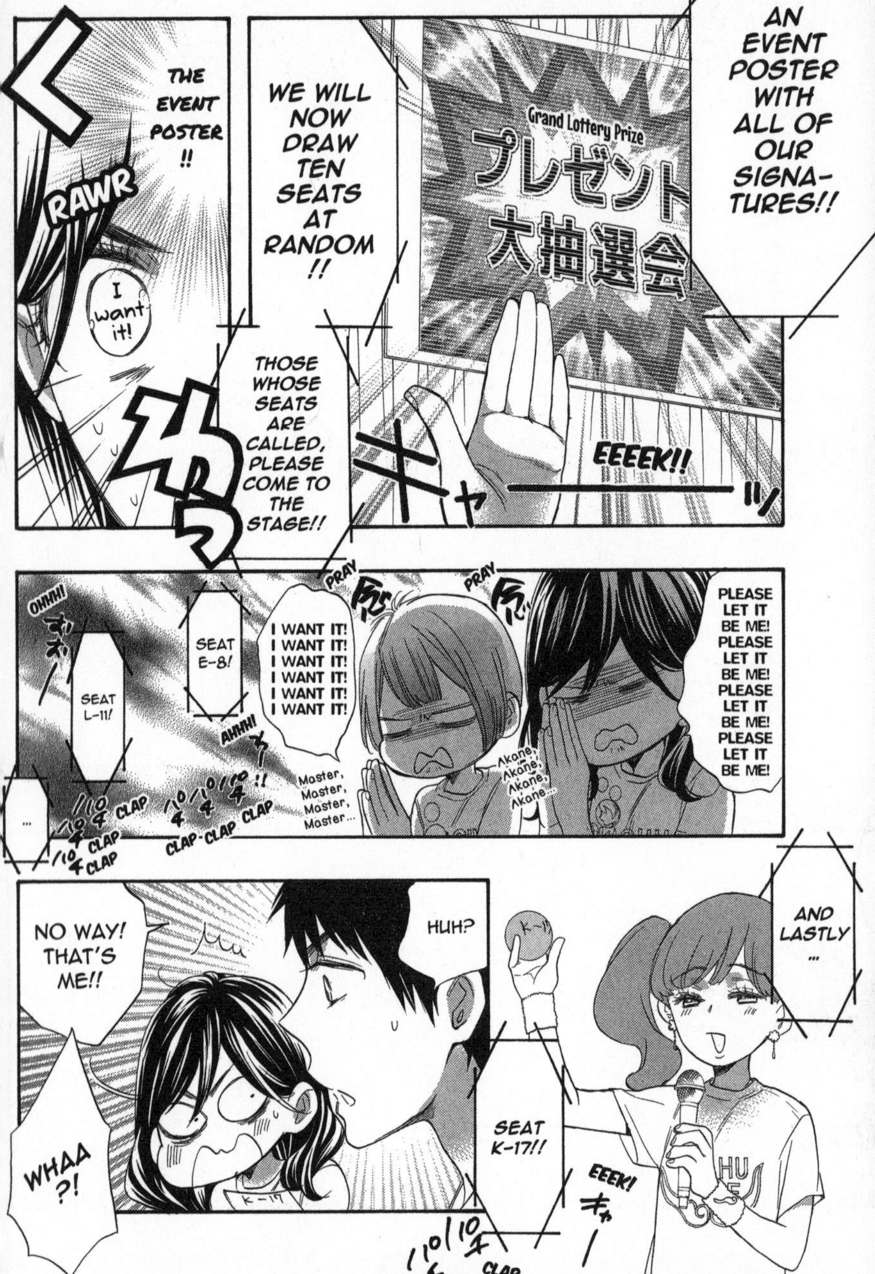
AN EVENT POSTER WITH ALL OF OUR SIGNATURES!!
Grand Lottery Prize
プレゼント大抽選会
EEEEK!!
WE WILL NOW DRAW TEN SEATS AT RANDOM!!
THOSE WHOSE SEATS ARE CALLED, PLEASE COME TO THE STAGE!!
THE EVENT POSTER!!
RAWR
I want it!
PLEASE LET IT BE ME! PLEASE LET IT BE ME! PLEASE LET IT BE ME! PLEASE LET IT BE ME!
PRAY
Akane, Akane, Akane, Akane...
PRAY
I WANT IT! I WANT IT! I WANT IT! I WANT IT! I WANT IT! I WANT IT!
Master, Master, Master, Master...
SEAT E-8!
AHHH!
CLAP CLAP CLAP
SEAT L-11!
OHHH!
...
CLAP CLAP CLAP
AND LASTLY...
SEAT K-17!!
EEEK!
CLAP CLAP CLAP
HUH?
NO WAY! THAT'S ME!!
WHAA?!

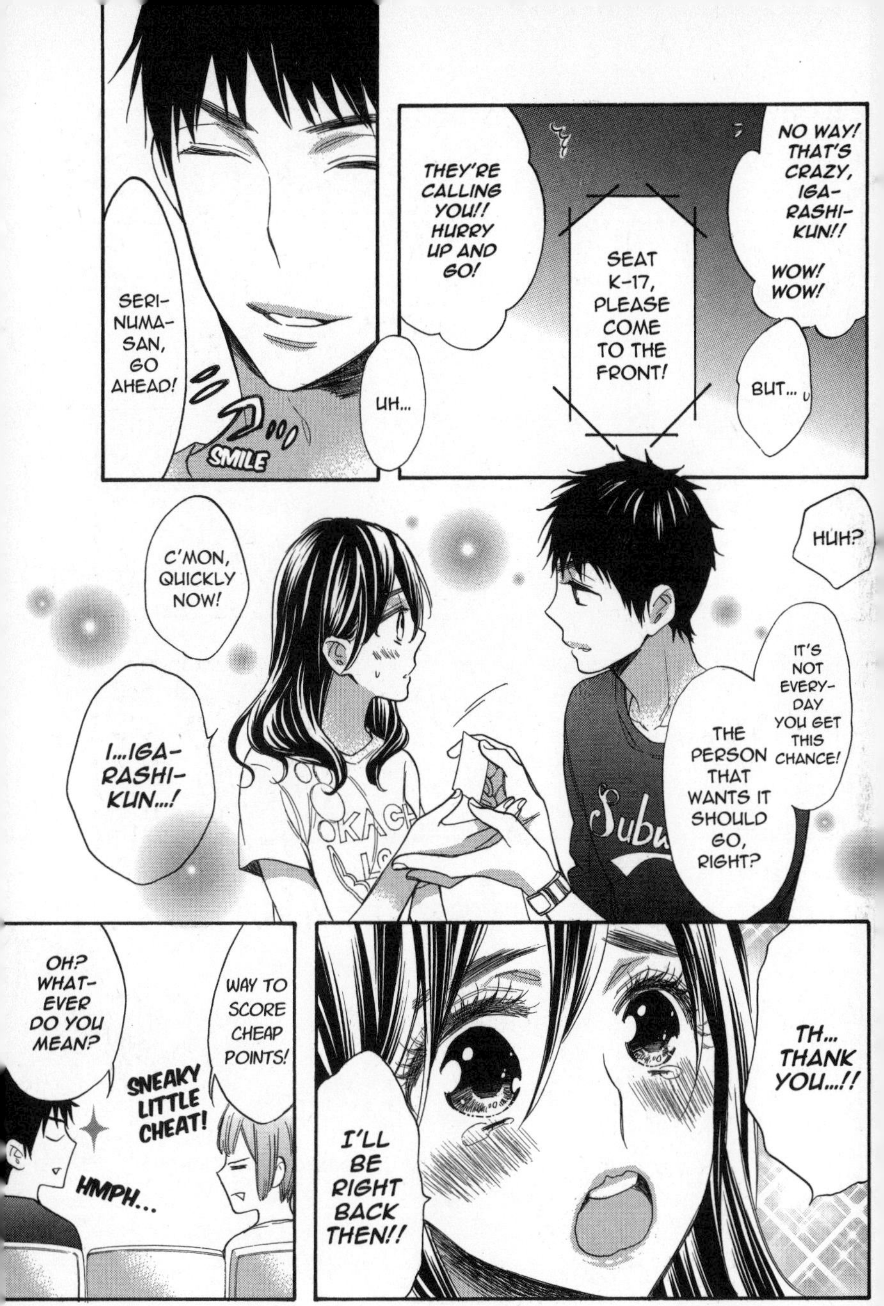
NO WAY! THAT'S CRAZY, IGA-RASHI-KUN!!
WOW! WOW!
SEAT K-17, PLEASE COME TO THE FRONT!
THEY'RE CALLING YOU!! HURRY UP AND GO!
BUT...
UH...
SERI-NUMA-SAN, GO AHEAD!
SMILE
HUH?
IT'S NOT EVERY-DAY YOU GET THIS CHANCE!
THE PERSON THAT WANTS IT SHOULD GO, RIGHT?
C'MON, QUICKLY NOW!
I...IGA-RASHI-KUN...!
TH... THANK YOU...!!
I'LL BE RIGHT BACK THEN!!
WAY TO SCORE CHEAP POINTS!
OH? WHAT-EVER DO YOU MEAN?
SNEAKY LITTLE CHEAT!
HMPH...

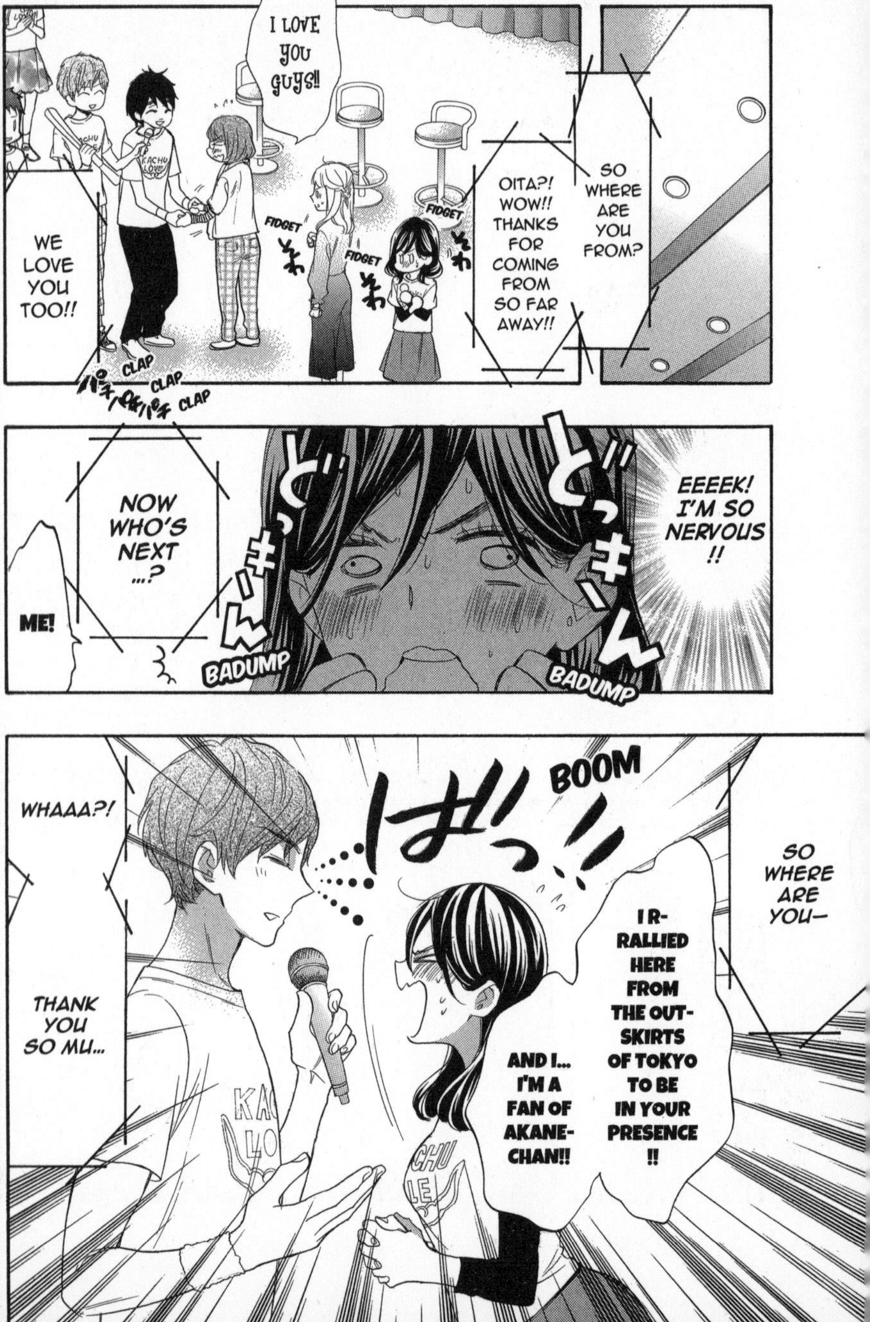
SO WHERE ARE YOU FROM?
OITA?! WOW!! THANKS FOR COMING FROM SO FAR AWAY!!
I LOVE YOU GUYS!!
FIDGET
FIDGET
FIDGET
WE LOVE YOU TOO!!
CLAP
CLAP
CLAP
EEEEK! I'M SO NERVOUS!!
BADUMP
NOW WHO'S NEXT ...?
BADUMP
ME!
SO WHERE ARE YOU—
BOOM
I R-RALLIED HERE FROM THE OUT-SKIRTS OF TOKYO TO BE IN YOUR PRESENCE!!
AND I... I'M A FAN OF AKANE-CHAN!!
WHAAA?!
THANK YOU SO MU...

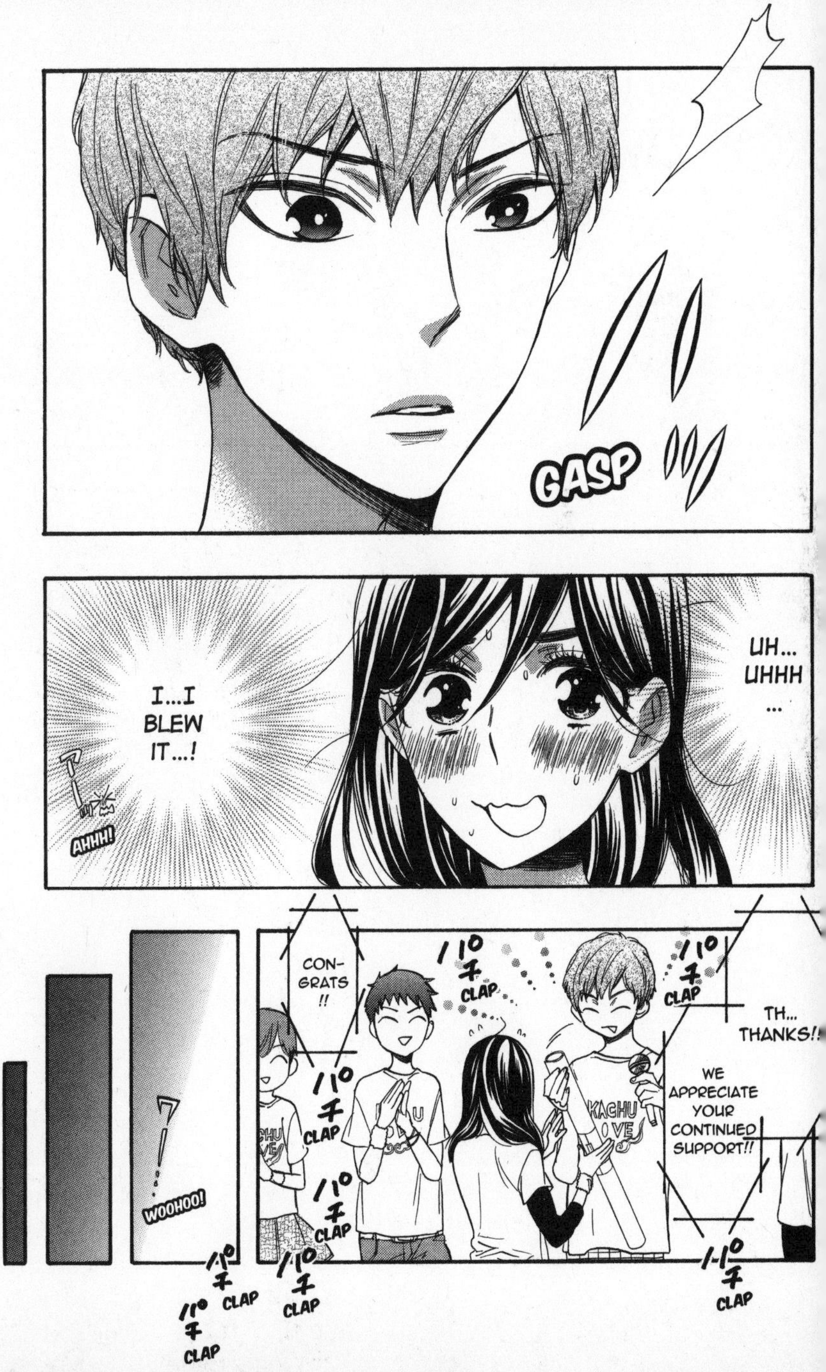
GASP
UH... UHHH ...
I...I BLEW IT...!
AHHH!
CLAP
TH... THANKS!!
WE APPRECIATE YOUR CONTINUED SUPPORT!!
CLAP
CLAP
CON-GRATS !!
CLAP
CLAP
WOOHOO!
CLAP
CLAP
CLAP

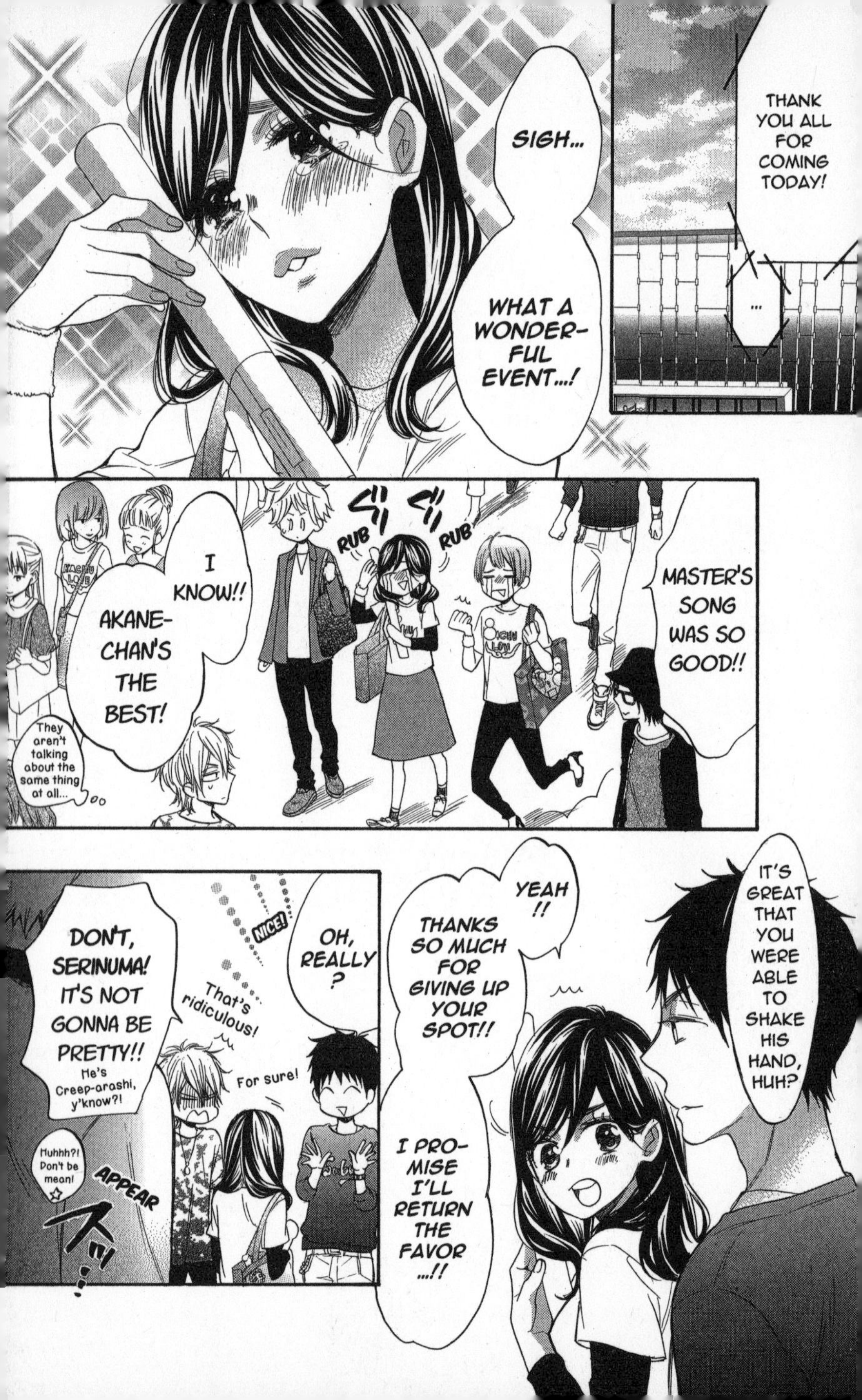
THANK YOU ALL FOR COMING TODAY!
...
SIGH...
WHAT A WONDER-FUL EVENT...!
MASTER'S SONG WAS SO GOOD!!
RUB
RUB
I KNOW!!
AKANE-CHAN'S THE BEST!
They aren't talking about the same thing at all...
IT'S GREAT THAT YOU WERE ABLE TO SHAKE HIS HAND, HUH?
YEAH!!
THANKS SO MUCH FOR GIVING UP YOUR SPOT!!
I PRO-MISE I'LL RETURN THE FAVOR...!!
OH, REALLY?
NICE!
That's ridiculous!
For sure!
DON'T, SERINUMA! IT'S NOT GONNA BE PRETTY!!
He's Creep-arashi, y'know?!
Huhhh?! Don't be mean! ☆
APPEAR

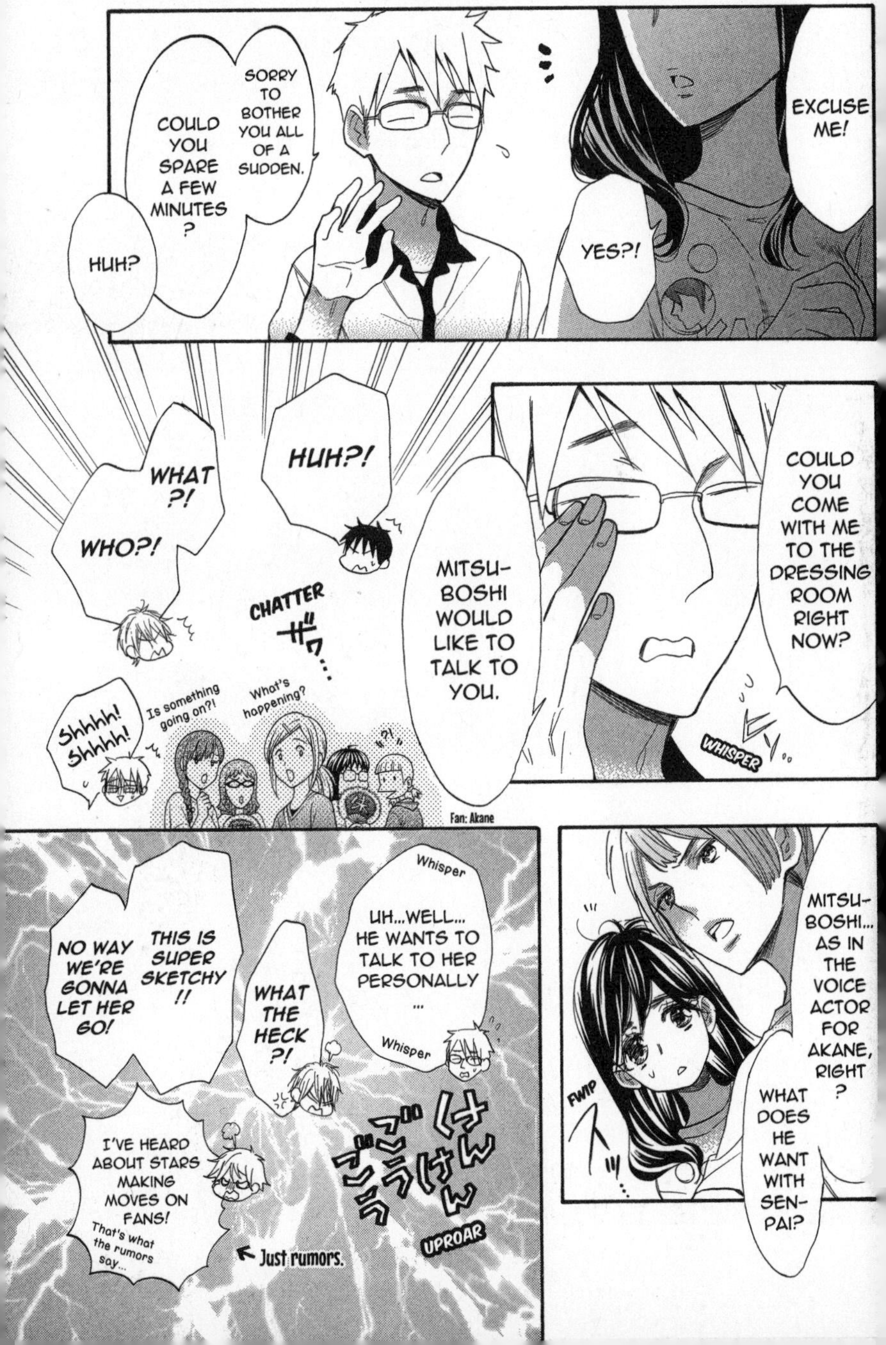
EXCUSE ME!
YES?!
SORRY TO BOTHER YOU ALL OF A SUDDEN.
COULD YOU SPARE A FEW MINUTES?
HUH?
COULD YOU COME WITH ME TO THE DRESSING ROOM RIGHT NOW?
WHISPER
MITSU-BOSHI WOULD LIKE TO TALK TO YOU.
HUH?!
WHAT?!
WHO?!
CHATTER
What's happening?
Is something going on?!
Shhhh! Shhhh!
Fan: Akane
MITSU-BOSHI... AS IN THE VOICE ACTOR FOR AKANE, RIGHT?
WHAT DOES HE WANT WITH SEN-PAI?
FWIP
Whisper
UH...WELL... HE WANTS TO TALK TO HER PERSONALLY...
Whisper
WHAT THE HECK?!
THIS IS SUPER SKETCHY!!
NO WAY WE'RE GONNA LET HER GO!
UPROAR
I'VE HEARD ABOUT STARS MAKING MOVES ON FANS!
That's what the rumors say...
Just rumors.

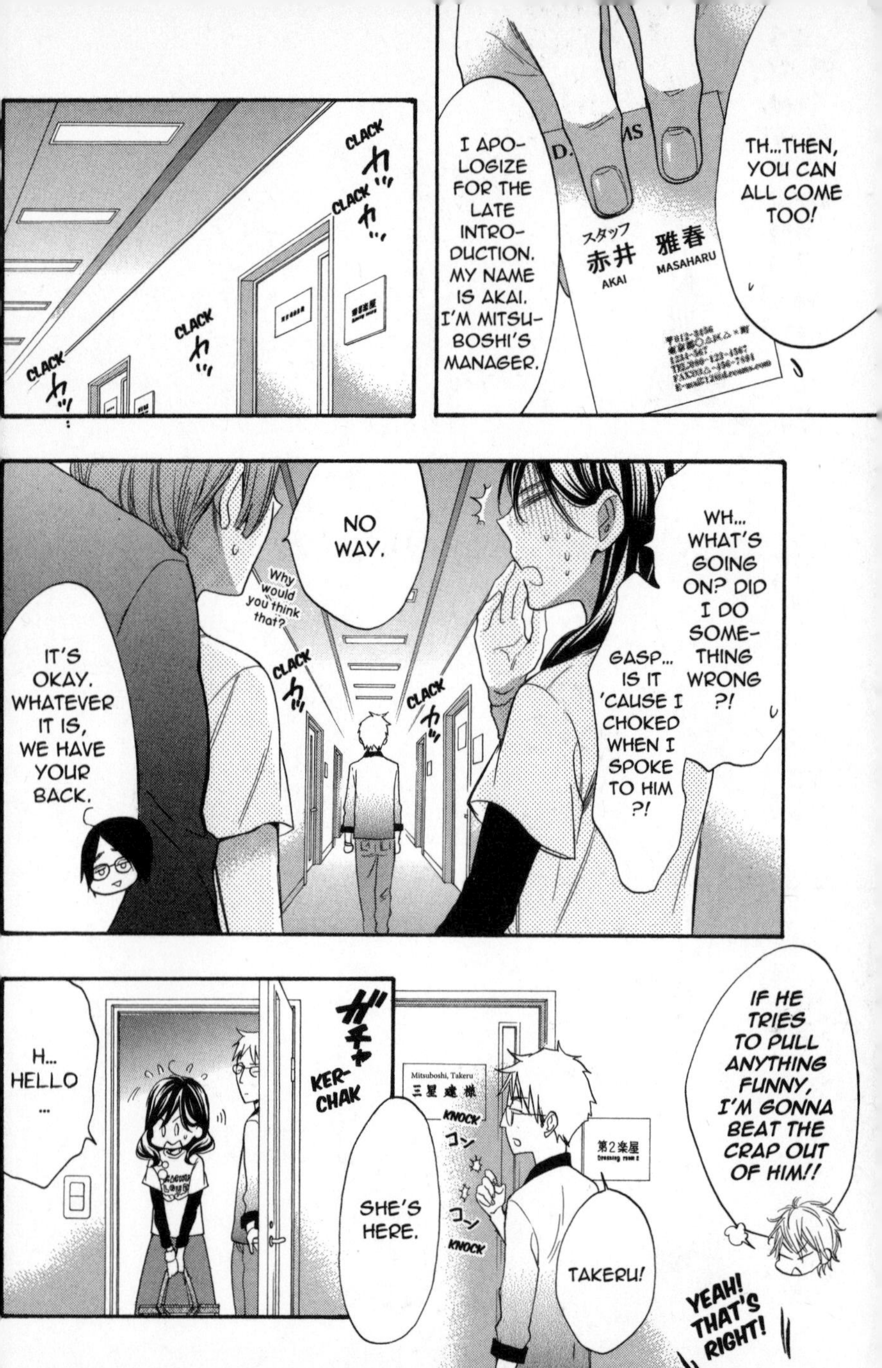
TH...THEN, YOU CAN ALL COME TOO!
I APOLOGIZE FOR THE LATE INTRODUCTION. MY NAME IS AKAI. I'M MITSUBOSHI'S MANAGER.
スタッフ
赤井 雅春
AKAI
MASAHARU
CLACK
CLACK
CLACK
CLACK
WH... WHAT'S GOING ON? DID I DO SOMETHING WRONG?!
GASP... IS IT 'CAUSE I CHOKED WHEN I SPOKE TO HIM?!
NO WAY.
Why would you think that?
IT'S OKAY. WHATEVER IT IS, WE HAVE YOUR BACK.
CLACK
CLACK
IF HE TRIES TO PULL ANYTHING FUNNY, I'M GONNA BEAT THE CRAP OUT OF HIM!!
YEAH! THAT'S RIGHT!
TAKERU!
第2楽屋
Dressing room 2
Mitsuboshi, Takeru
三星建様
KNOCK
KNOCK
SHE'S HERE.
KER-CHAK
H... HELLO ...

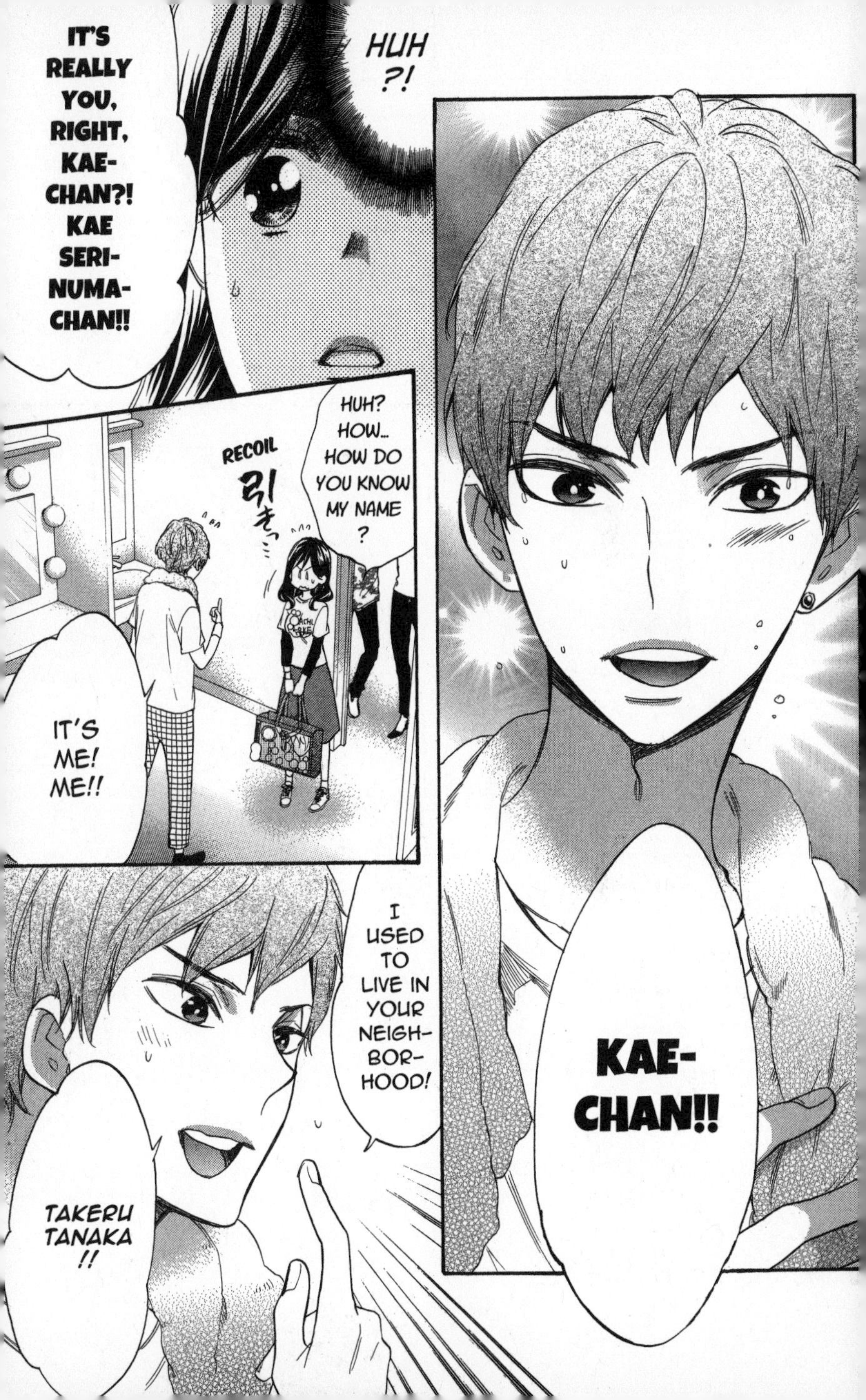
KAE-CHAN!!
HUH?!
IT'S REALLY YOU, RIGHT, KAE-CHAN?! KAE SERI-NUMA-CHAN!!
HUH? HOW... HOW DO YOU KNOW MY NAME?
RECOIL
IT'S ME! ME!!
I USED TO LIVE IN YOUR NEIGH-BOR-HOOD!
TAKERU TANAKA!!

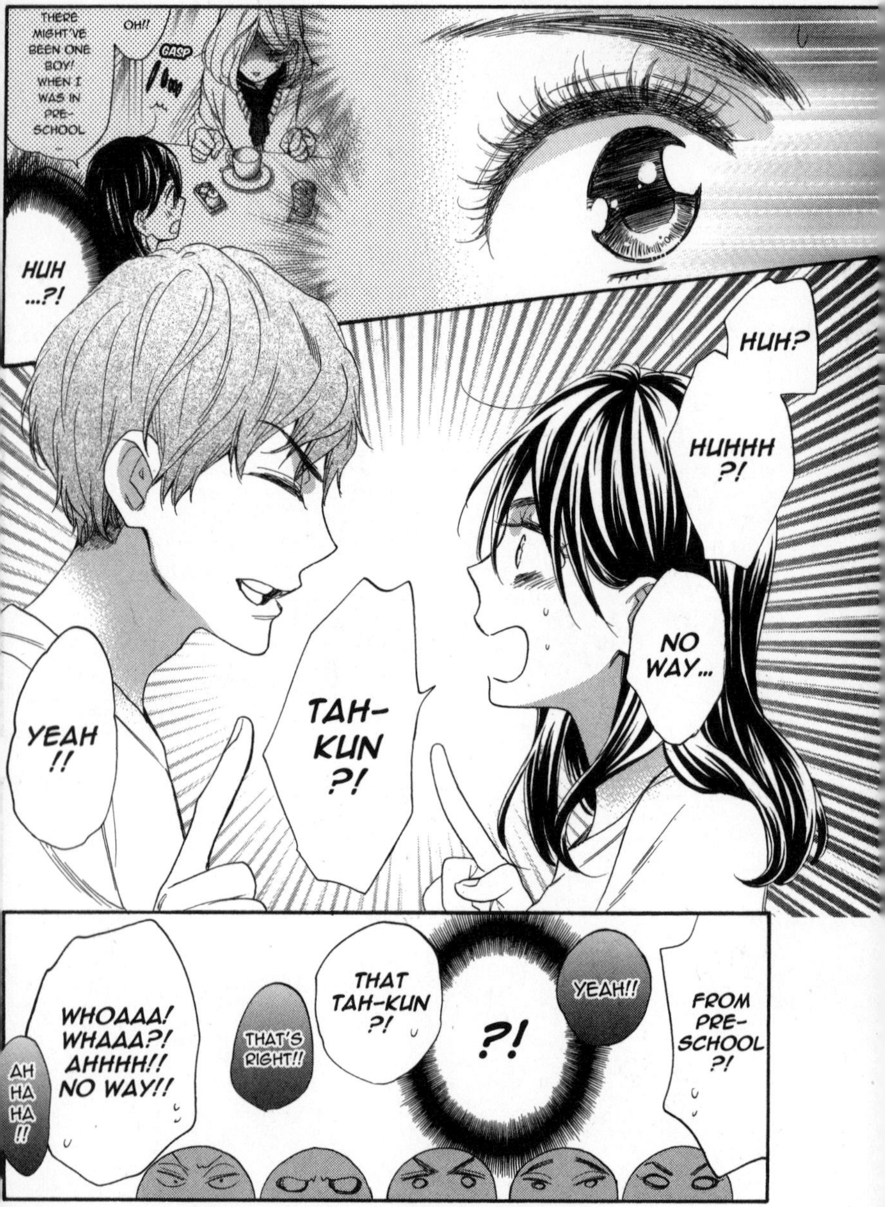
GASP
OH!!
THERE MIGHT'VE BEEN ONE BOY! WHEN I WAS IN PRE-SCHOOL...
HUH ...?!
HUH?
HUHHH ?!
NO WAY...
TAH-KUN ?!
YEAH !!
FROM PRE-SCHOOL ?!
YEAH!!
?!
THAT TAH-KUN ?!
THAT'S RIGHT!!
WHOAAA! WHAAA?! AHHHH!! NO WAY!!
AH HA HA !!

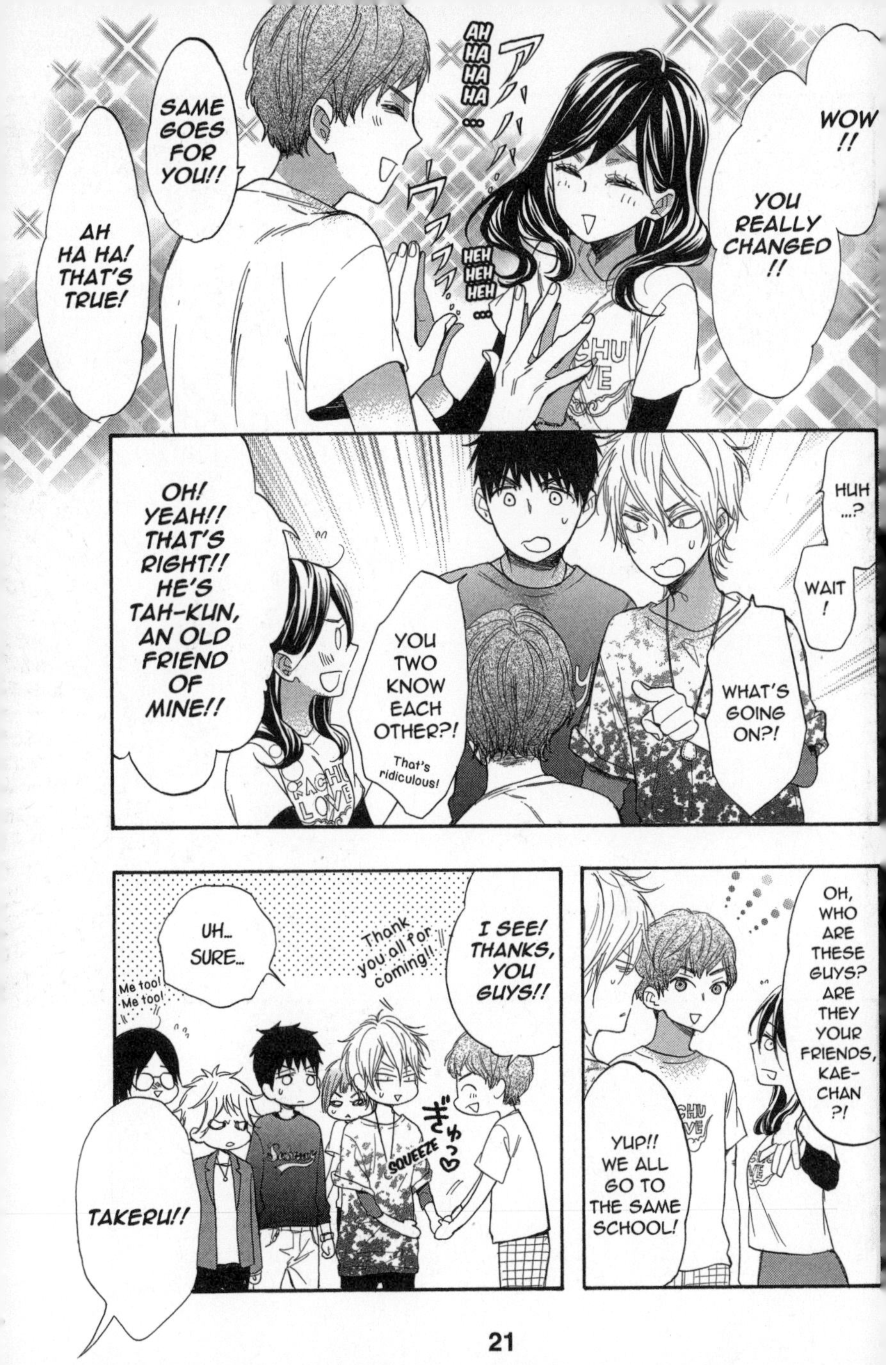
WOW!! YOU REALLY CHANGED!!
AH HA HA HA...
HEH HEH HEH...
SAME GOES FOR YOU!!
AH HA HA! THAT'S TRUE!
HUH...? WAIT!
WHAT'S GOING ON?!
YOU TWO KNOW EACH OTHER?!
That's ridiculous!
OH! YEAH!! THAT'S RIGHT!! HE'S TAH-KUN, AN OLD FRIEND OF MINE!!
OH, WHO ARE THESE GUYS? ARE THEY YOUR FRIENDS, KAE-CHAN?!
YUP!! WE ALL GO TO THE SAME SCHOOL!
I SEE! THANKS, YOU GUYS!!
Thank you all for coming!!
UH... SURE...
Me too! Me too!
SQUEEZE
TAKERU!!

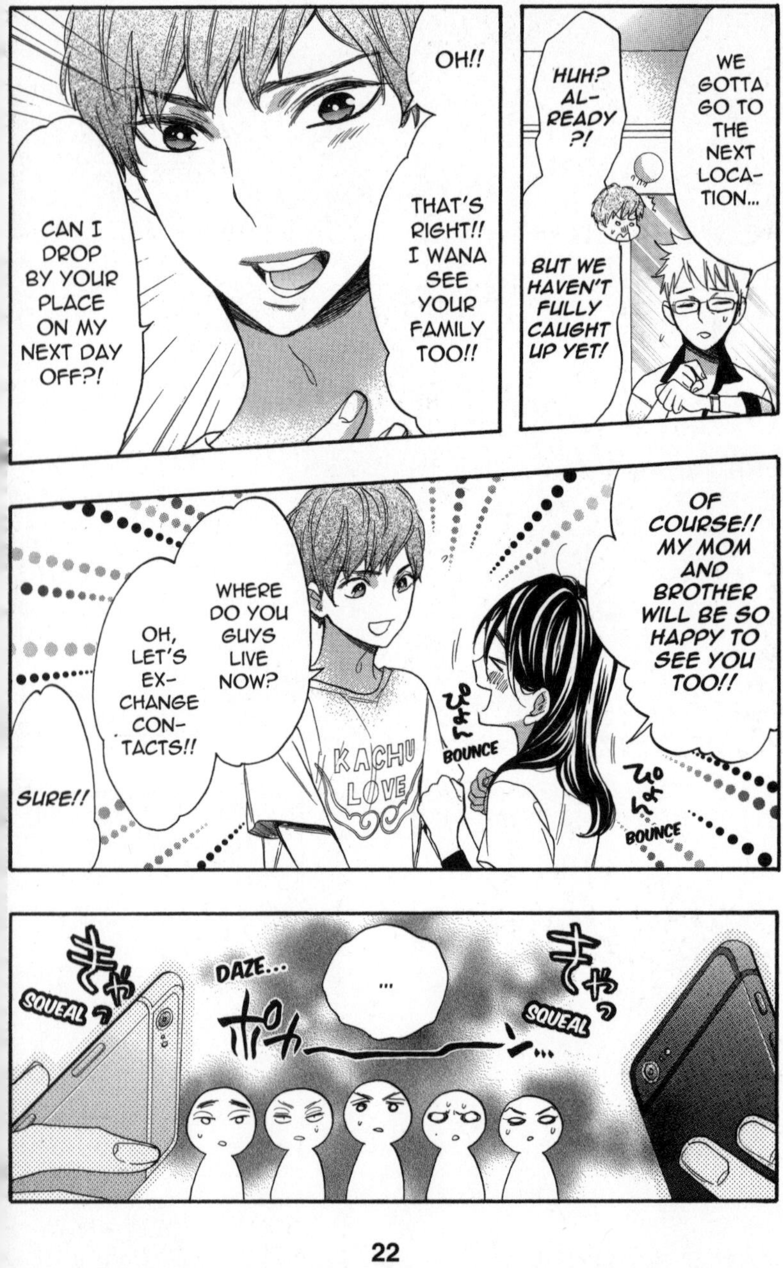
WE GOTTA GO TO THE NEXT LOCATION...
HUH? ALREADY?!
BUT WE HAVEN'T FULLY CAUGHT UP YET!
OH!!
THAT'S RIGHT!! I WANA SEE YOUR FAMILY TOO!!
CAN I DROP BY YOUR PLACE ON MY NEXT DAY OFF?!
OF COURSE!! MY MOM AND BROTHER WILL BE SO HAPPY TO SEE YOU TOO!!
ぴょん
BOUNCE
ぴょん
BOUNCE
WHERE DO YOU GUYS LIVE NOW?
OH, LET'S EXCHANGE CONTACTS!!
SURE!!
きゃっ
SQUEAL
...
DAZE...
ポカーン...
きゃっ
SQUEAL

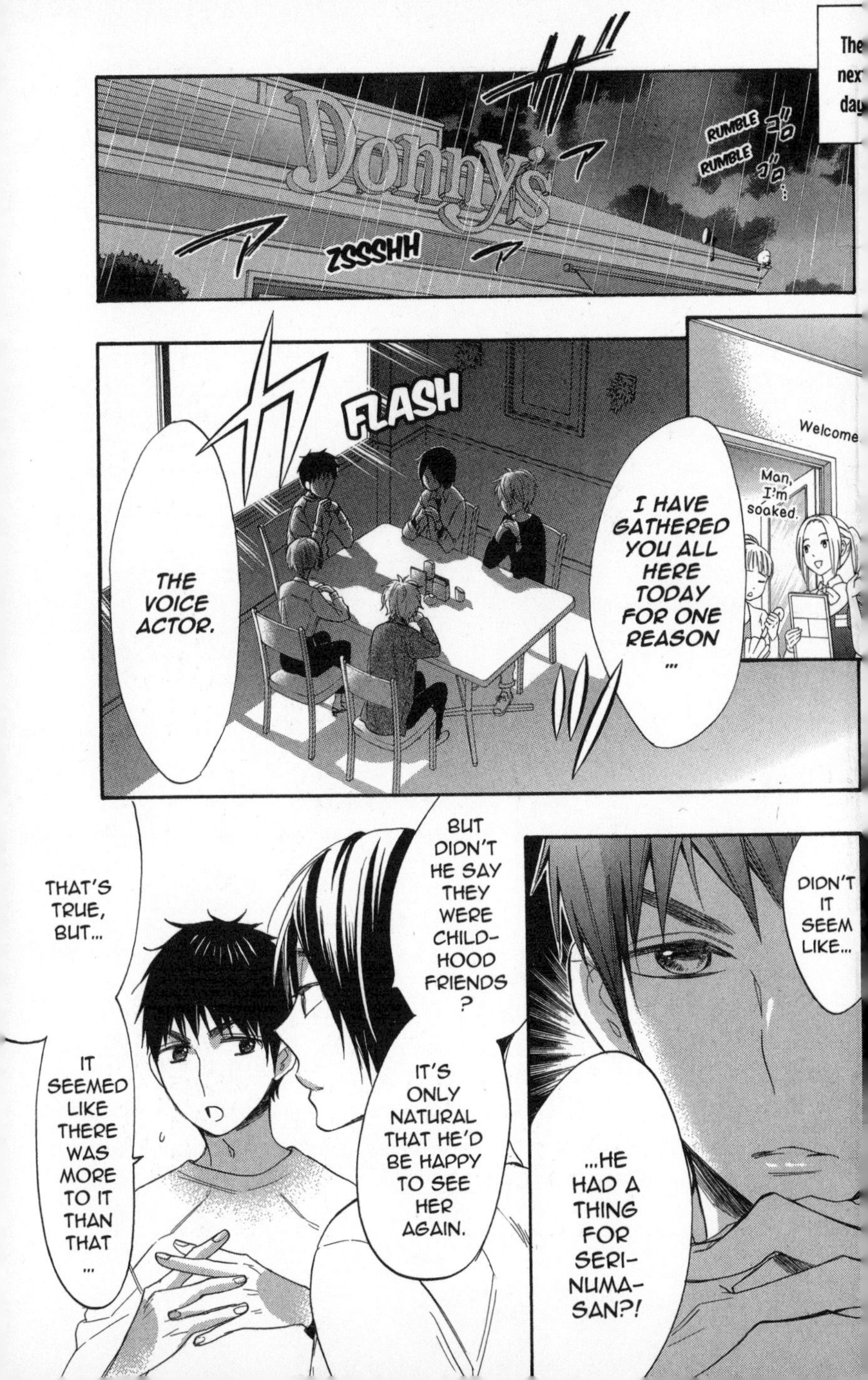

The next day
RUMBLE ゴロ
RUMBLE ゴロ…
Donny's
ZSSSHH
FLASH
Welcome
Man, I'm soaked.
I HAVE GATHERED YOU ALL HERE TODAY FOR ONE REASON…
THE VOICE ACTOR.
DIDN'T IT SEEM LIKE…
…HE HAD A THING FOR SERI-NUMA-SAN?!
BUT DIDN'T HE SAY THEY WERE CHILD-HOOD FRIENDS?
THAT'S TRUE, BUT…
IT'S ONLY NATURAL THAT HE'D BE HAPPY TO SEE HER AGAIN.
IT SEEMED LIKE THERE WAS MORE TO IT THAN THAT…

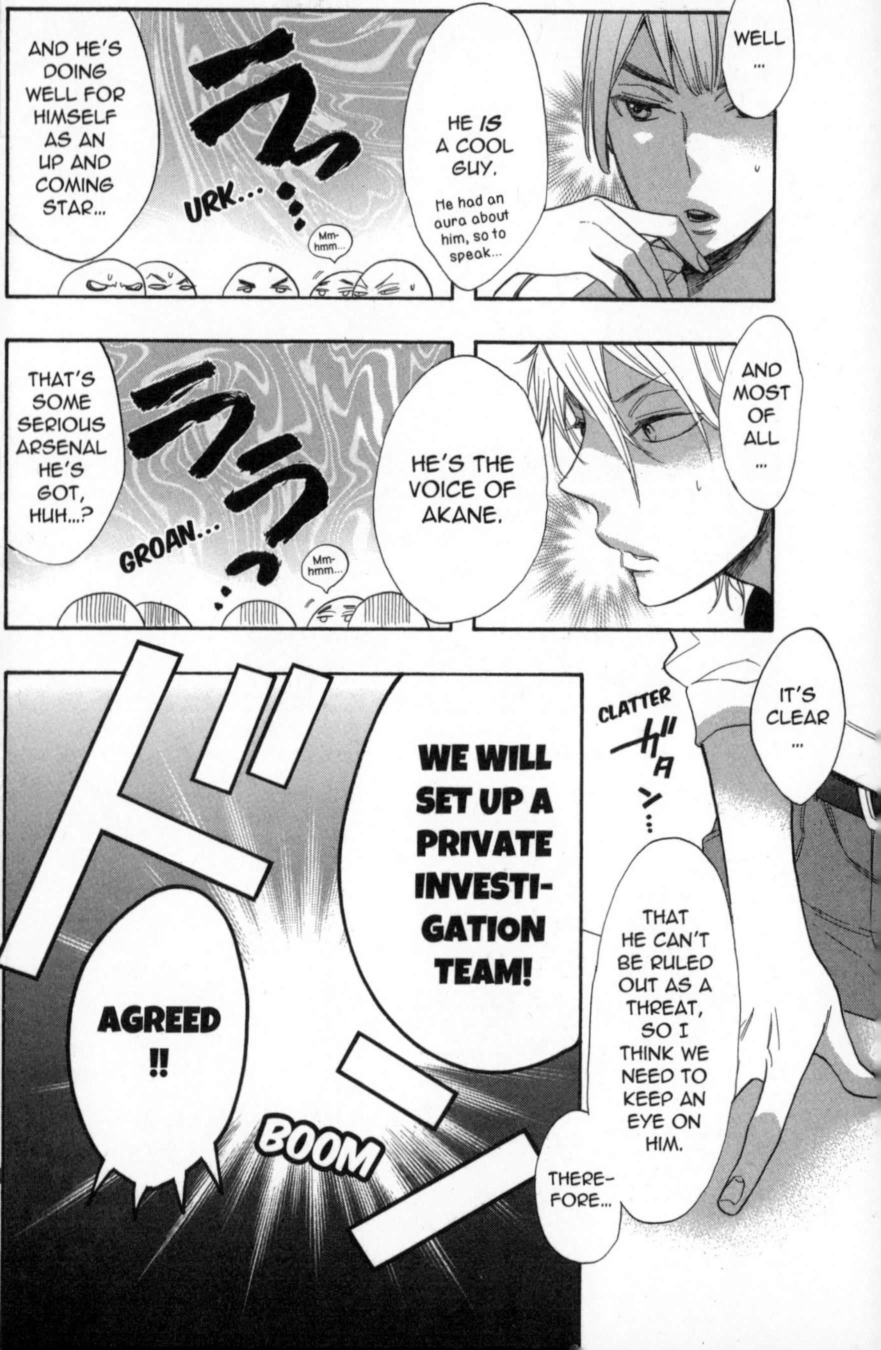
WELL ...
HE *IS* A COOL GUY.
He had an aura about him, so to speak...
AND HE'S DOING WELL FOR HIMSELF AS AN UP AND COMING STAR...
URK...
Mm-hmm...
AND MOST OF ALL ...
HE'S THE VOICE OF AKANE.
THAT'S SOME SERIOUS ARSENAL HE'S GOT, HUH...?
GROAN...
Mm-hmm...
IT'S CLEAR ...
CLATTER
THAT HE CAN'T BE RULED OUT AS A THREAT, SO I THINK WE NEED TO KEEP AN EYE ON HIM.
THEREFORE...
WE WILL SET UP A PRIVATE INVESTIGATION TEAM!
BOOM
AGREED !!

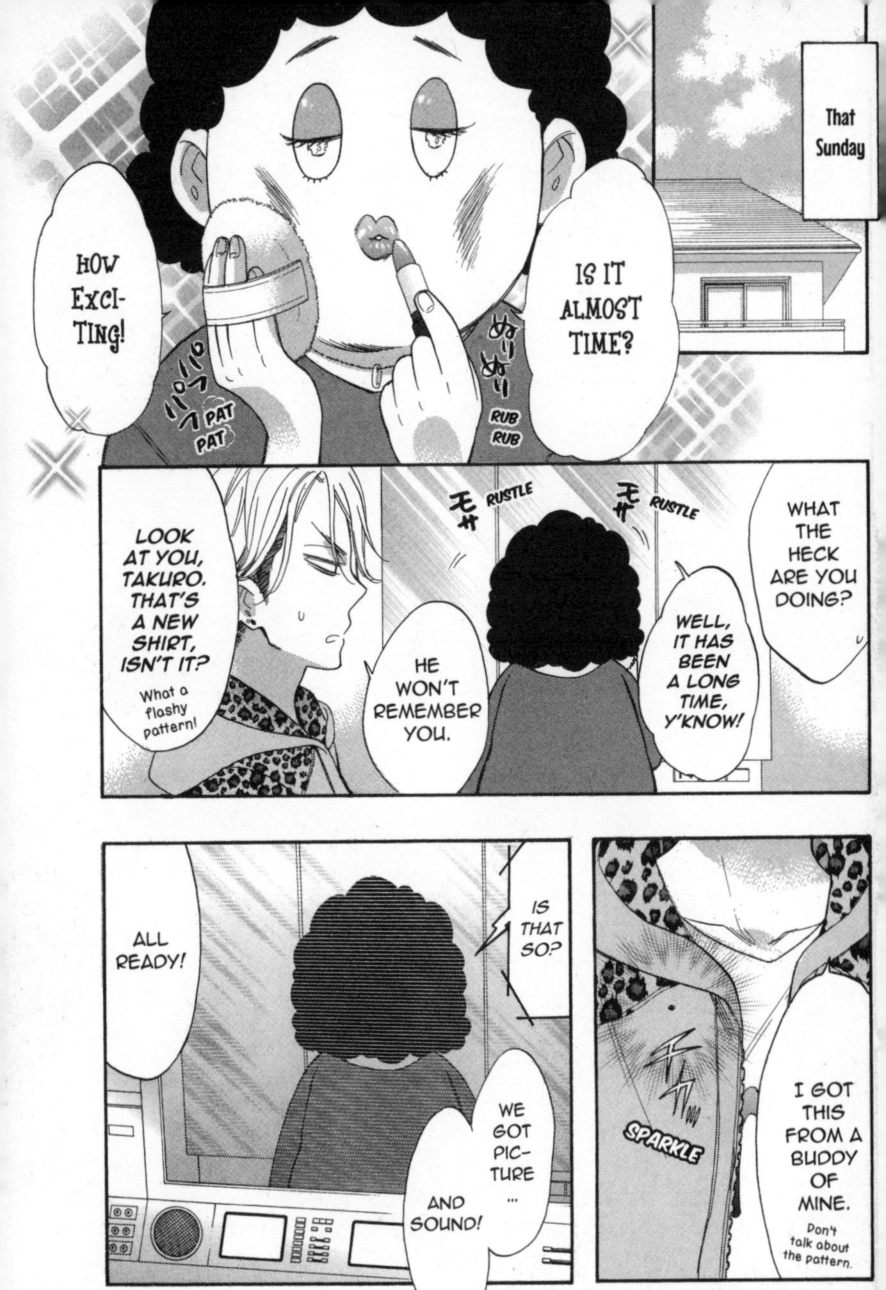
That Sunday
IS IT ALMOST TIME?
RUB RUB
PAT PAT
HOW EXCI-TING!
WHAT THE HECK ARE YOU DOING?
RUSTLE
RUSTLE
WELL, IT HAS BEEN A LONG TIME, Y'KNOW!
HE WON'T REMEMBER YOU.
LOOK AT YOU, TAKURO. THAT'S A NEW SHIRT, ISN'T IT?
What a flashy pattern!
SPARKLE
I GOT THIS FROM A BUDDY OF MINE.
Don't talk about the pattern.
IS THAT SO?
ALL READY!
WE GOT PIC-TURE...
AND SOUND!

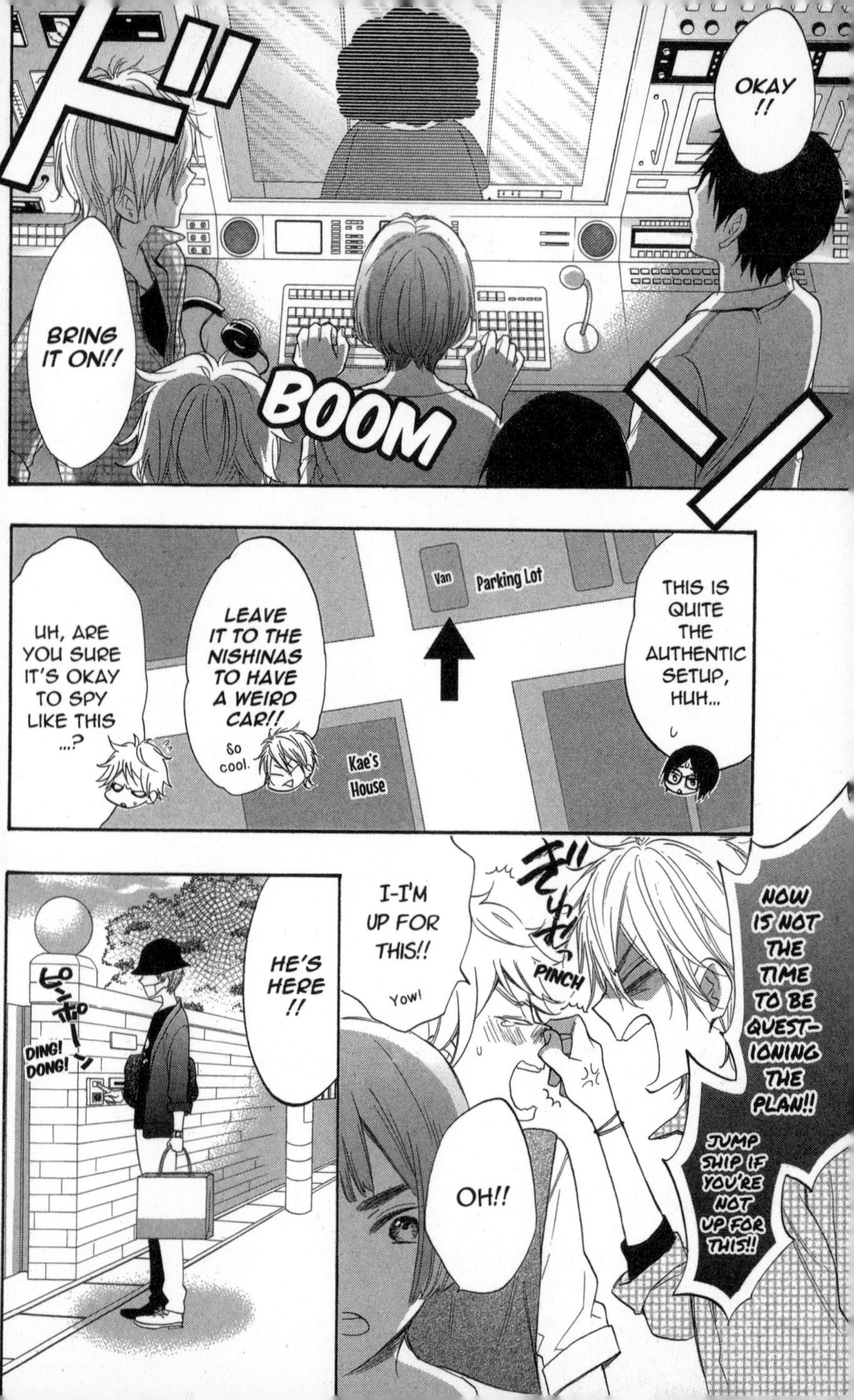
OKAY!!
BRING IT ON!!
BOOM
THIS IS QUITE THE AUTHENTIC SETUP, HUH...
Van
Parking Lot
Kae's House
LEAVE IT TO THE NISHINAS TO HAVE A WEIRD CAR!!
So cool.
UH, ARE YOU SURE IT'S OKAY TO SPY LIKE THIS ...?
NOW IS NOT THE TIME TO BE QUESTIONING THE PLAN!!
JUMP SHIP IF YOU'RE NOT UP FOR THIS!!
PINCH
I-I'M UP FOR THIS!!
Yow!
OH!!
HE'S HERE!!
DING! DONG!

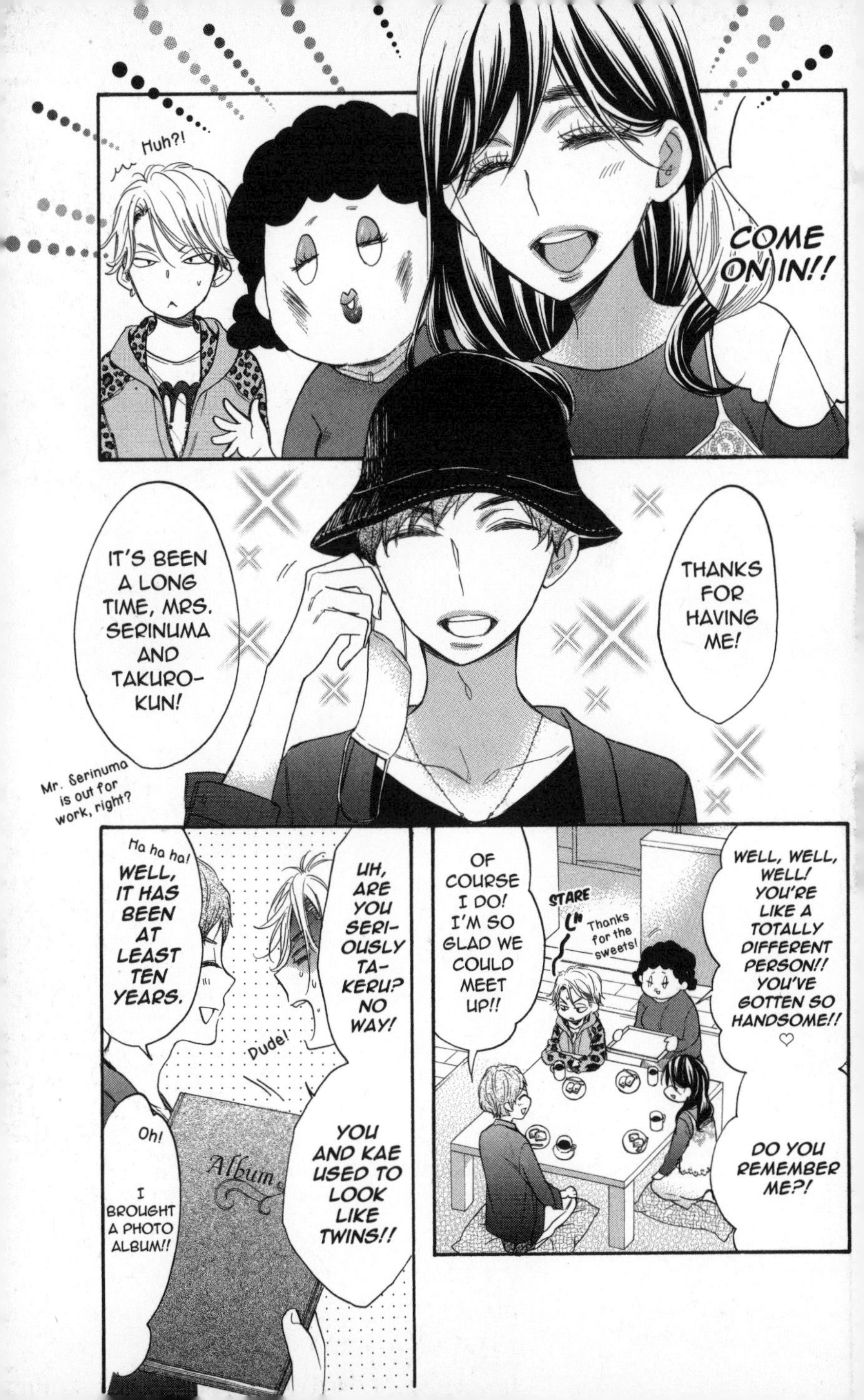
COME ON IN!!
Huh?!
THANKS FOR HAVING ME!
IT'S BEEN A LONG TIME, MRS. SERINUMA AND TAKURO-KUN!
Mr. Serinuma is out for work, right?
WELL, WELL, WELL! YOU'RE LIKE A TOTALLY DIFFERENT PERSON!! YOU'VE GOTTEN SO HANDSOME!! ♡
DO YOU REMEMBER ME?!
OF COURSE I DO! I'M SO GLAD WE COULD MEET UP!!
STARE
Thanks for the sweets!
UH, ARE YOU SERIOUSLY TAKERU? NO WAY!
Ha ha ha! WELL, IT HAS BEEN AT LEAST TEN YEARS.
Dude!
YOU AND KAE USED TO LOOK LIKE TWINS!!
Oh! I BROUGHT A PHOTO ALBUM!!
Album

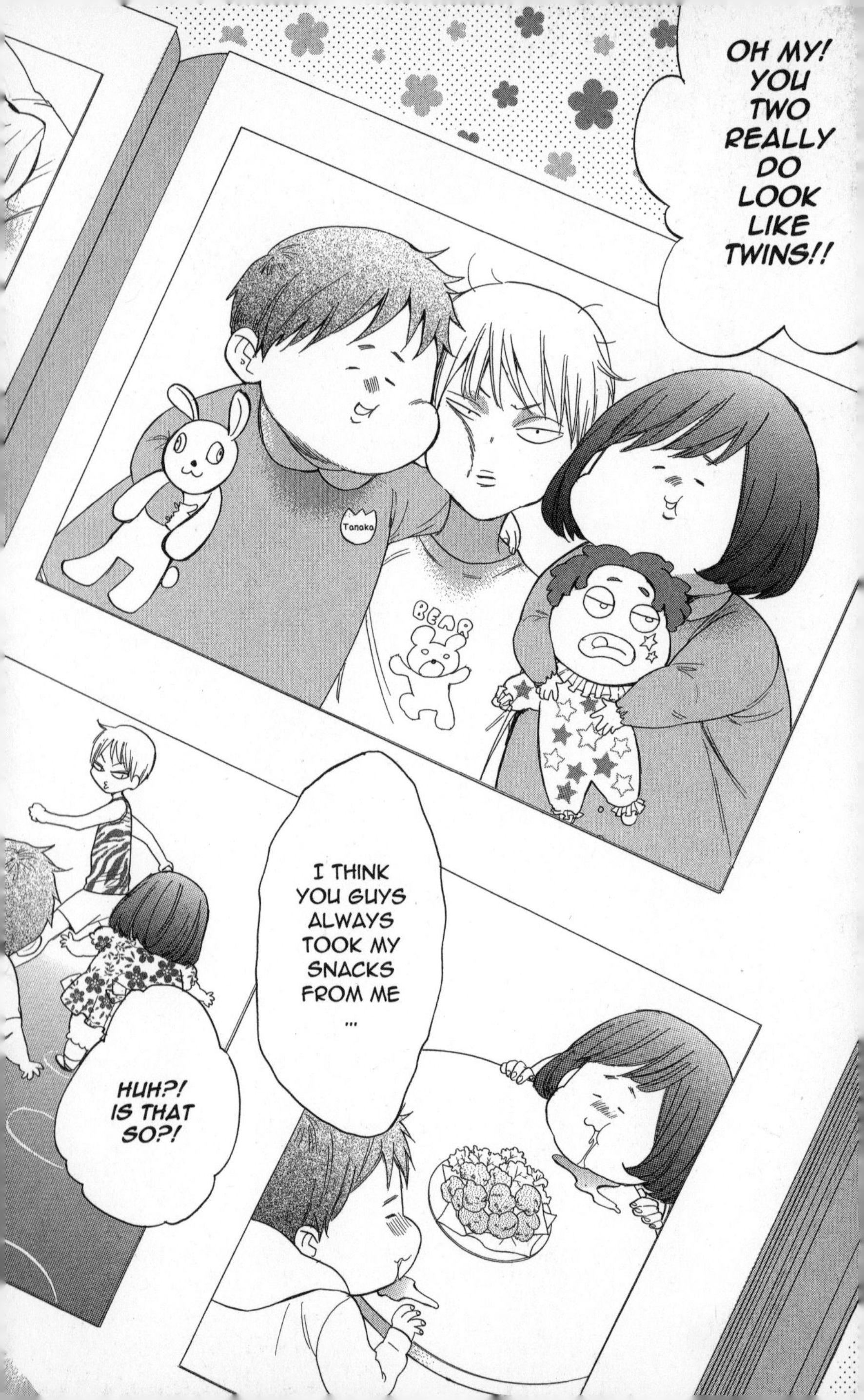
OH MY! YOU TWO REALLY DO LOOK LIKE TWINS!!
Tanaka
BEAR
I THINK YOU GUYS ALWAYS TOOK MY SNACKS FROM ME ...
HUH?! IS THAT SO?!

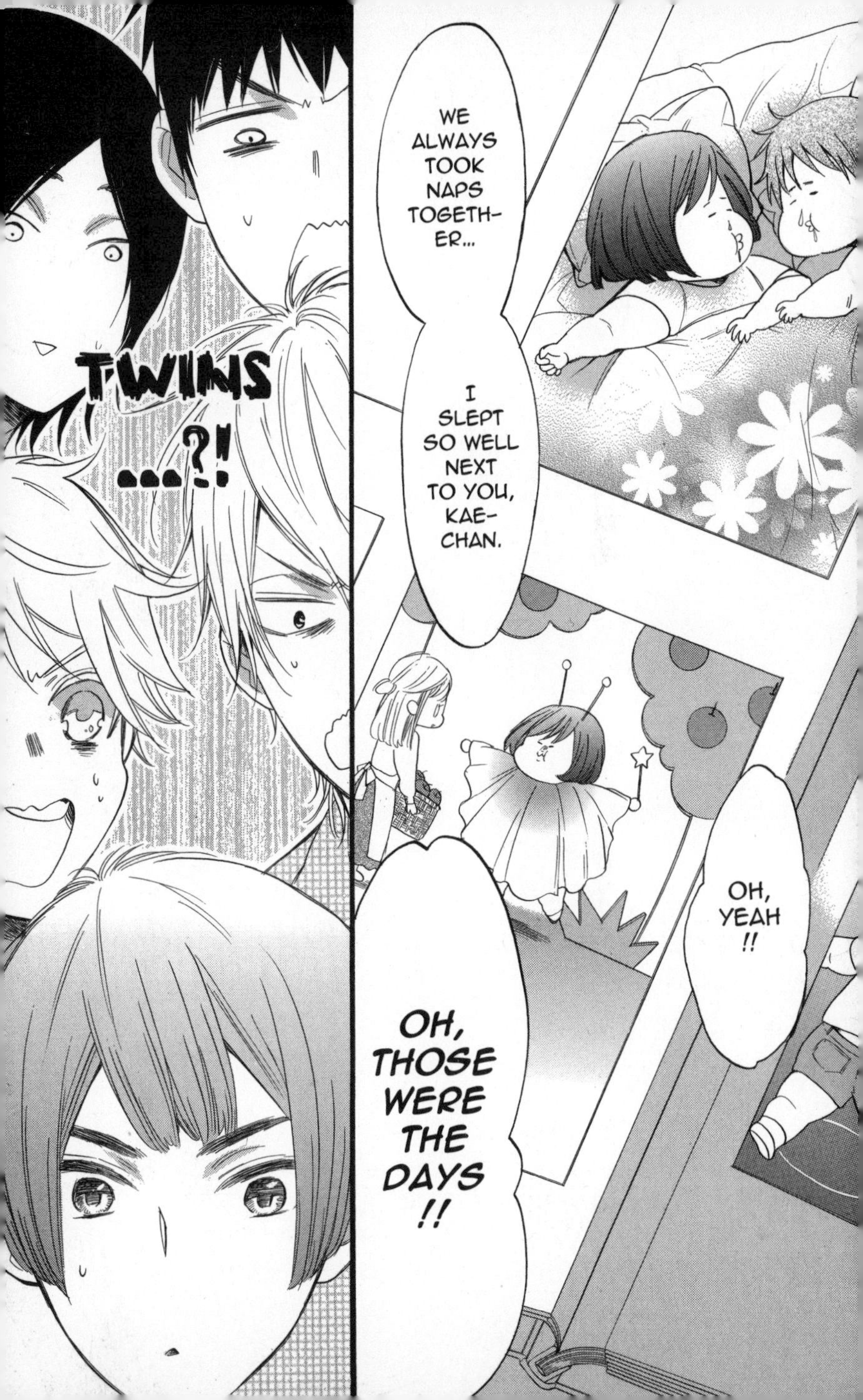
WE ALWAYS TOOK NAPS TOGETH-ER...
I SLEPT SO WELL NEXT TO YOU, KAE-CHAN.
OH, YEAH !!
OH, THOSE WERE THE DAYS !!
TWINS ...?!

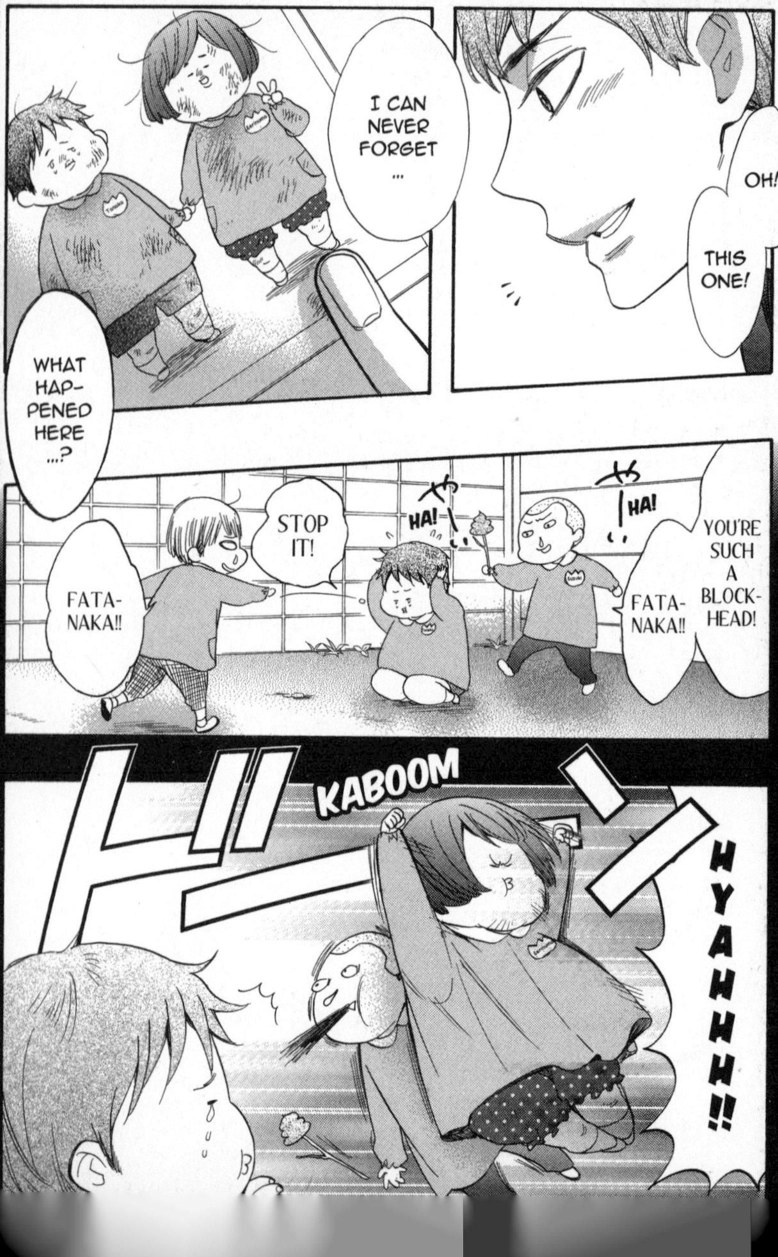
OH!
THIS ONE!
I CAN NEVER FORGET ...
WHAT HAPPENED HERE ...?
YOU'RE SUCH A BLOCKHEAD!
FATA-NAKA!!
HA!
HA!
STOP IT!
FATA-NAKA!!
KABOOM
HYAHHHH!!

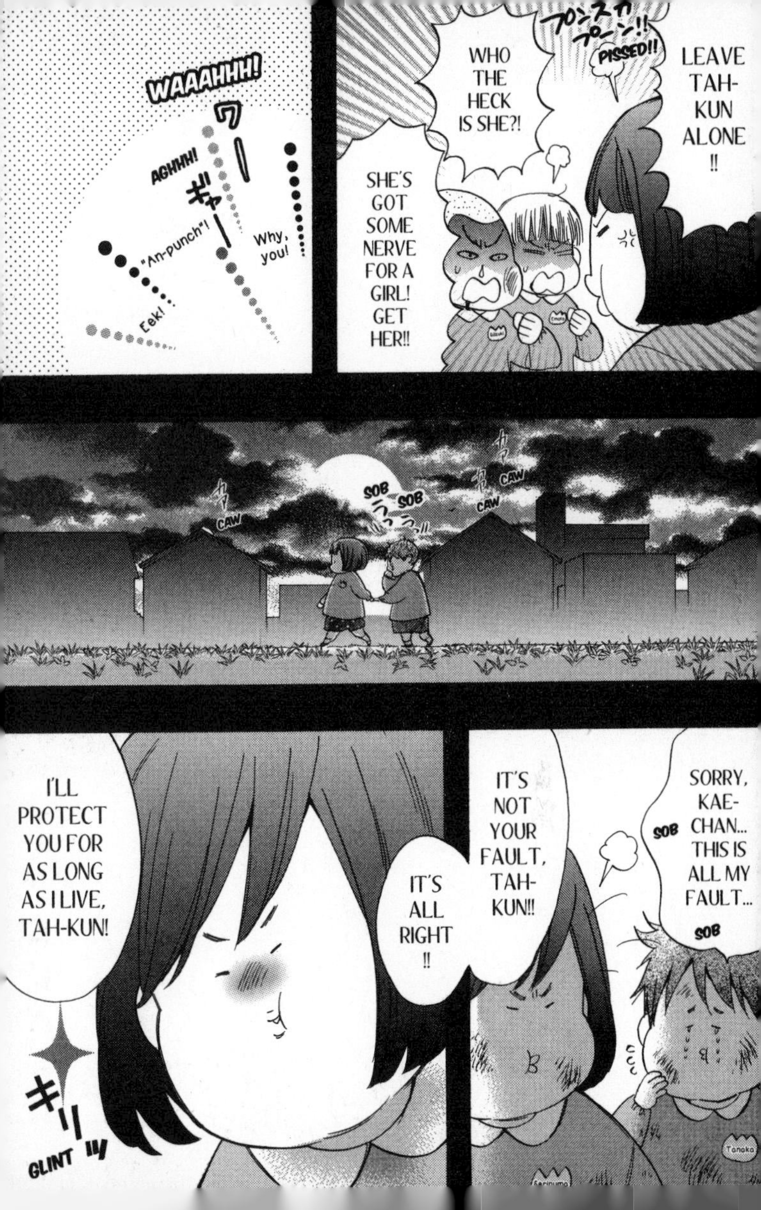
LEAVE TAH-KUN ALONE!!
プンスカプーン!!
PISSED!!
WHO THE HECK IS SHE?!
SHE'S GOT SOME NERVE FOR A GIRL! GET HER!!
WAAAHHH!
ワー
AGHHH!
ギャー
"An-punch"!
Why, you!
Eek!
CAW
CAW
SOB
SOB
CAW
SORRY, KAE-CHAN... THIS IS ALL MY FAULT...
SOB
SOB
IT'S NOT YOUR FAULT, TAH-KUN!!
IT'S ALL RIGHT!!
I'LL PROTECT YOU FOR AS LONG AS I LIVE, TAH-KUN!
GLINT

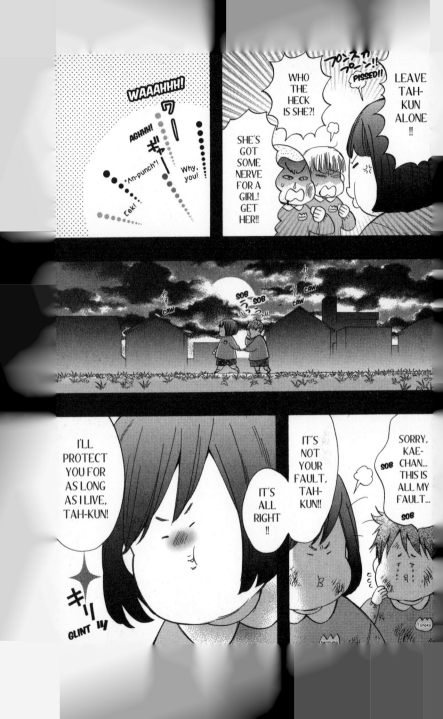

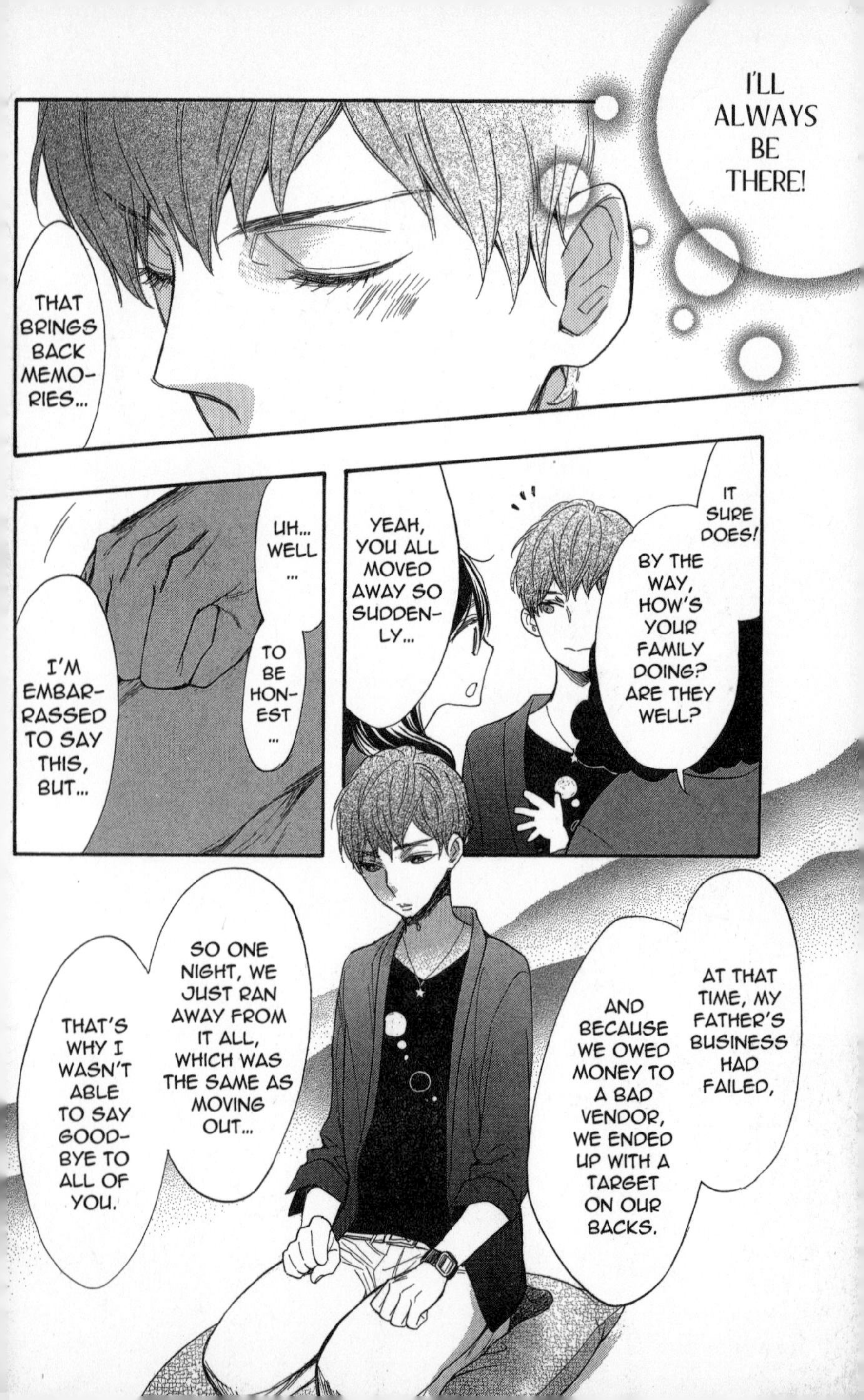
I'LL ALWAYS BE THERE!
THAT BRINGS BACK MEMORIES...
IT SURE DOES!
BY THE WAY, HOW'S YOUR FAMILY DOING? ARE THEY WELL?
YEAH, YOU ALL MOVED AWAY SO SUDDENLY...
UH... WELL...
TO BE HONEST...
I'M EMBARRASSED TO SAY THIS, BUT...
AT THAT TIME, MY FATHER'S BUSINESS HAD FAILED,
AND BECAUSE WE OWED MONEY TO A BAD VENDOR, WE ENDED UP WITH A TARGET ON OUR BACKS.
SO ONE NIGHT, WE JUST RAN AWAY FROM IT ALL, WHICH WAS THE SAME AS MOVING OUT...
THAT'S WHY I WASN'T ABLE TO SAY GOODBYE TO ALL OF YOU.

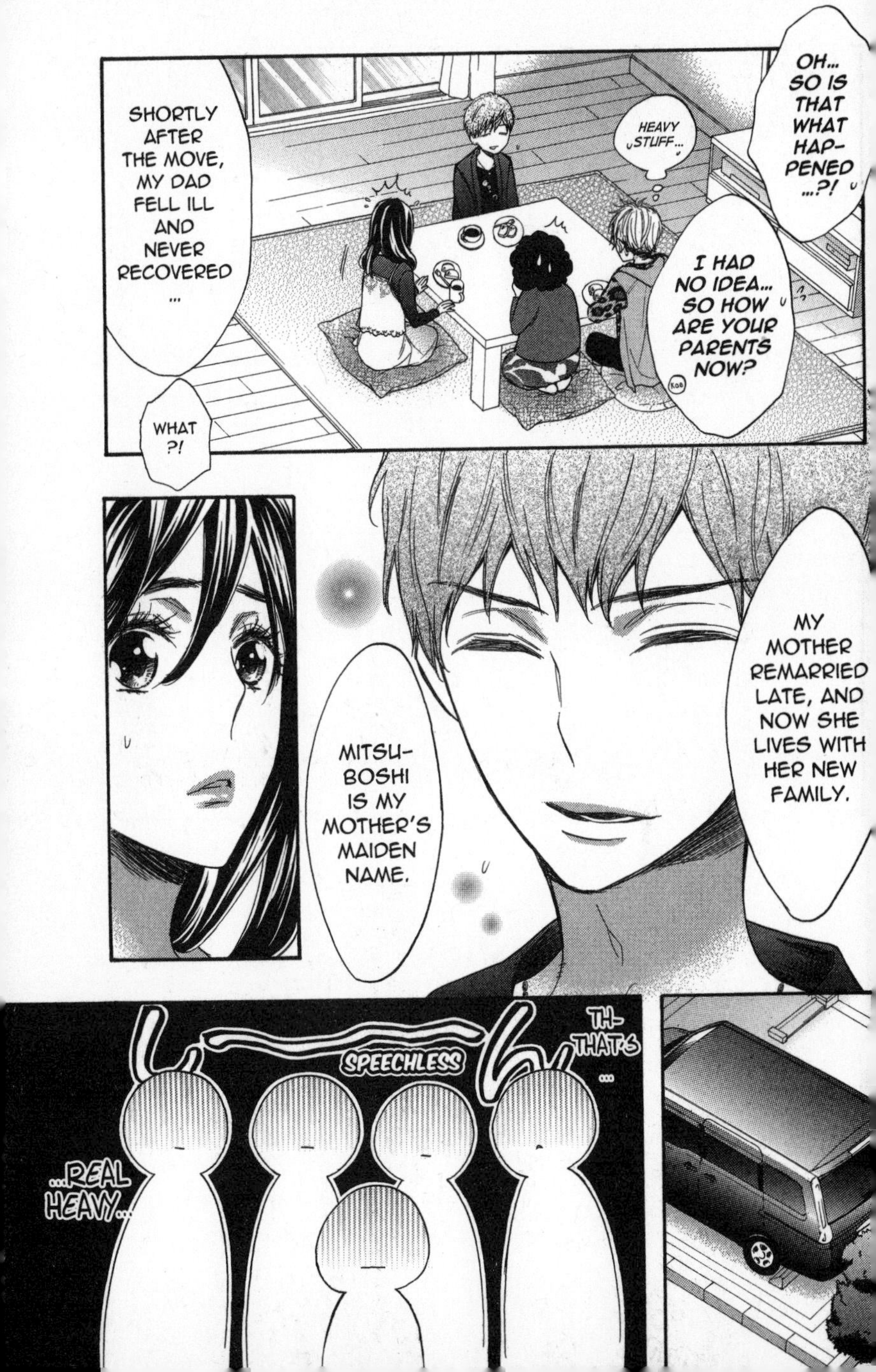
OH... SO IS THAT WHAT HAPPENED ...?!
HEAVY STUFF...
I HAD NO IDEA... SO HOW ARE YOUR PARENTS NOW?
SHORTLY AFTER THE MOVE, MY DAD FELL ILL AND NEVER RECOVERED ...
WHAT ?!
MY MOTHER REMARRIED LATE, AND NOW SHE LIVES WITH HER NEW FAMILY.
MITSU-BOSHI IS MY MOTHER'S MAIDEN NAME.
TH-THAT'S ...
SPEECHLESS
...REAL HEAVY...

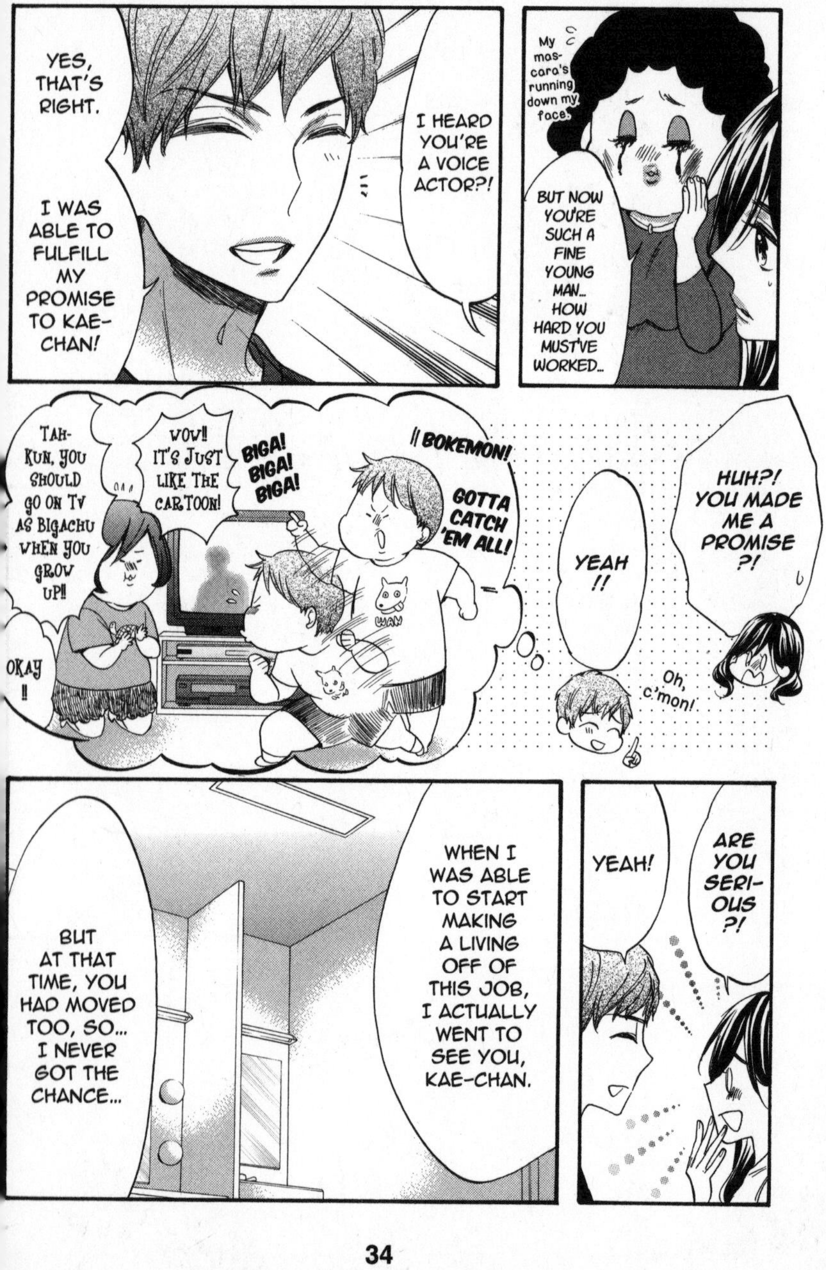
My mas-cara's running down my face.
BUT NOW YOU'RE SUCH A FINE YOUNG MAN... HOW HARD YOU MUST'VE WORKED...
I HEARD YOU'RE A VOICE ACTOR?!
YES, THAT'S RIGHT.
I WAS ABLE TO FULFILL MY PROMISE TO KAE-CHAN!
HUH?! YOU MADE ME A PROMISE?!
YEAH!!
Oh, c'mon!
BOKEMON!
GOTTA CATCH 'EM ALL!
BIGA! BIGA! BIGA!
WOW!! IT'S JUST LIKE THE CARTOON!
TAH-KUN, YOU SHOULD GO ON TV AS BIGACHU WHEN YOU GROW UP!!
OKAY!!
ARE YOU SERI-OUS?!
YEAH!
WHEN I WAS ABLE TO START MAKING A LIVING OFF OF THIS JOB, I ACTUALLY WENT TO SEE YOU, KAE-CHAN.
BUT AT THAT TIME, YOU HAD MOVED TOO, SO... I NEVER GOT THE CHANCE...

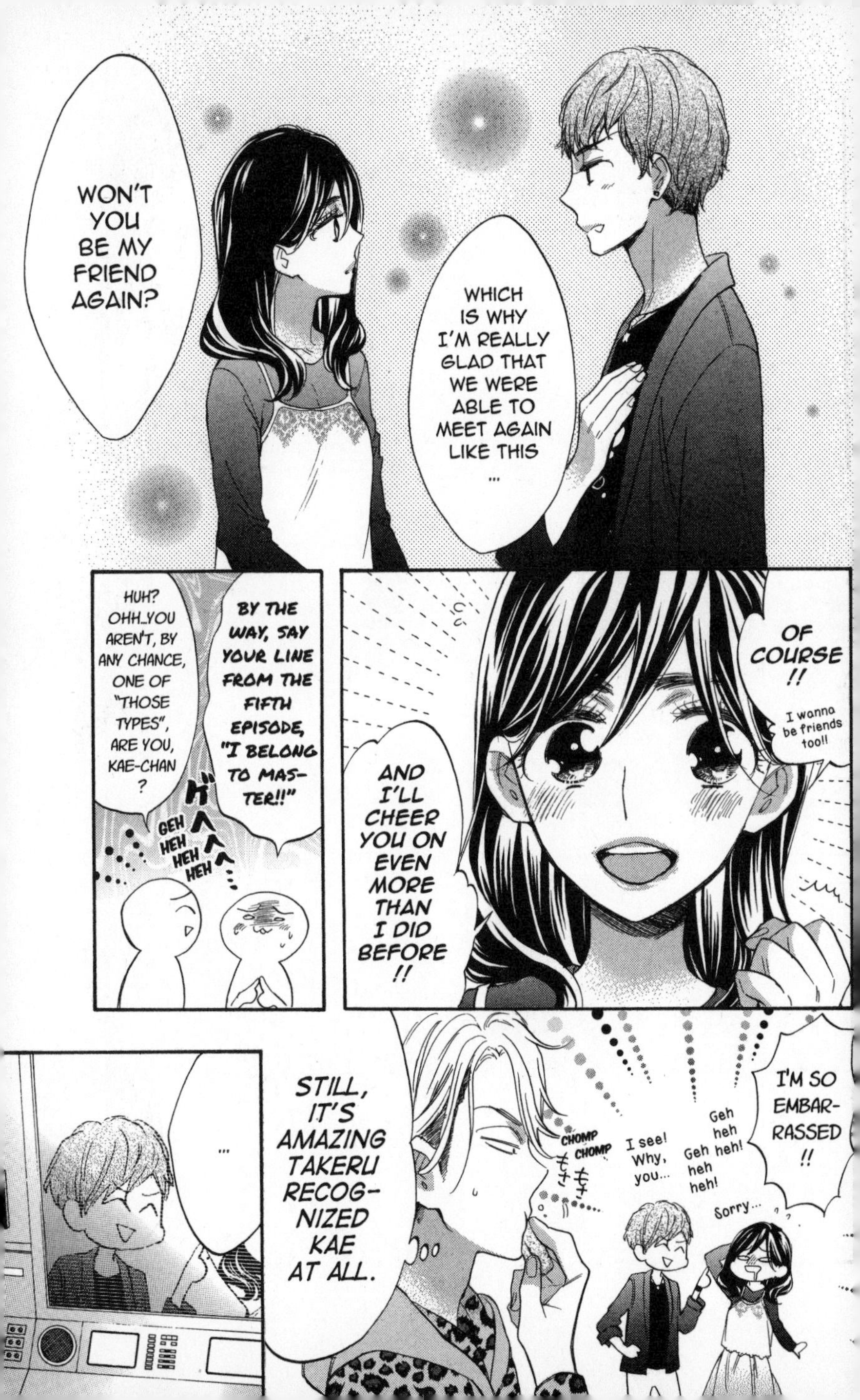
WHICH IS WHY I'M REALLY GLAD THAT WE WERE ABLE TO MEET AGAIN LIKE THIS ...
WON'T YOU BE MY FRIEND AGAIN?
OF COURSE!!
I wanna be friends too!!
AND I'LL CHEER YOU ON EVEN MORE THAN I DID BEFORE!!
BY THE WAY, SAY YOUR LINE FROM THE FIFTH EPISODE, "I BELONG TO MASTER!!"
HUH? OHH...YOU AREN'T, BY ANY CHANCE, ONE OF "THOSE TYPES", ARE YOU, KAE-CHAN?
GEH HEH HEH HEH
I'M SO EMBARRASSED!!
Geh heh Geh heh heh! heh heh!
I see! Why, you...
Sorry...
CHOMP CHOMP
STILL, IT'S AMAZING TAKERU RECOGNIZED KAE AT ALL.
...

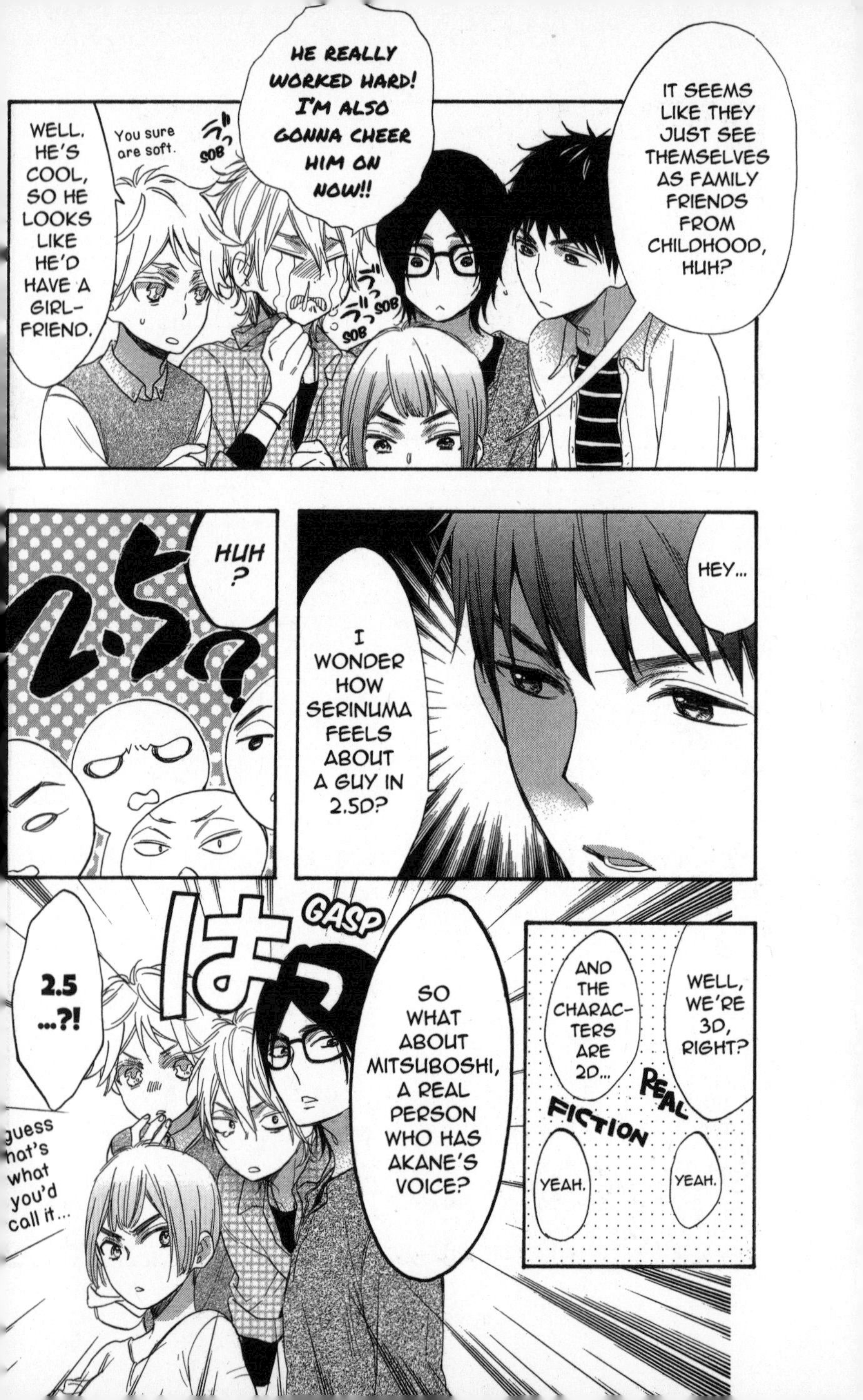
IT SEEMS LIKE THEY JUST SEE THEMSELVES AS FAMILY FRIENDS FROM CHILDHOOD, HUH?
HE REALLY WORKED HARD! I'M ALSO GONNA CHEER HIM ON NOW!!
SOB
SOB
SOB
You sure are soft.
WELL. HE'S COOL, SO HE LOOKS LIKE HE'D HAVE A GIRL- FRIEND.
HEY...
I WONDER HOW SERINUMA FEELS ABOUT A GUY IN 2.5D?
HUH?
2.5?
WELL, WE'RE 3D, RIGHT?
AND THE CHARAC- TERS ARE 2D...
REAL
FICTION
YEAH.
YEAH.
SO WHAT ABOUT MITSUBOSHI, A REAL PERSON WHO HAS AKANE'S VOICE?
GASP
はっ
2.5 ...?!
guess hat's what you'd call it...

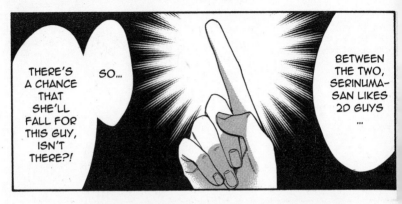

BETWEEN THE TWO, SERINUMA-SAN LIKES 2D GUYS ...
SO...
THERE'S A CHANCE THAT SHE'LL FALL FOR THIS GUY, ISN'T THERE?!
...
...OH...
WELL, I MEAN, HE'S A POPULAR VOICE ACTOR, RIGHT?! THEY COME FROM DIFFERENT WORLDS.
EVEN IF SHE LIKES HIM, HE'S STILL A CELEBRITY, Y'KNOW!
THAT'S RIGHT!
IT'S NOT LIKE THEY'LL SEE EACH OTHER EVERY DAY LIKE WE DO AT SCHOOL!
No way!
AND SENPAI AND I BOTH MAINLY LIKE THE CHARACTERS, NOT THEIR VOICE ACTORS!
SENPAI IS FOR SURE INTO 2D GUYS!
AND THAT SHOULD MAKE US HAPPY?!!

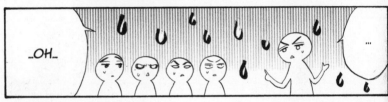

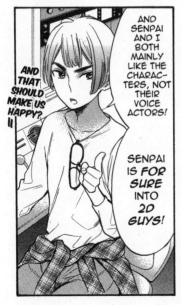

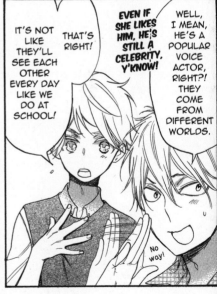

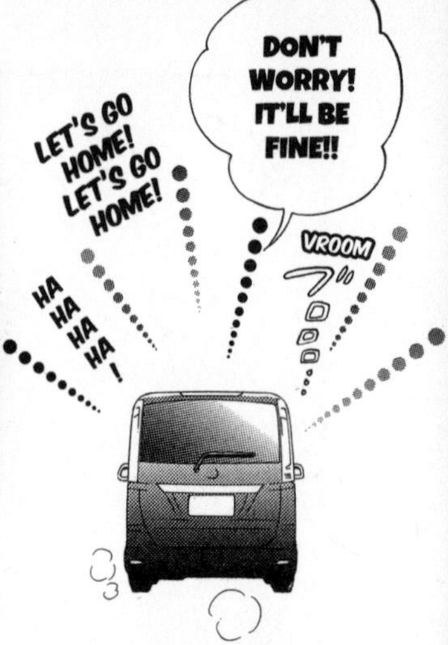
DON'T WORRY! IT'LL BE FINE!!
VROOM
LET'S GO HOME! LET'S GO HOME!
HA HA HA HA!
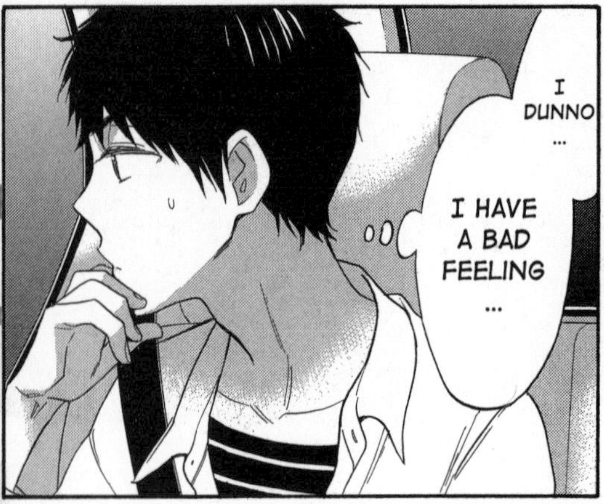
I DUNNO ...
I HAVE A BAD FEELING ...
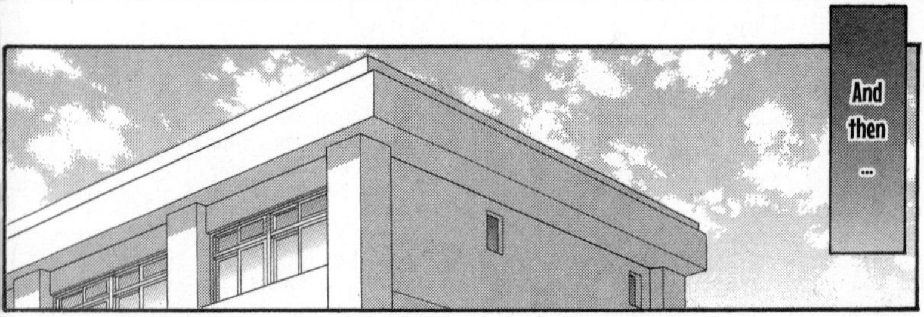
And then ...
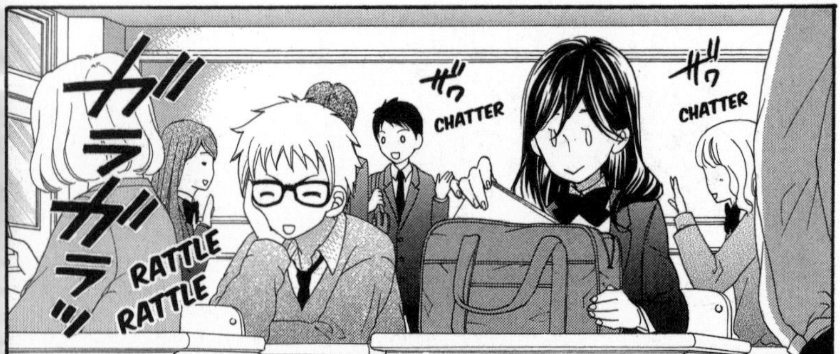
CHATTER
CHATTER
RATTLE RATTLE

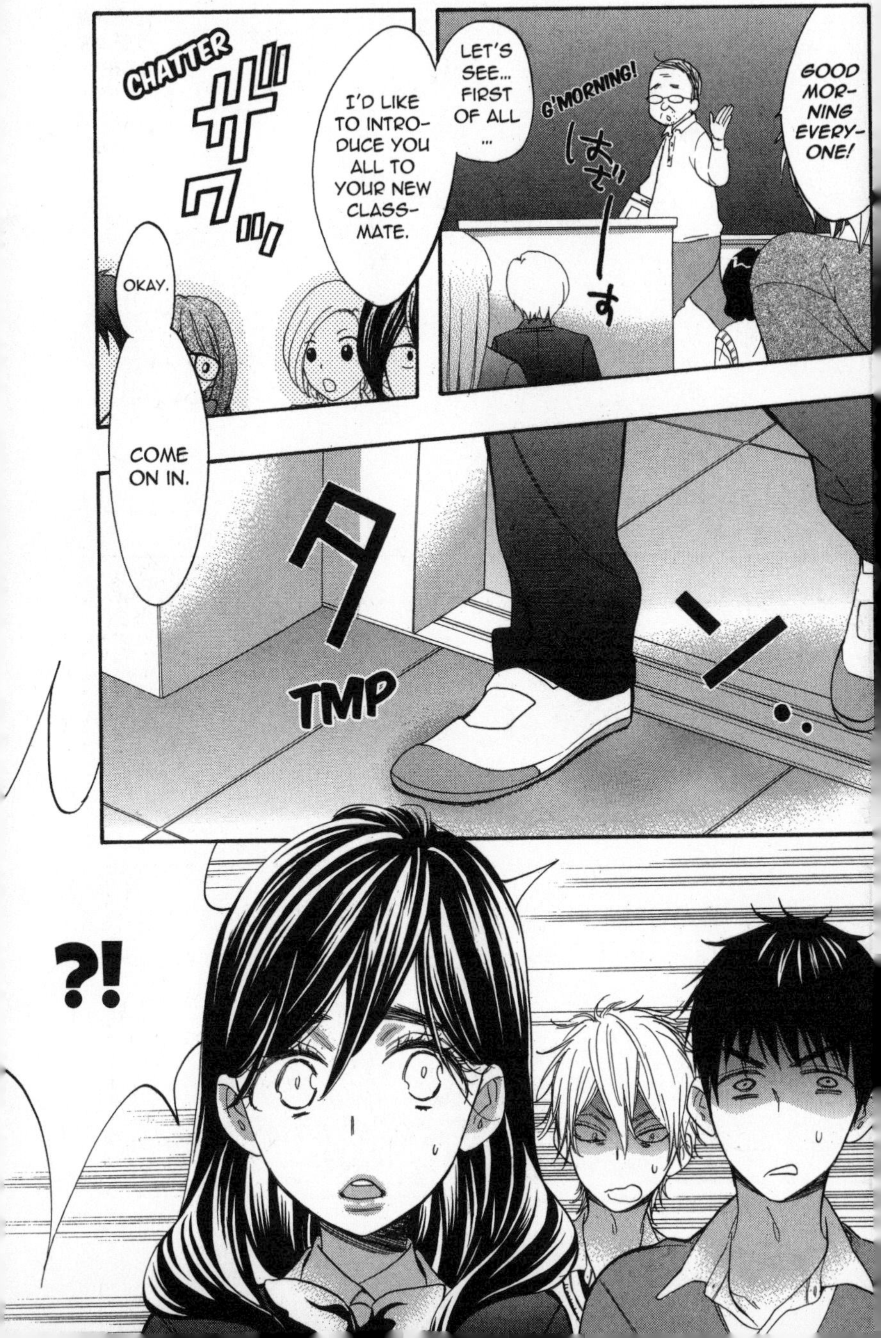
GOOD MORNING EVERYONE!
G'MORNING!
LET'S SEE... FIRST OF ALL ...
I'D LIKE TO INTRODUCE YOU ALL TO YOUR NEW CLASSMATE.
CHATTER
OKAY.
COME ON IN.
TMP
?!

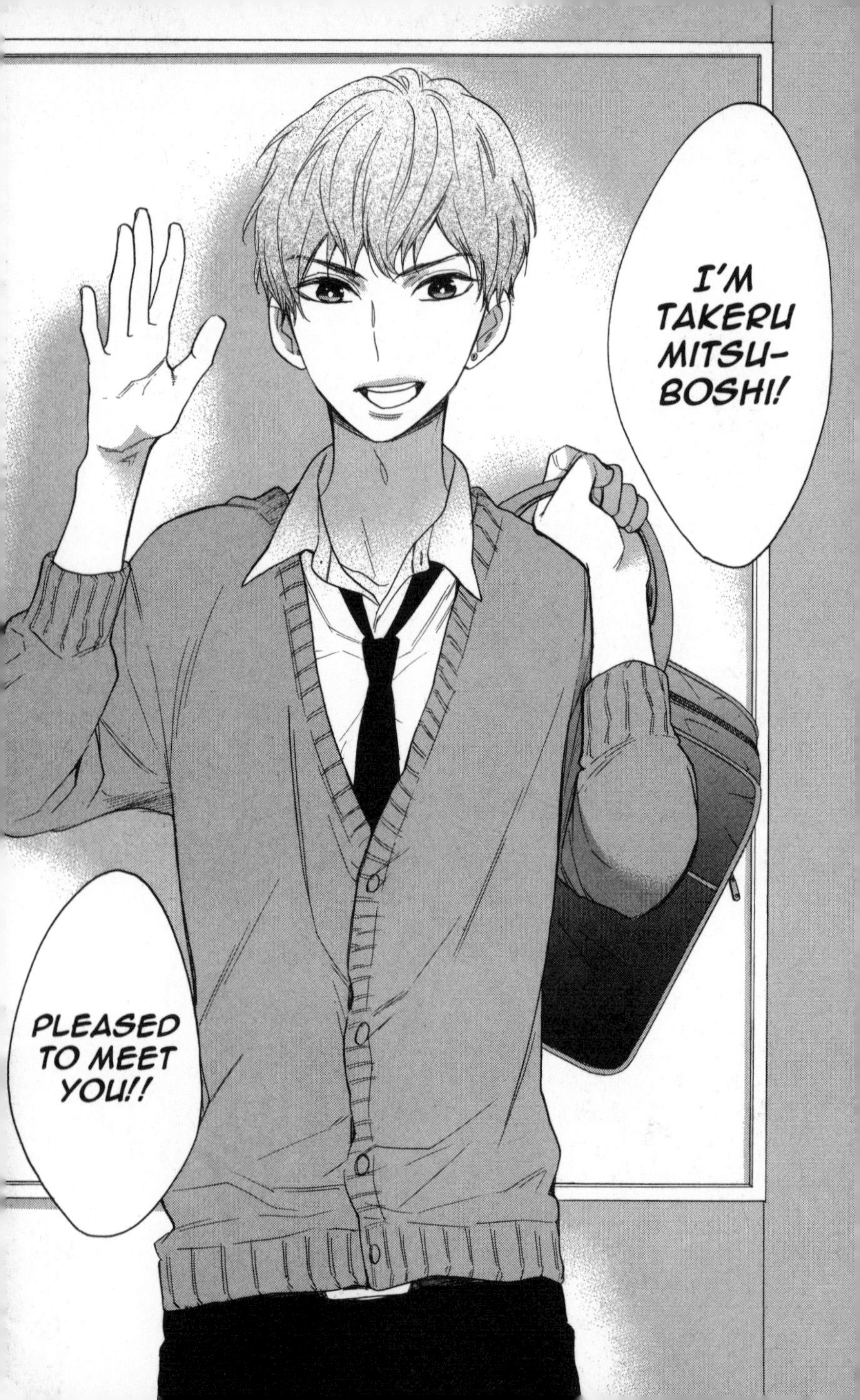
I'M TAKERU MITSU-BOSHI!
PLEASED TO MEET YOU!!

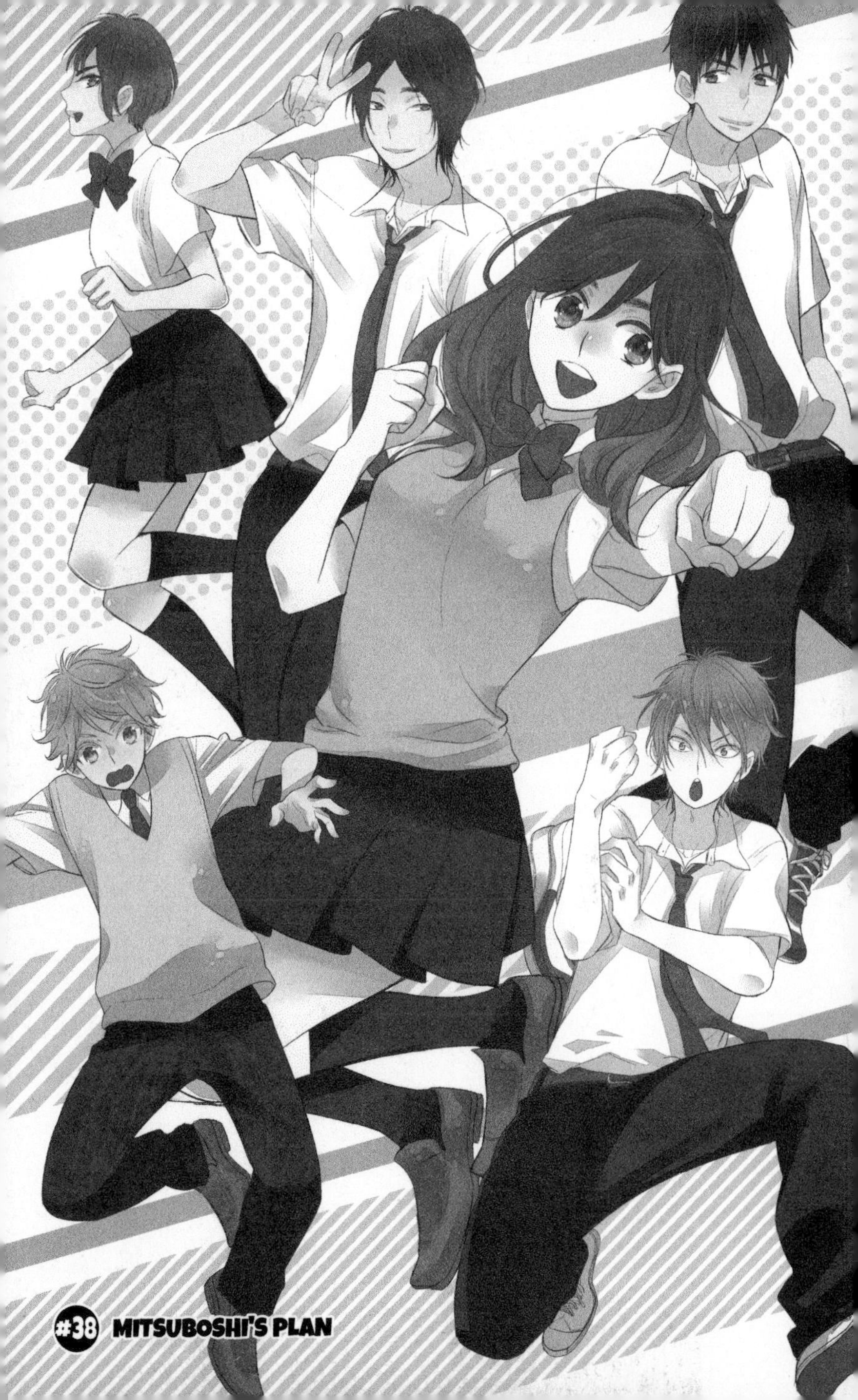

#38 MITSUBOSHI'S PLAN

KiSS HiM, NOT ME!

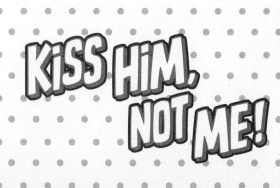

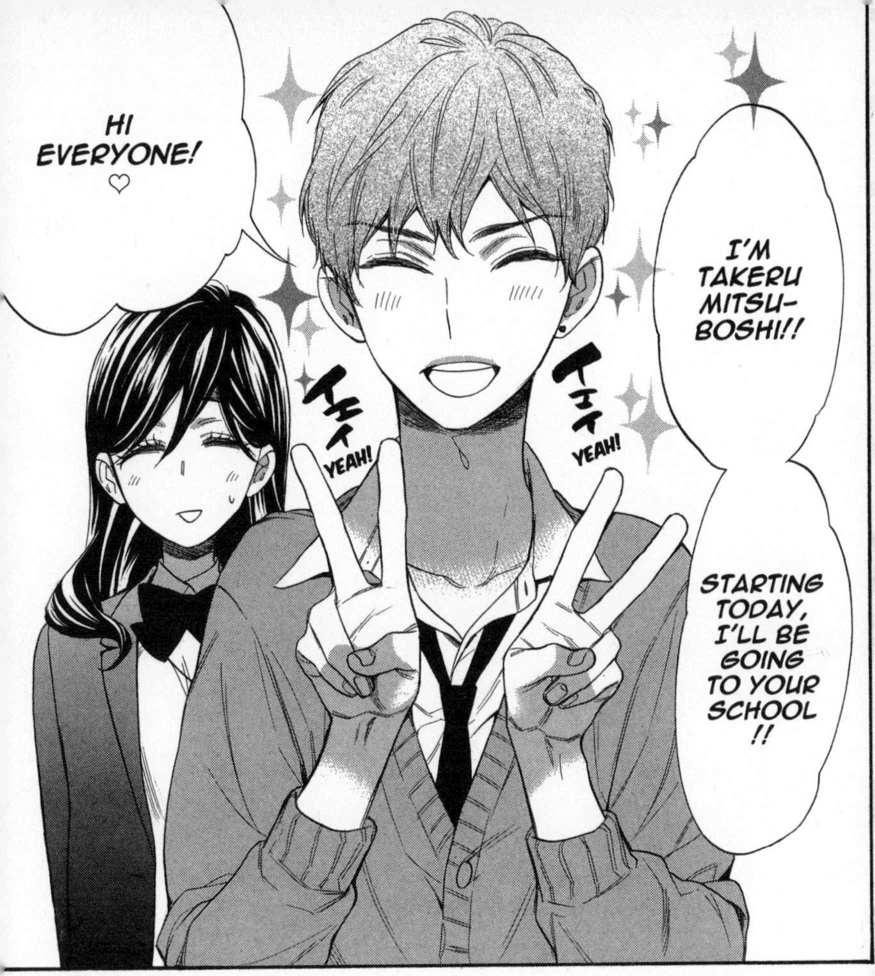
I'M TAKERU MITSU-BOSHI!!
STARTING TODAY, I'LL BE GOING TO YOUR SCHOOL !!
イェイ YEAH!
イェイ YEAH!
HI EVERYONE! ♡

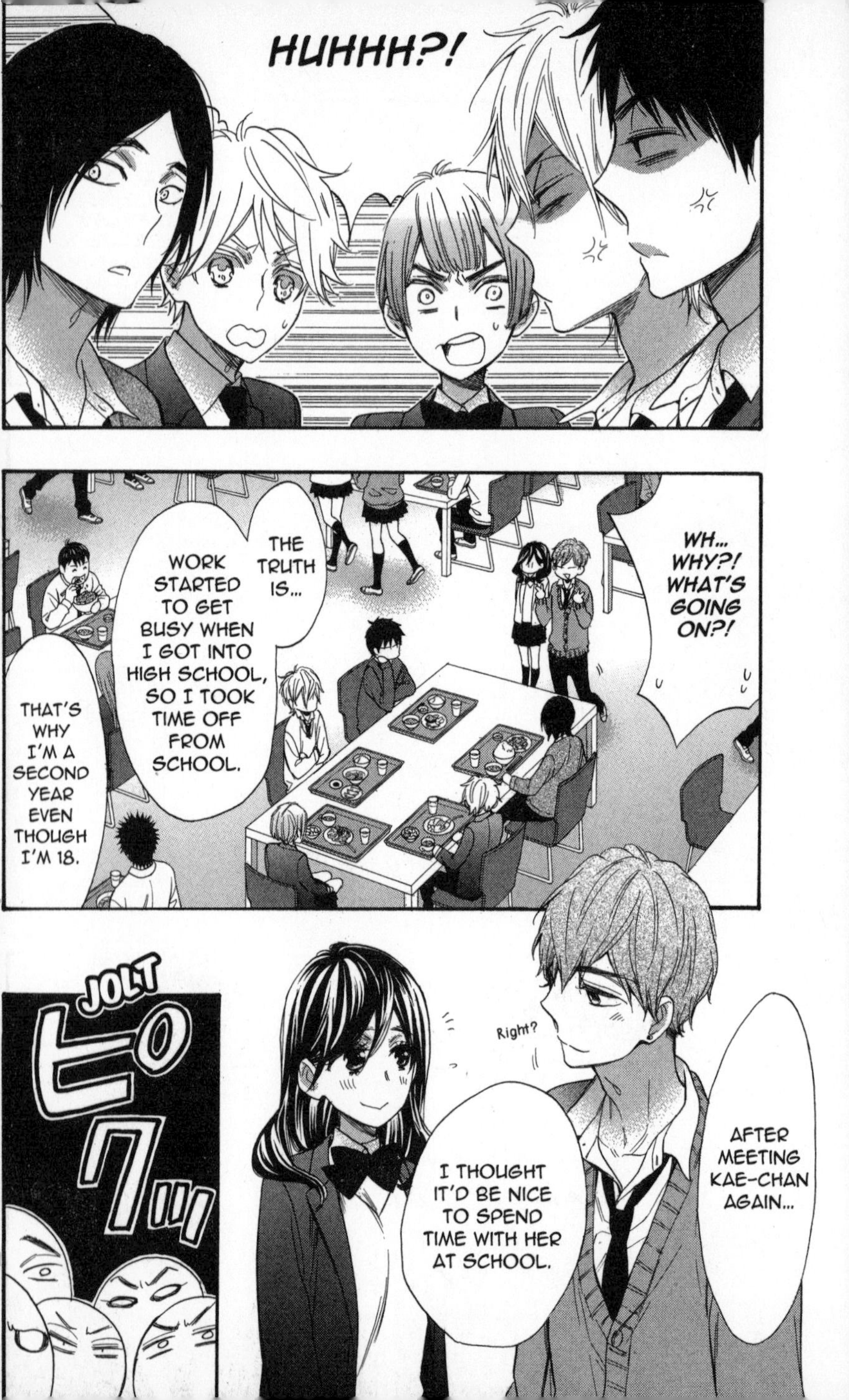
HUHHH?!
WH... WHY?! WHAT'S GOING ON?!
THE TRUTH IS...
WORK STARTED TO GET BUSY WHEN I GOT INTO HIGH SCHOOL, SO I TOOK TIME OFF FROM SCHOOL.
THAT'S WHY I'M A SECOND YEAR EVEN THOUGH I'M 18.
AFTER MEETING KAE-CHAN AGAIN...
I THOUGHT IT'D BE NICE TO SPEND TIME WITH HER AT SCHOOL.
Right?
JOLT
ビクッ

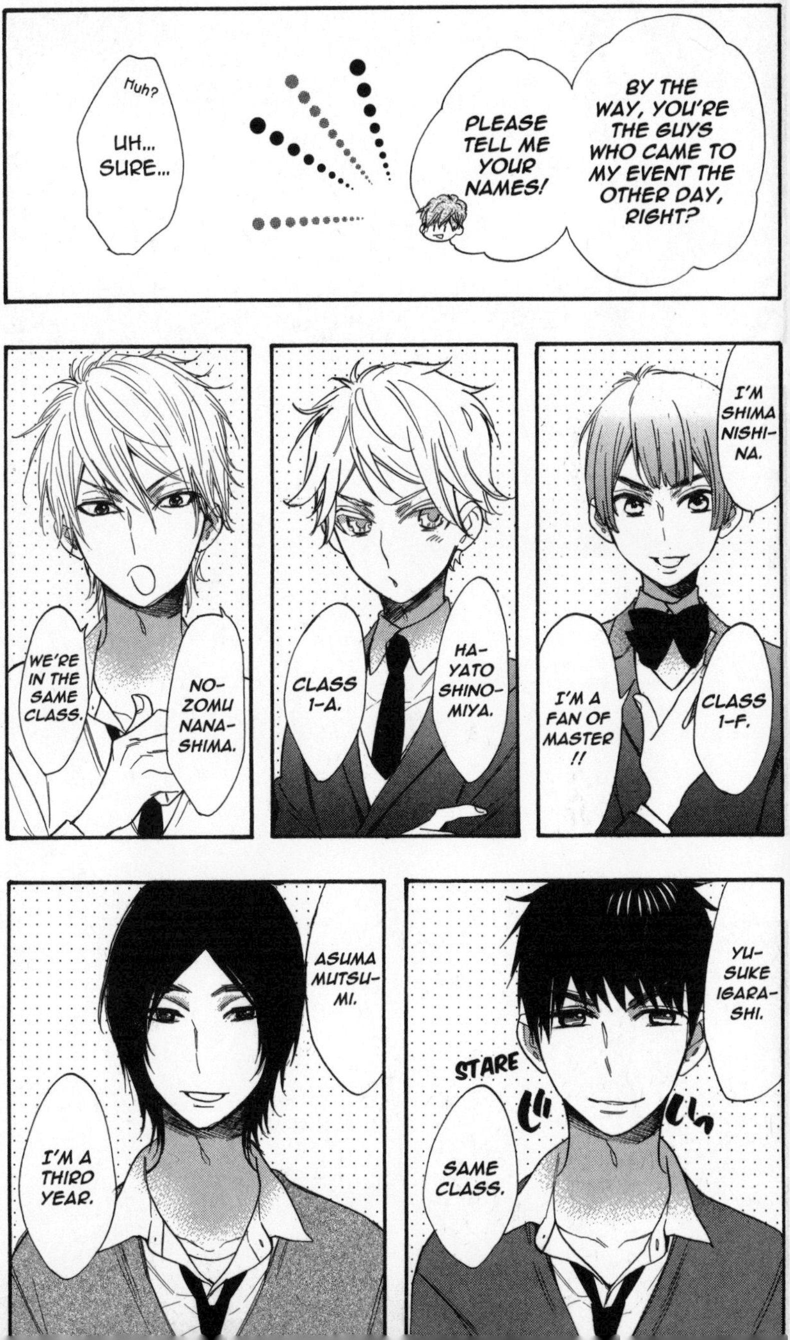
BY THE WAY, YOU'RE THE GUYS WHO CAME TO MY EVENT THE OTHER DAY, RIGHT?
PLEASE TELL ME YOUR NAMES!
Huh?
UH... SURE...
I'M SHIMA NISHI-NA.
CLASS 1-F.
I'M A FAN OF MASTER !!
HA-YATO SHINO-MIYA.
CLASS 1-A.
NO-ZOMU NANA-SHIMA.
WE'RE IN THE SAME CLASS.
YU-SUKE IGARA-SHI.
STARE
SAME CLASS.
ASUMA MUTSU-MI.
I'M A THIRD YEAR.

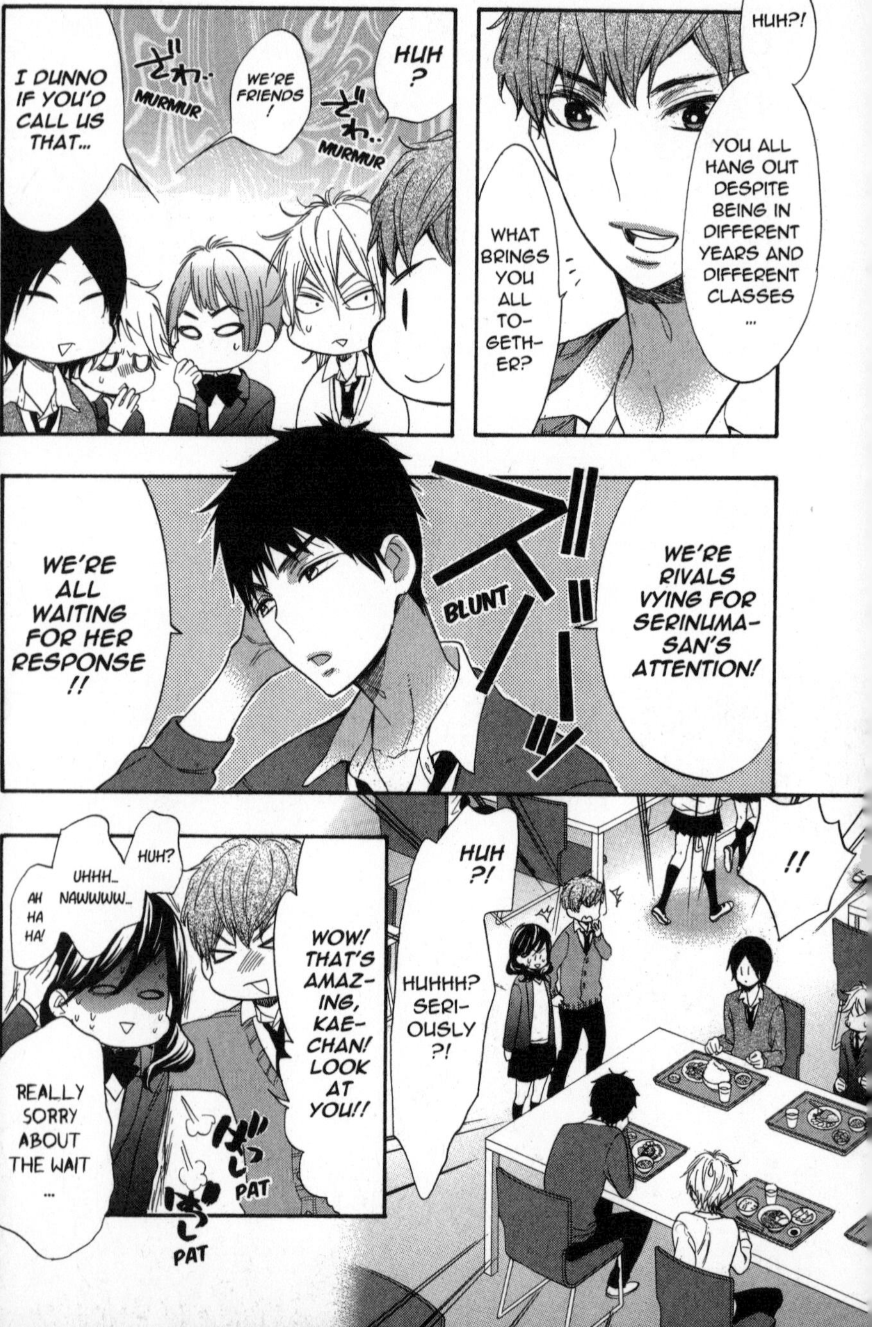
HUH?!
YOU ALL HANG OUT DESPITE BEING IN DIFFERENT YEARS AND DIFFERENT CLASSES ...
WHAT BRINGS YOU ALL TO-GETH-ER?
HUH ?
ざわ.. MURMUR
WE'RE FRIENDS !
ざわ.. MURMUR
I DUNNO IF YOU'D CALL US THAT...
WE'RE RIVALS VYING FOR SERINUMA-SAN'S ATTENTION!
BLUNT
WE'RE ALL WAITING FOR HER RESPONSE !!
!!
HUH ?!
HUHHH? SERI-OUSLY ?!
WOW! THAT'S AMAZ-ING, KAE-CHAN! LOOK AT YOU!!
HUH?
UHHH... NAWWWW...
AH HA HA!
REALLY SORRY ABOUT THE WAIT ...
ぱしっ PAT
ぱしっ PAT

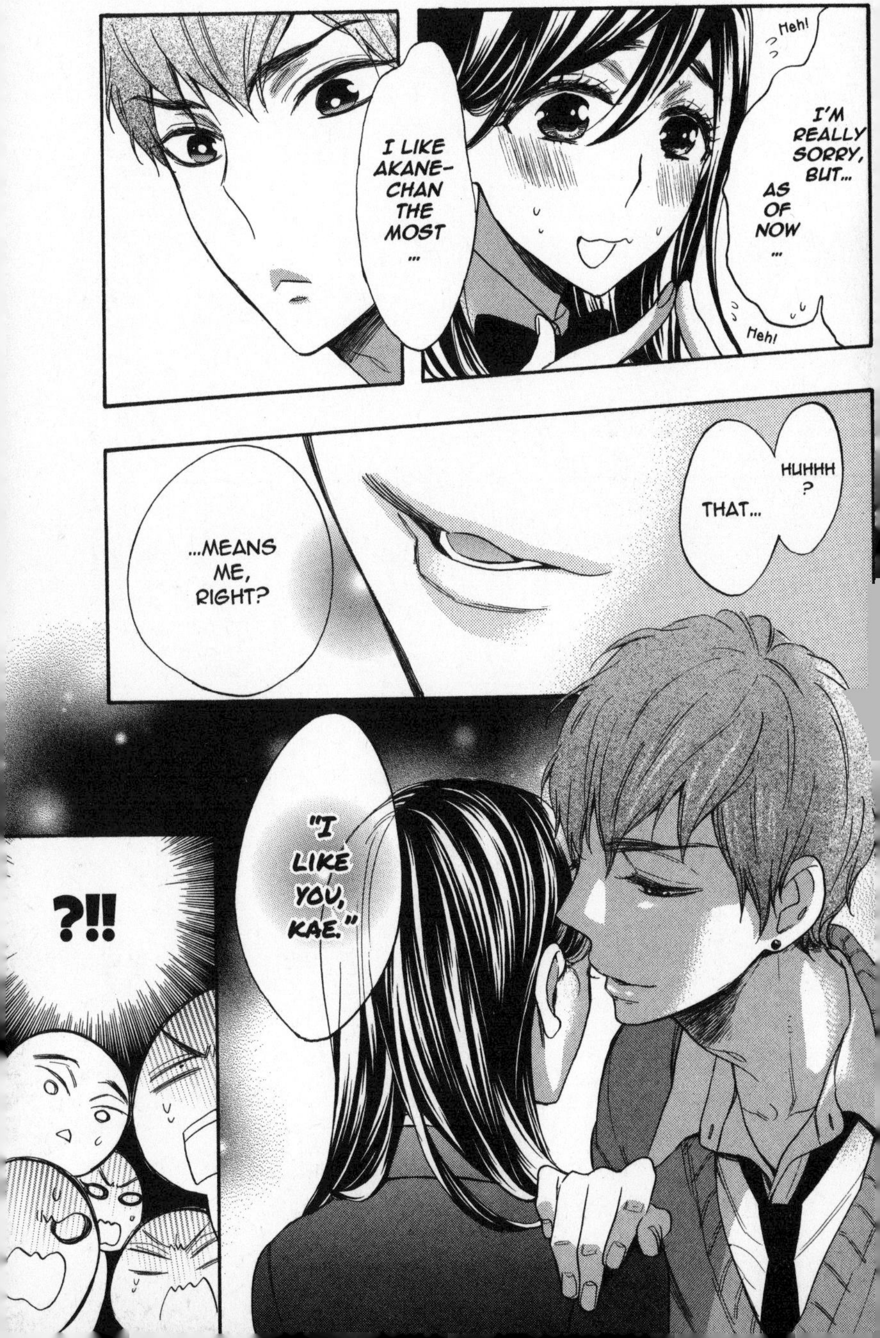

Heh!
I'M REALLY SORRY, BUT...
AS OF NOW...
Heh!
I LIKE AKANE-CHAN THE MOST...
HUHHH?
THAT...
...MEANS ME, RIGHT?
"I LIKE YOU, KAE."
?!!

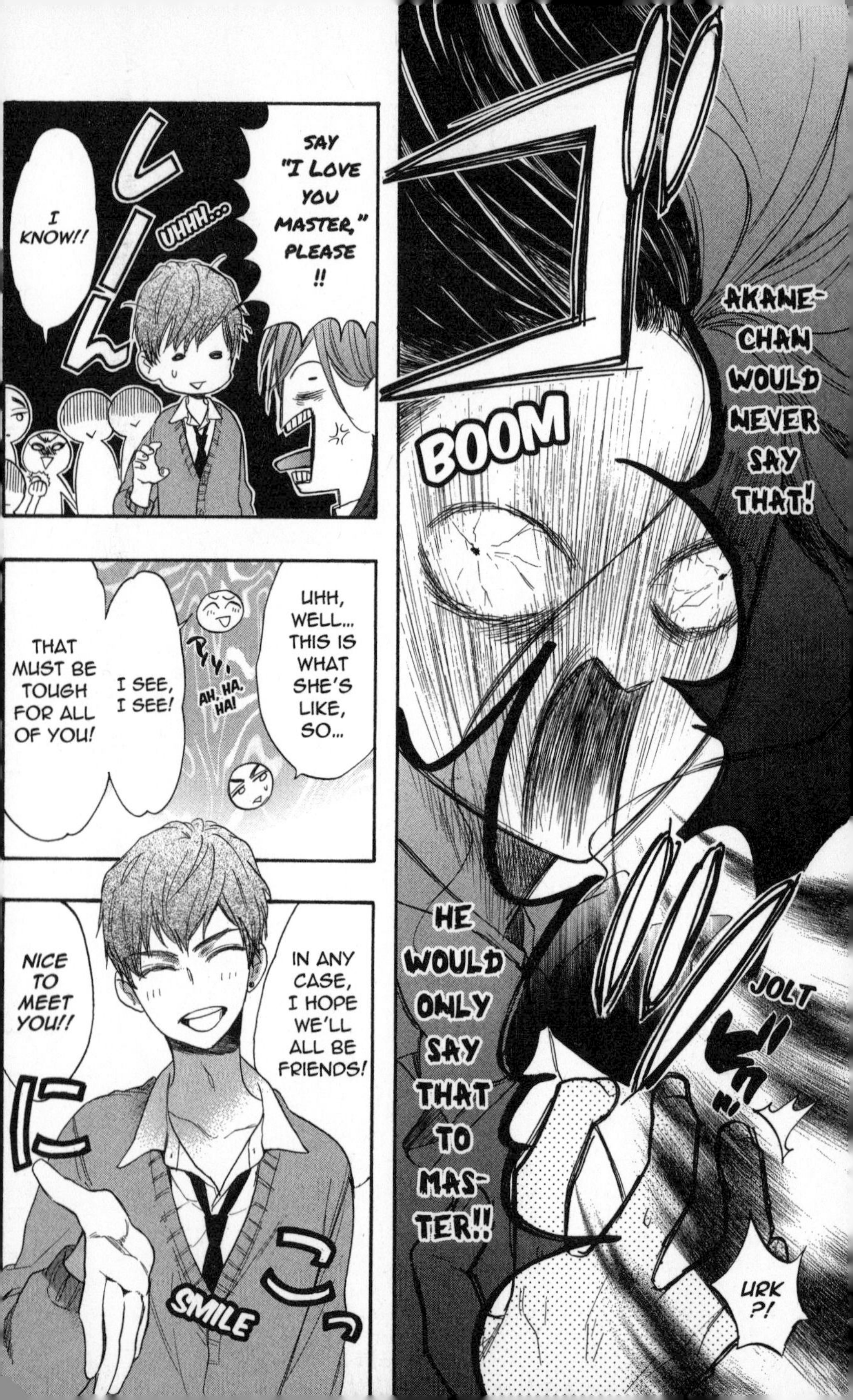
AKANE-CHAN WOULD NEVER SAY THAT!
BOOM
JOLT
HE WOULD ONLY SAY THAT TO MASTER!!
URK ?!
SAY "I LOVE YOU MASTER," PLEASE !!
UHHH...
I KNOW!!
UHH, WELL... THIS IS WHAT SHE'S LIKE, SO...
AH, HA, HA!
I SEE, I SEE!
THAT MUST BE TOUGH FOR ALL OF YOU!
IN ANY CASE, I HOPE WE'LL ALL BE FRIENDS!
NICE TO MEET YOU!!
SMILE

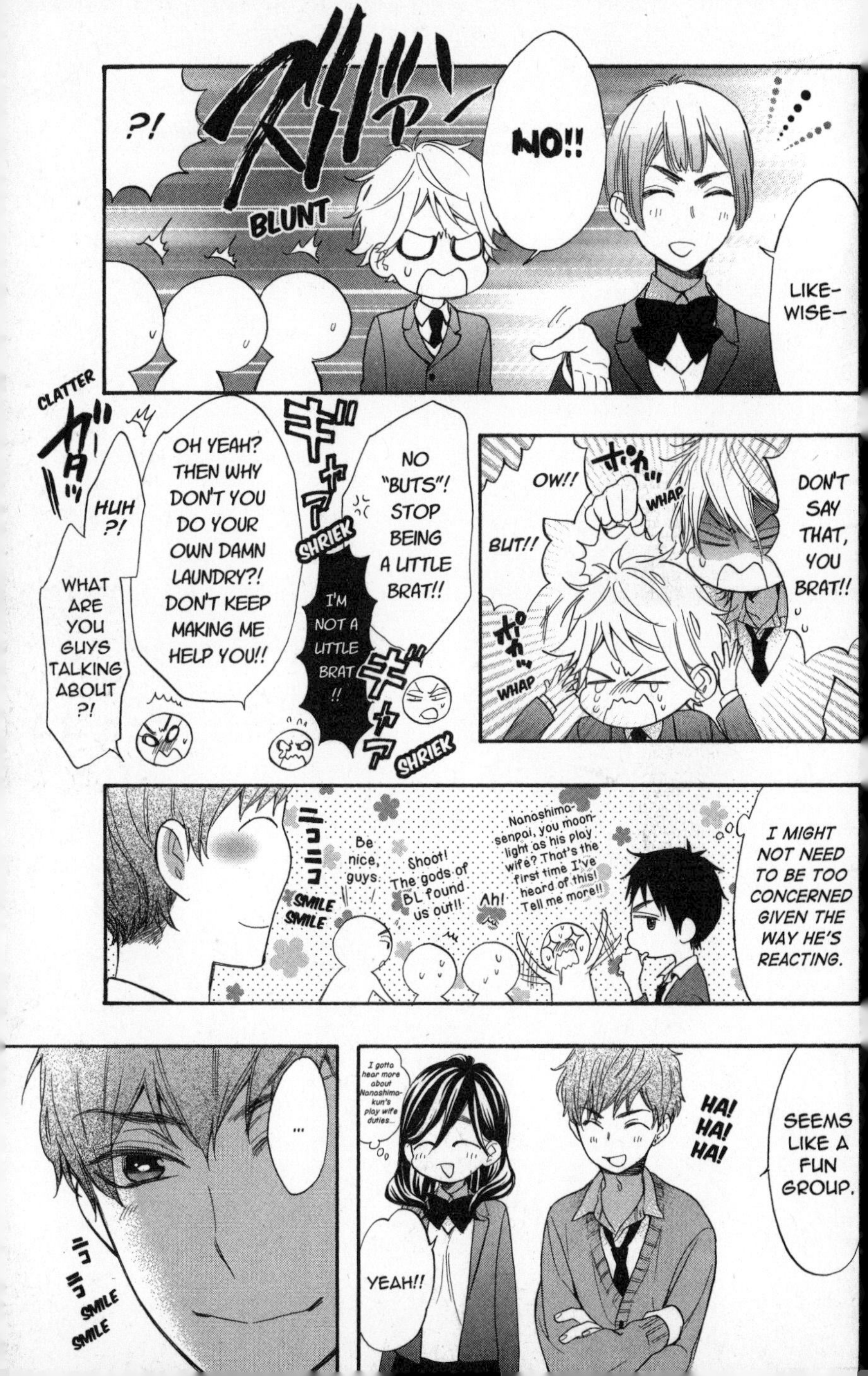
LIKE-WISE—
NO!!
?!
BLUNT
DON'T SAY THAT, YOU BRAT!!
WHAP
OW!!
BUT!!
WHAP
NO "BUTS"! STOP BEING A LITTLE BRAT!!
SHRIEK
I'M NOT A LITTLE BRAT!!
SHRIEK
OH YEAH? THEN WHY DON'T YOU DO YOUR OWN DAMN LAUNDRY?! DON'T KEEP MAKING ME HELP YOU!!
HUH?!
WHAT ARE YOU GUYS TALKING ABOUT?!
CLATTER
I MIGHT NOT NEED TO BE TOO CONCERNED GIVEN THE WAY HE'S REACTING.
Nanashima-senpai, you moonlight as his play wife? That's the first time I've heard of this! Tell me more!!
Ah!
Shoot! The gods of BL found us out!!
Be nice, guys.
SMILE SMILE
SEEMS LIKE A FUN GROUP.
HA! HA! HA!
I gotta hear more about Nanashima-kun's play wife duties...
YEAH!!
...
SMILE SMILE

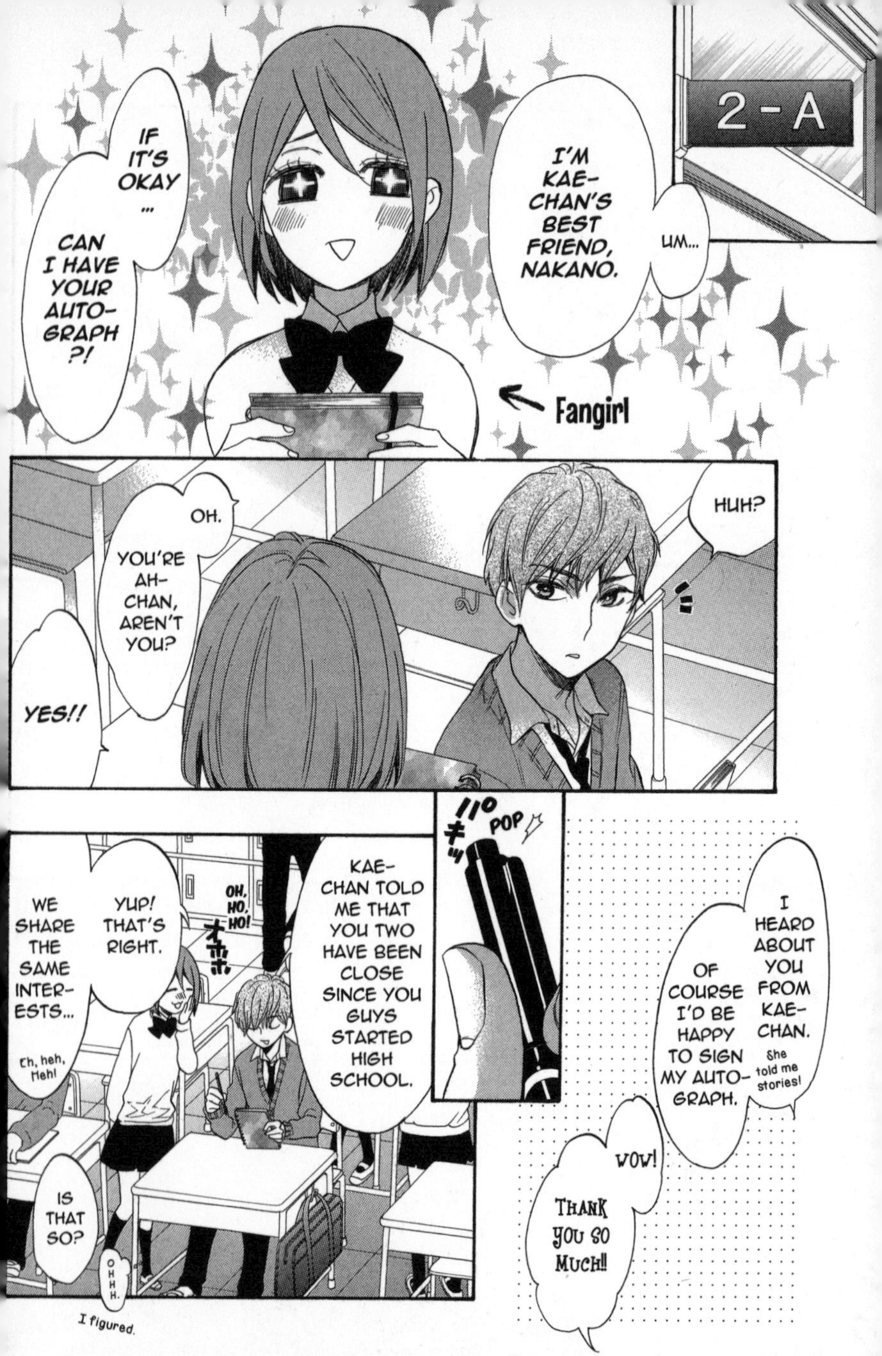
2-A
UM...
I'M KAE-CHAN'S BEST FRIEND, NAKANO.
Fangirl
IF IT'S OKAY... CAN I HAVE YOUR AUTOGRAPH?!
HUH?
OH. YOU'RE AH-CHAN, AREN'T YOU?
YES!!
POP
I HEARD ABOUT YOU FROM KAE-CHAN.
She told me stories!
OF COURSE I'D BE HAPPY TO SIGN MY AUTOGRAPH.
WOW!
THANK YOU SO MUCH!!
KAE-CHAN TOLD ME THAT YOU TWO HAVE BEEN CLOSE SINCE YOU GUYS STARTED HIGH SCHOOL.
YUP! THAT'S RIGHT.
OH, HO, HO!
WE SHARE THE SAME INTERESTS...
Eh, heh, Heh!
IS THAT SO?
OHHH.
I figured.

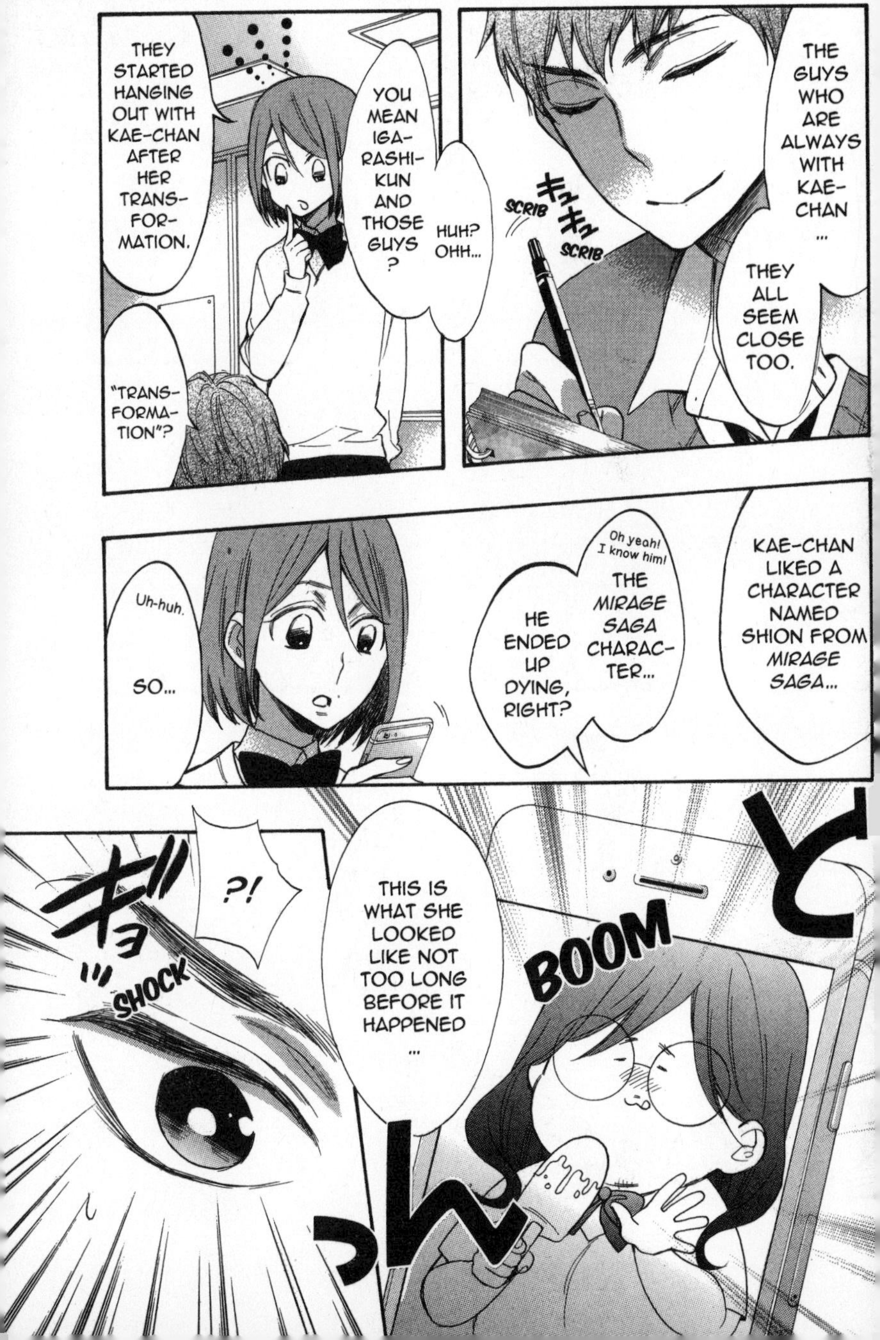
THE GUYS WHO ARE ALWAYS WITH KAE-CHAN ...
THEY ALL SEEM CLOSE TOO.
SCRIB SCRIB
HUH? OHH...
YOU MEAN IGA-RASHI-KUN AND THOSE GUYS ?
THEY STARTED HANGING OUT WITH KAE-CHAN AFTER HER TRANS-FOR-MATION.
"TRANS-FORMA-TION"?
KAE-CHAN LIKED A CHARACTER NAMED SHION FROM MIRAGE SAGA...
Oh yeah! I know him!
THE MIRAGE SAGA CHARAC-TER...
HE ENDED UP DYING, RIGHT?
Uh-huh.
SO...
BOOM
THIS IS WHAT SHE LOOKED LIKE NOT TOO LONG BEFORE IT HAPPENED ...
?!
SHOCK

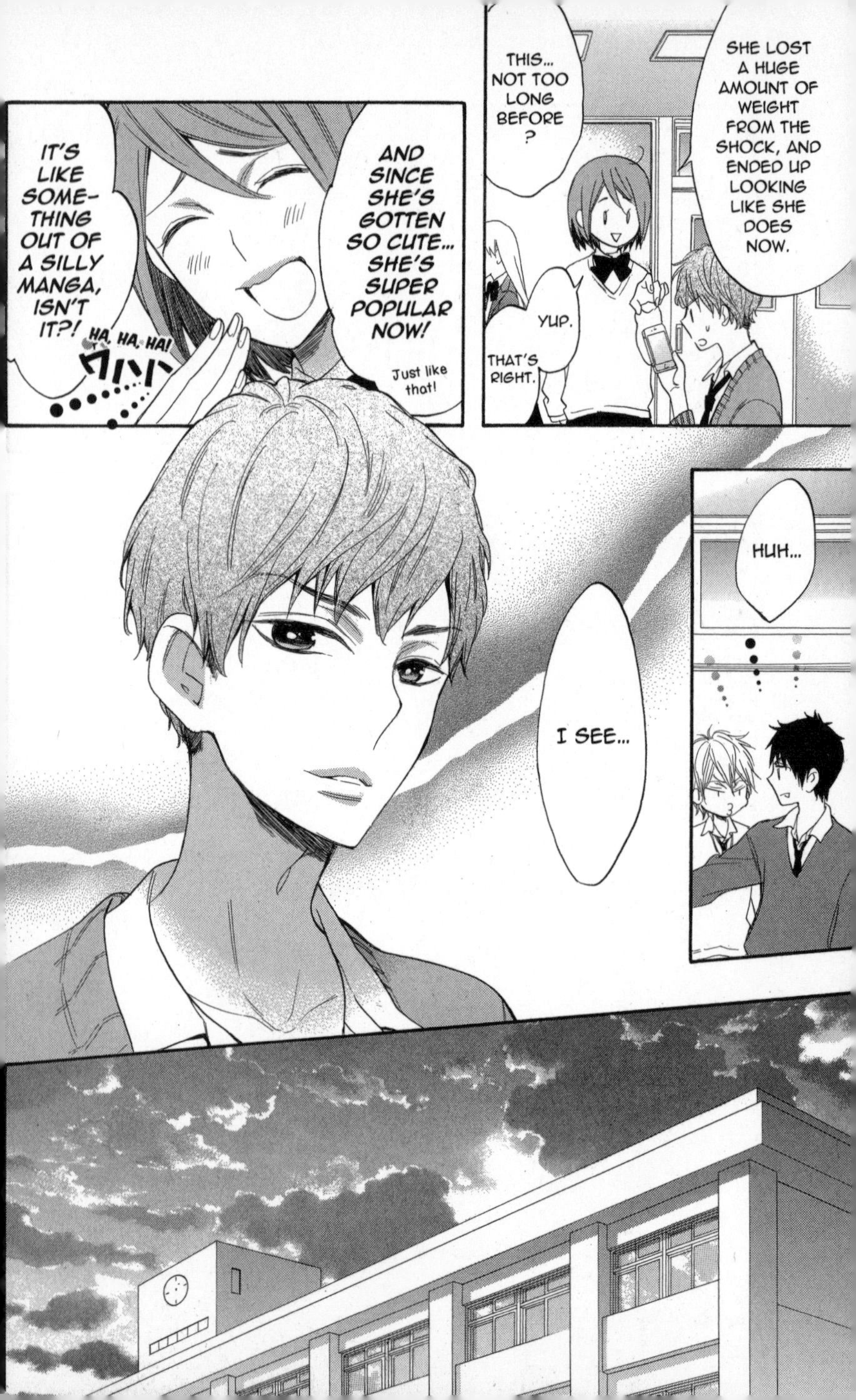
SHE LOST A HUGE AMOUNT OF WEIGHT FROM THE SHOCK, AND ENDED UP LOOKING LIKE SHE DOES NOW.
THIS... NOT TOO LONG BEFORE?
YUP.
THAT'S RIGHT.
AND SINCE SHE'S GOTTEN SO CUTE... SHE'S SUPER POPULAR NOW!
Just like that!
IT'S LIKE SOME-THING OUT OF A SILLY MANGA, ISN'T IT?!
HA, HA, HA!
ワハハ
HUH...
I SEE...

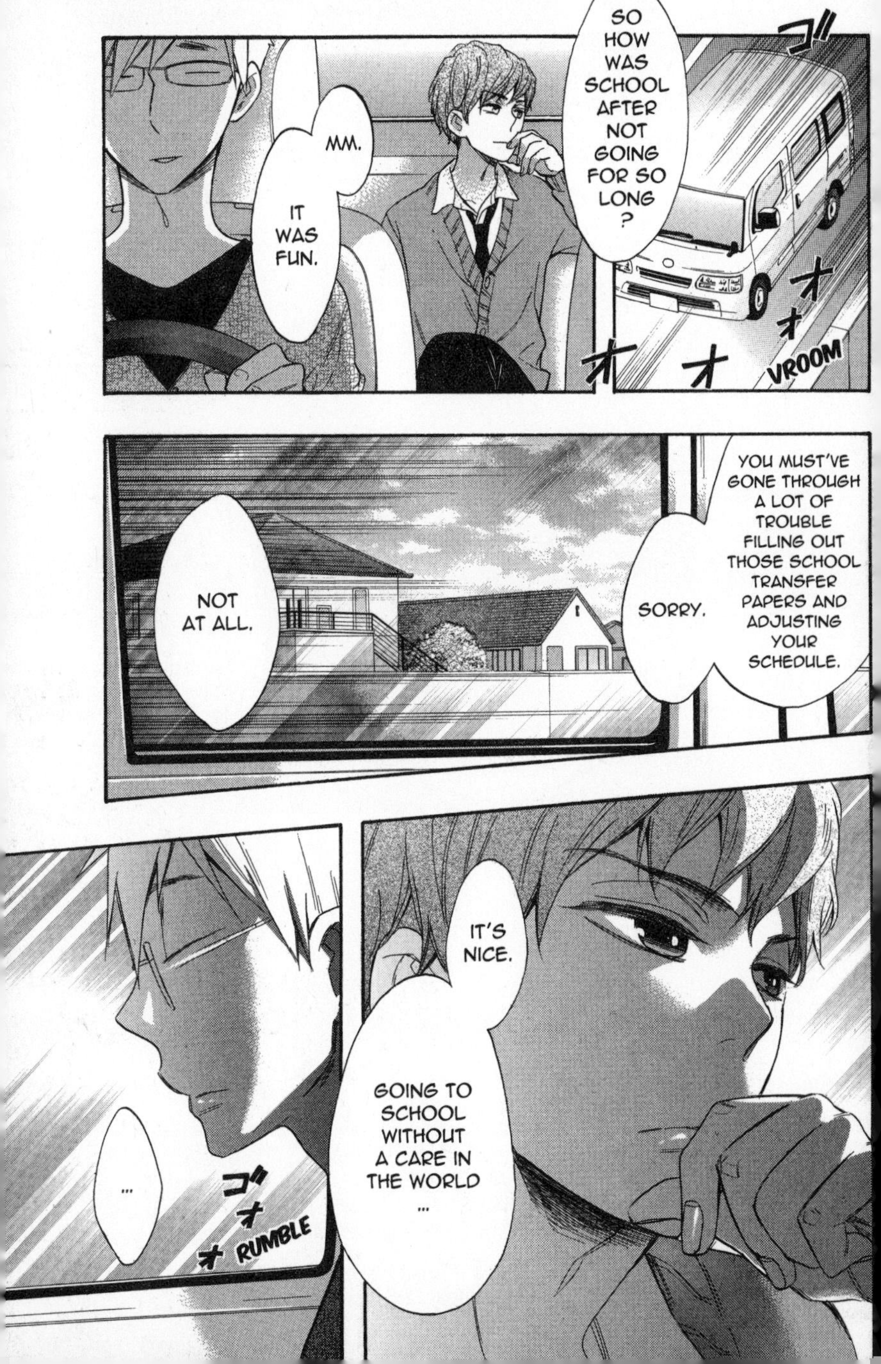

ゴオオオオ
VROOM
SO HOW WAS SCHOOL AFTER NOT GOING FOR SO LONG?
MM.
IT WAS FUN.
YOU MUST'VE GONE THROUGH A LOT OF TROUBLE FILLING OUT THOSE SCHOOL TRANSFER PAPERS AND ADJUSTING YOUR SCHEDULE.
SORRY.
NOT AT ALL.
IT'S NICE.
GOING TO SCHOOL WITHOUT A CARE IN THE WORLD...
...
ゴオオ
RUMBLE

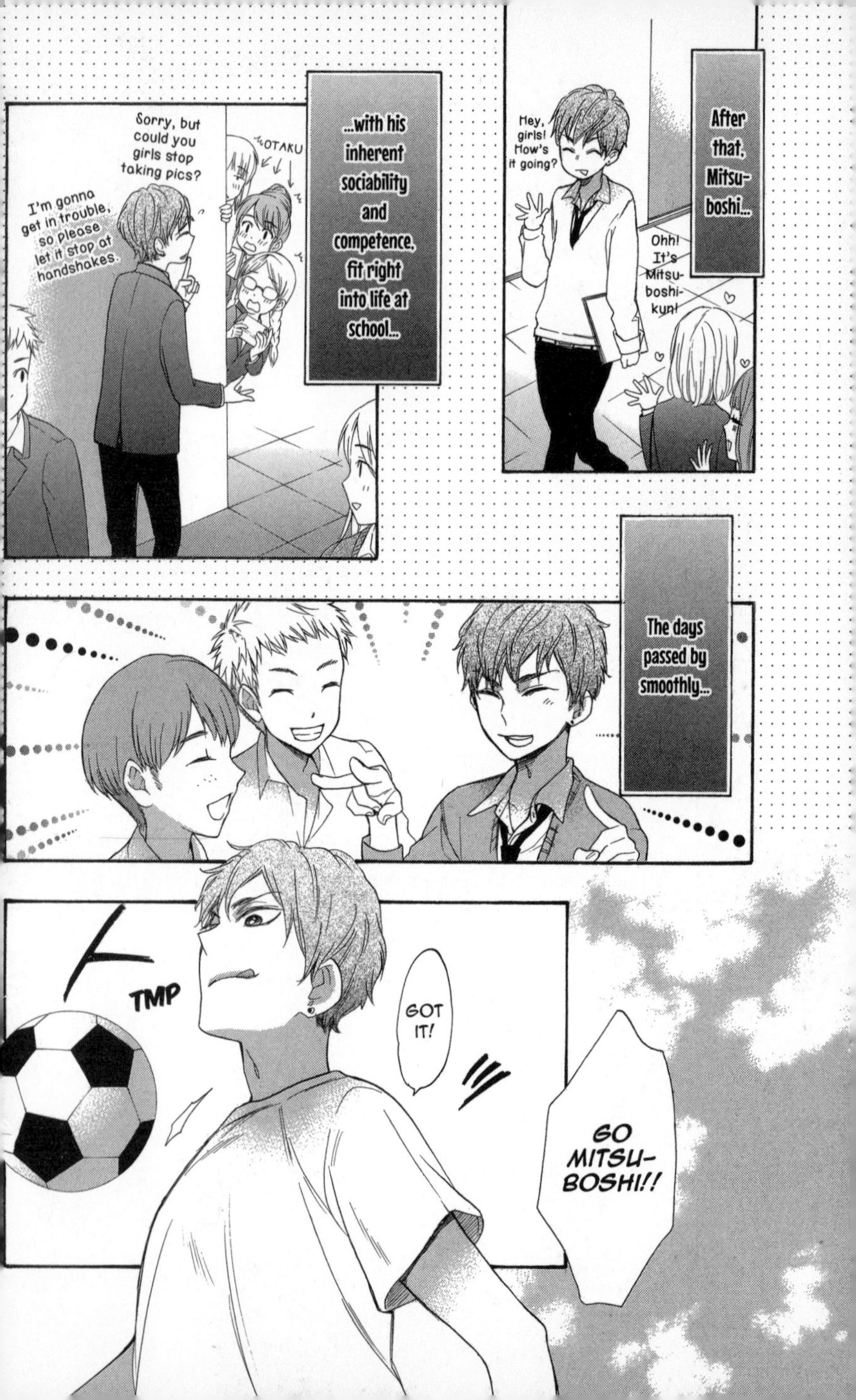
After that, Mitsu-boshi...
Hey, girls! How's it going?
Ohh! It's Mitsu-boshi-kun!
...with his inherent sociability and competence, fit right into life at school...
Sorry, but could you girls stop taking pics?
OTAKU
I'm gonna get in trouble, so please let it stop at handshakes.
The days passed by smoothly...
GO MITSU-BOSHI!!
GOT IT!
TMP

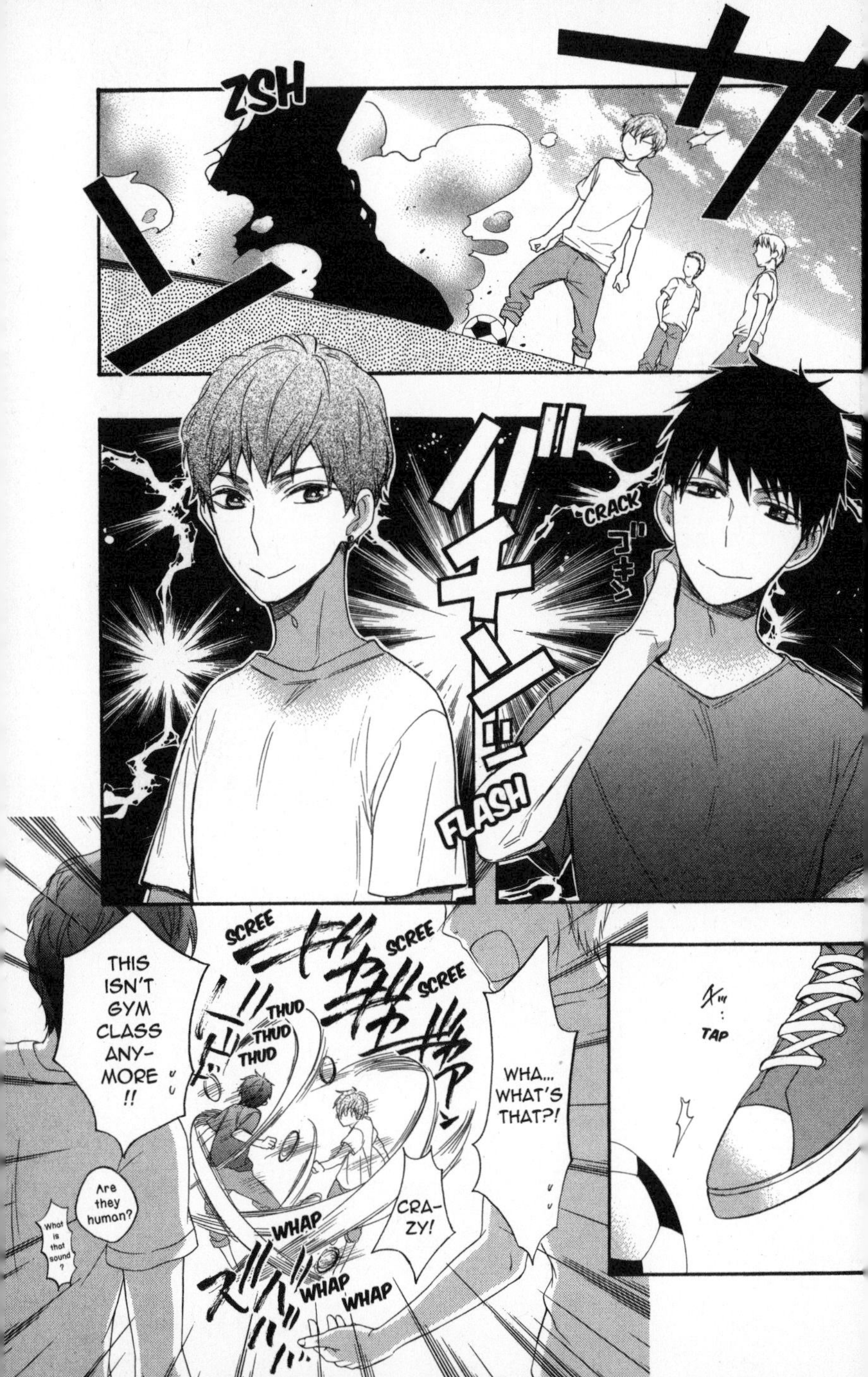
ZSH
CRACK
ゴキン
FLASH
TAP
WHA... WHAT'S THAT?!
CRA-ZY!
SCREE
SCREE
SCREE
THUD
THUD
THUD
THIS ISN'T GYM CLASS ANY-MORE!!
Are they human?
What is that sound?
WHAP
WHAP
WHAP

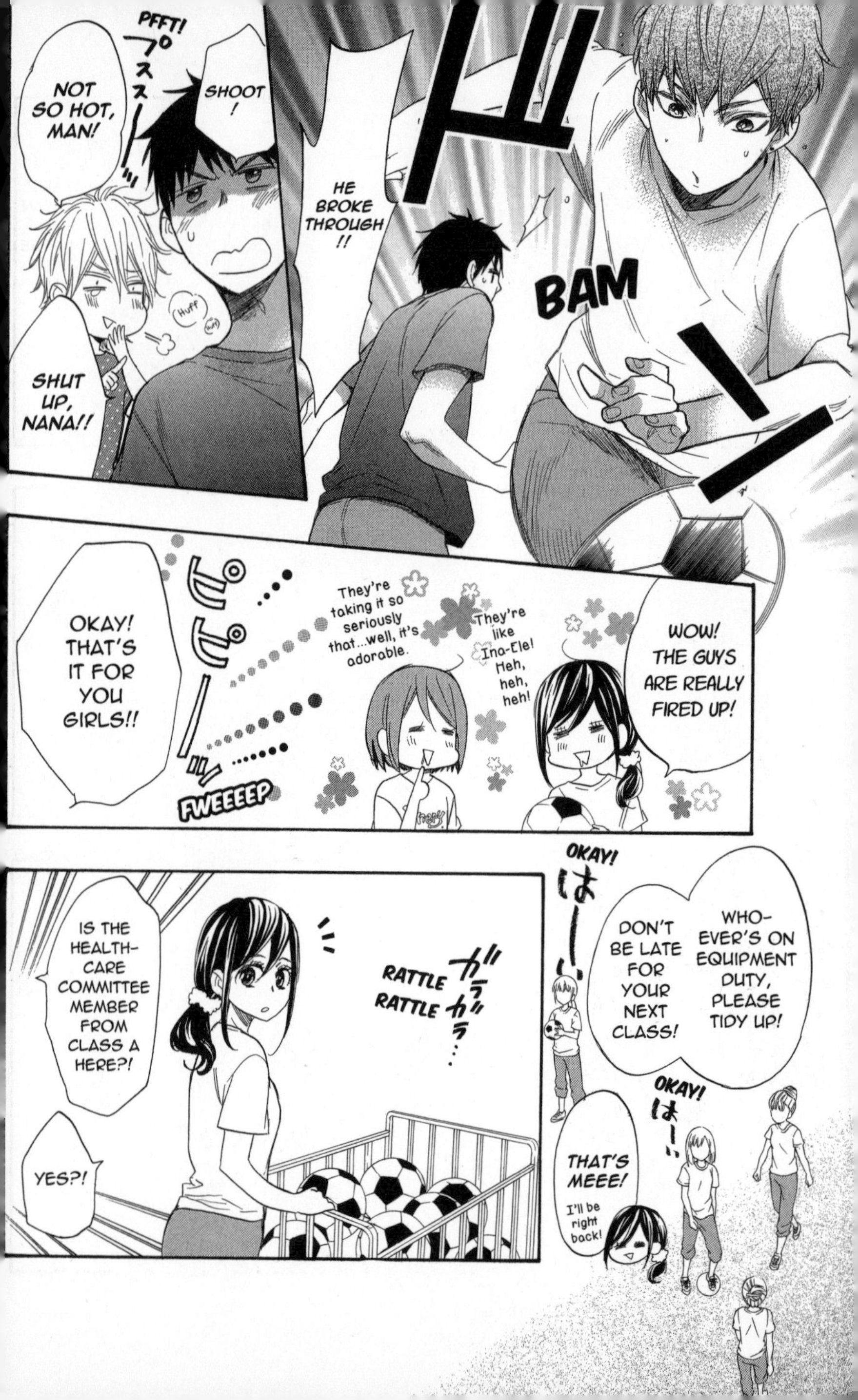

BAM
HE BROKE THROUGH!!
SHOOT!
PFFT! プスー
NOT SO HOT, MAN!
Huff Huff
SHUT UP, NANA!!
WOW! THE GUYS ARE REALLY FIRED UP!
They're like Ina-Ele! Heh, heh, heh!
They're taking it so seriously that...well, it's adorable.
ピピーッ
FWEEEEP
OKAY! THAT'S IT FOR YOU GIRLS!!
WHO-EVER'S ON EQUIPMENT DUTY, PLEASE TIDY UP!
DON'T BE LATE FOR YOUR NEXT CLASS!
OKAY! はーい
OKAY! はーい
THAT'S MEEE!
I'll be right back!
IS THE HEALTH-CARE COMMITTEE MEMBER FROM CLASS A HERE?!
RATTLE RATTLE ガラガラ...
YES?!

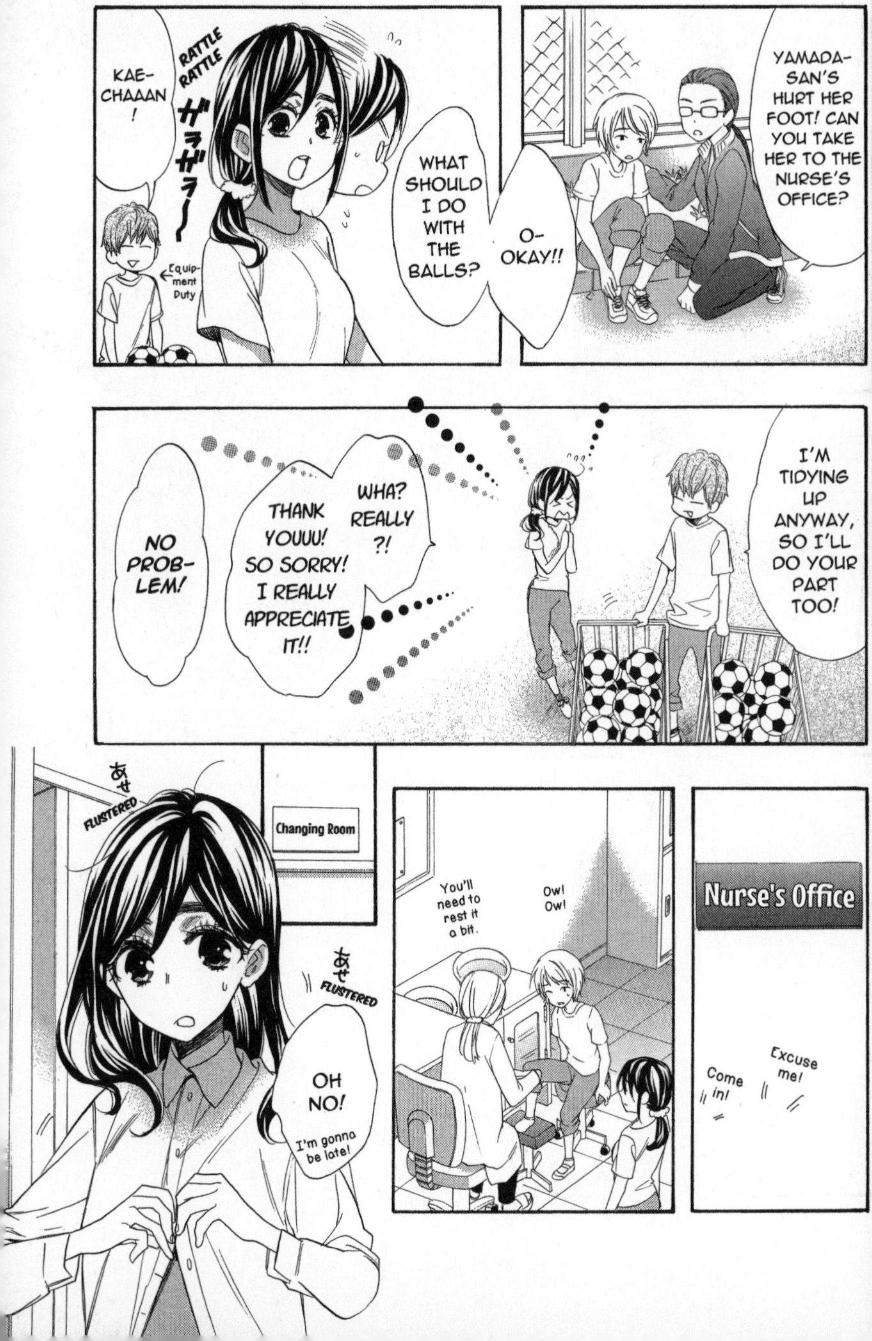
YAMADA-SAN'S HURT HER FOOT! CAN YOU TAKE HER TO THE NURSE'S OFFICE?
O-OKAY!!
WHAT SHOULD I DO WITH THE BALLS?
RATTLE RATTLE
ガラガラ~
KAE-CHAAAN!
Equipment Duty
I'M TIDYING UP ANYWAY, SO I'LL DO YOUR PART TOO!
WHA? REALLY?!
THANK YOUUU! SO SORRY! I REALLY APPRECIATE IT!!
NO PROB-LEM!
Nurse's Office
Excuse me!
Come in!
Ow! Ow!
You'll need to rest it a bit.
Changing Room
あせ
FLUSTERED
あせ
FLUSTERED
OH NO!
I'm gonna be late!

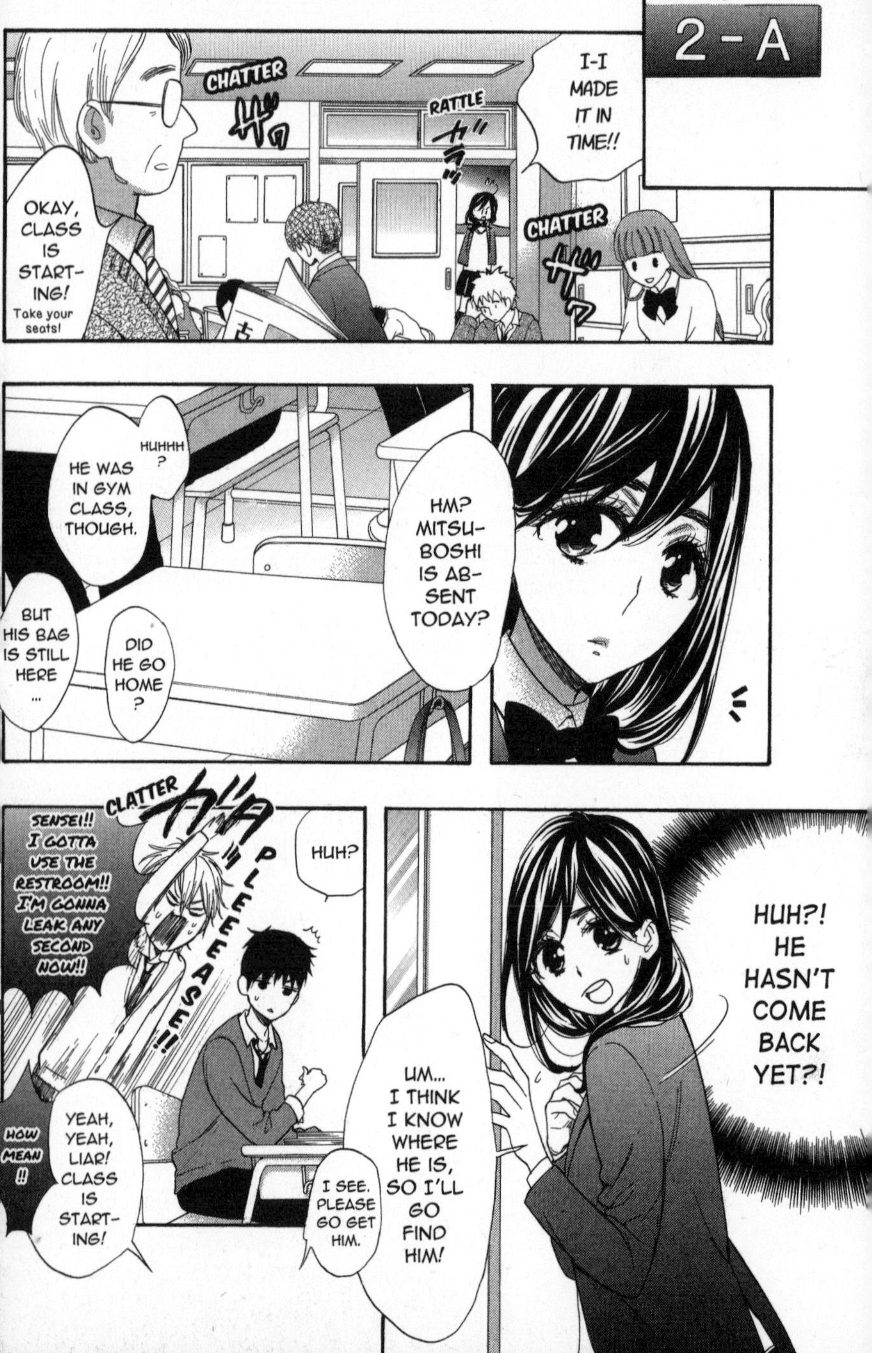
2-A
I-I MADE IT IN TIME!!
RATTLE
CHATTER
CHATTER
OKAY, CLASS IS START-ING!
Take your seats!
HM? MITSU-BOSHI IS AB-SENT TODAY?
HUHHH?
HE WAS IN GYM CLASS, THOUGH.
DID HE GO HOME?
BUT HIS BAG IS STILL HERE ...
HUH?! HE HASN'T COME BACK YET?!
UM... I THINK I KNOW WHERE HE IS, SO I'LL GO FIND HIM!
HUH?
CLATTER
SENSEI!! I GOTTA USE THE RESTROOM!! I'M GONNA LEAK ANY SECOND NOW!!
PLEEEASE!!
I SEE. PLEASE GO GET HIM.
YEAH, YEAH, LIAR! CLASS IS START-ING!
HOW MEAN!!

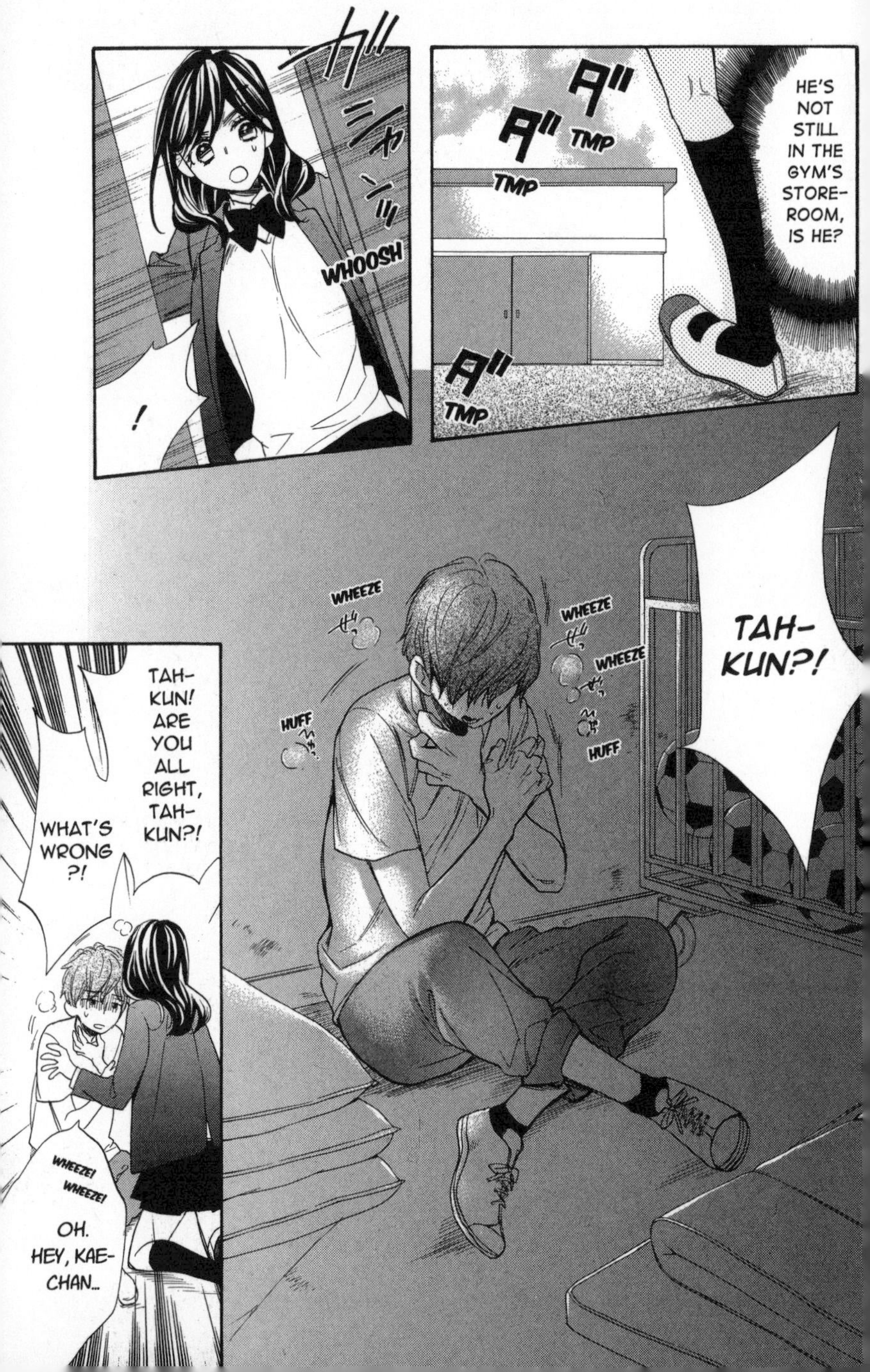
TMP
TMP
TMP
HE'S NOT STILL IN THE GYM'S STORE-ROOM, IS HE?
WHOOSH
!
TAH-KUN?!
WHEEZE
WHEEZE
WHEEZE
HUFF
HUFF
TAH-KUN! ARE YOU ALL RIGHT, TAH-KUN?!
WHAT'S WRONG?!
WHEEZE! WHEEZE!
OH. HEY, KAE-CHAN...

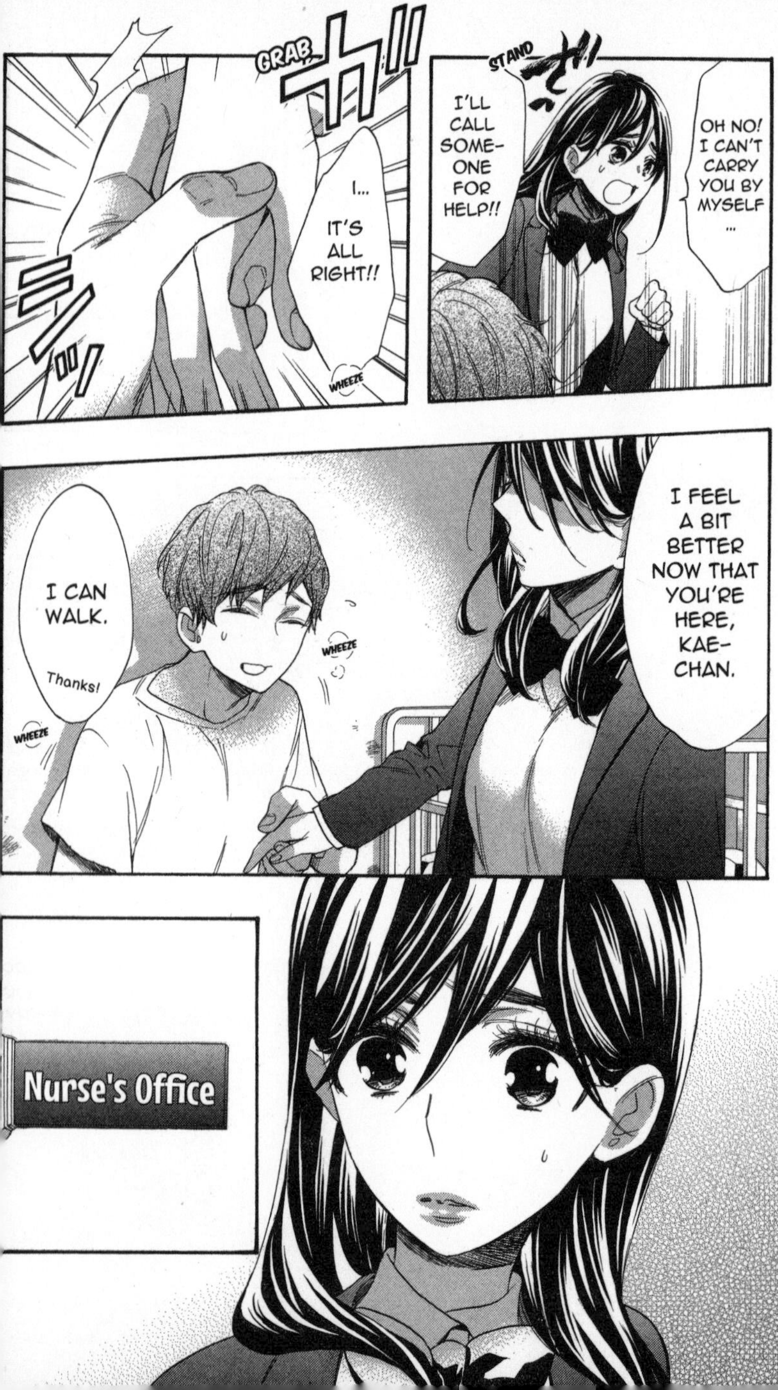
STAND
OH NO! I CAN'T CARRY YOU BY MYSELF...
I'LL CALL SOME-ONE FOR HELP!!
GRAB
I... IT'S ALL RIGHT!!
WHEEZE
I FEEL A BIT BETTER NOW THAT YOU'RE HERE, KAE-CHAN.
WHEEZE
I CAN WALK.
Thanks!
WHEEZE
Nurse's Office

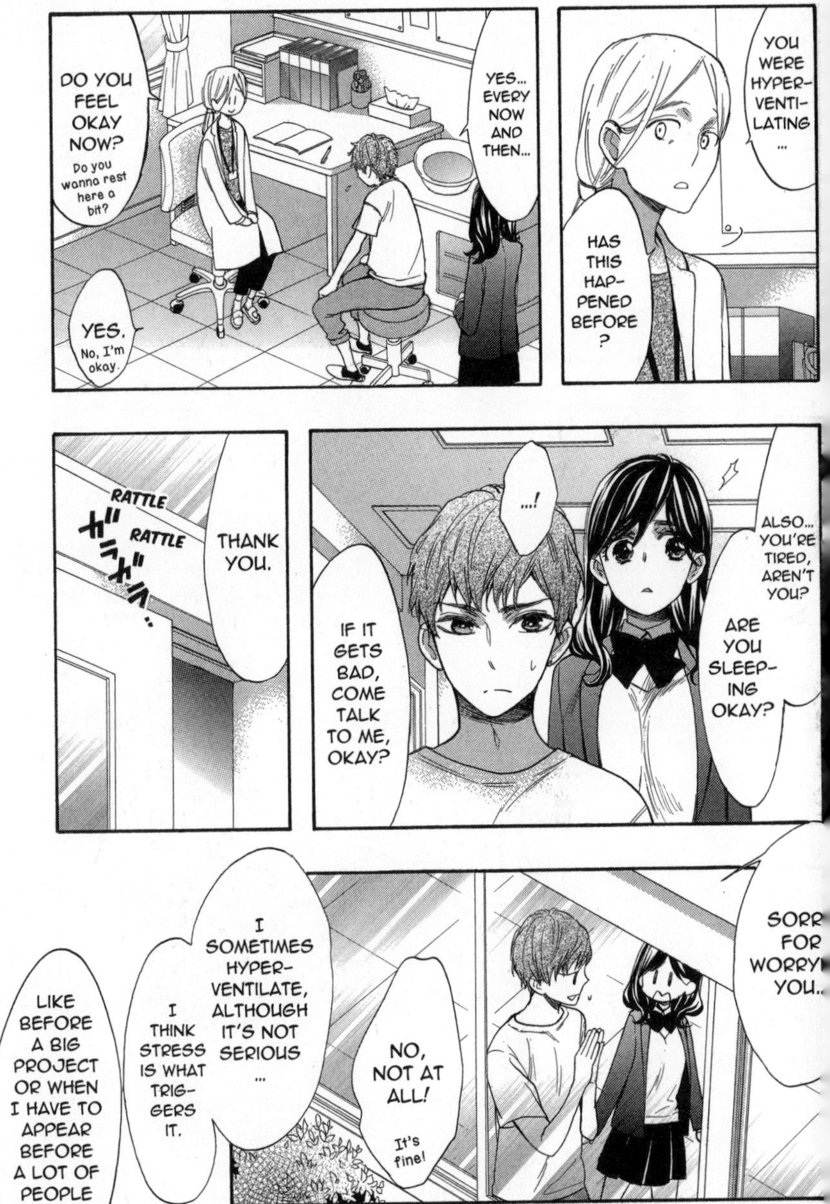
YOU WERE HYPER-VENTI-LATING ...
HAS THIS HAP-PENED BEFORE ?
YES... EVERY NOW AND THEN...
DO YOU FEEL OKAY NOW?
Do you wanna rest here a bit?
YES.
No, I'm okay.
ALSO... YOU'RE TIRED, AREN'T YOU?
ARE YOU SLEEP-ING OKAY?
...!
IF IT GETS BAD, COME TALK TO ME, OKAY?
THANK YOU.
RATTLE
RATTLE
SORR FOR WORRY YOU..
NO, NOT AT ALL!
It's fine!
I SOMETIMES HYPER-VENTILATE, ALTHOUGH IT'S NOT SERIOUS ...
I THINK STRESS IS WHAT TRIG-GERS IT.
LIKE BEFORE A BIG PROJECT OR WHEN I HAVE TO APPEAR BEFORE A LOT OF PEOPLE ...

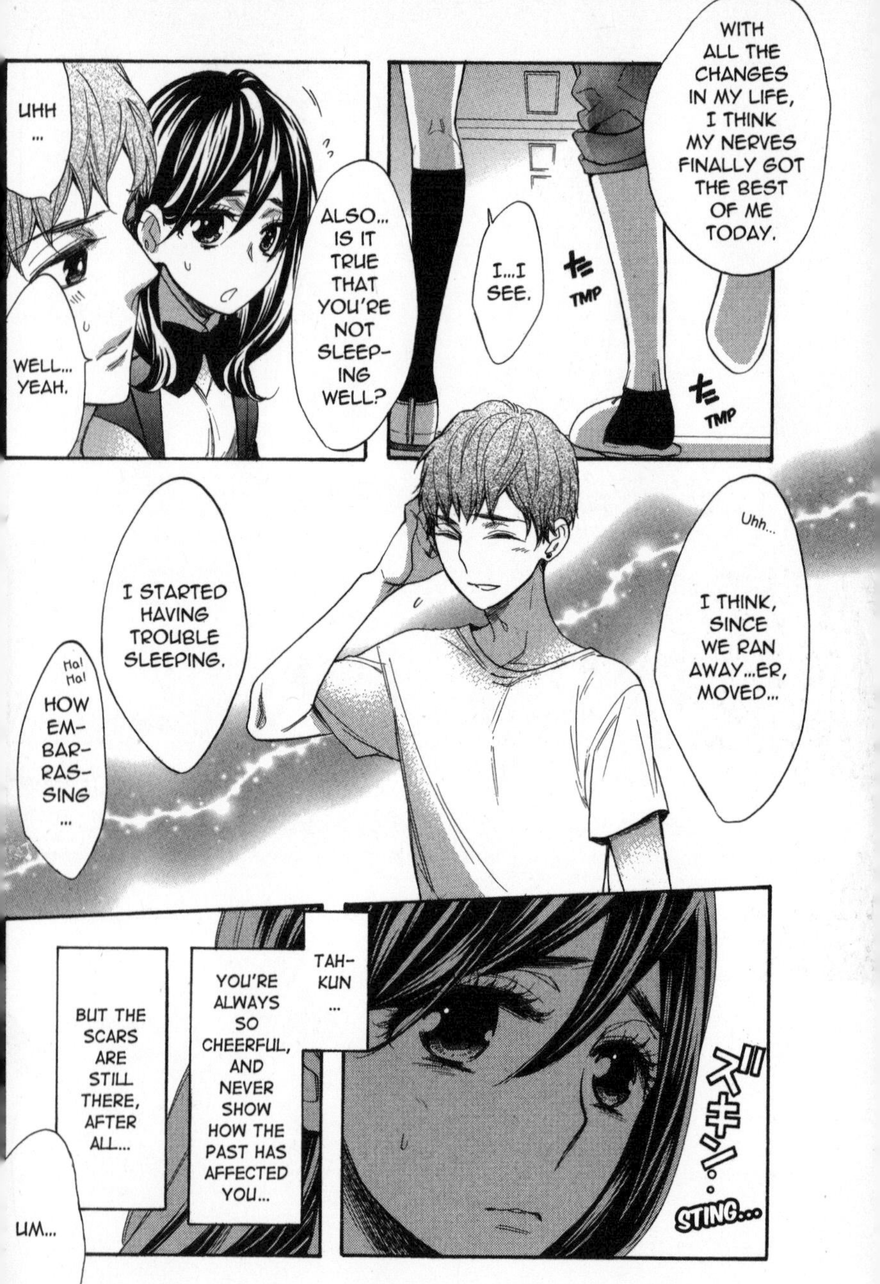
WITH ALL THE CHANGES IN MY LIFE, I THINK MY NERVES FINALLY GOT THE BEST OF ME TODAY.
TMP
TMP
I...I SEE.
ALSO... IS IT TRUE THAT YOU'RE NOT SLEEP-ING WELL?
UHH...
WELL... YEAH.
Uhh...
I THINK, SINCE WE RAN AWAY...ER, MOVED...
I STARTED HAVING TROUBLE SLEEPING.
Ha! Ha! HOW EM-BAR-RAS-SING...
STING...
TAH-KUN...
YOU'RE ALWAYS SO CHEERFUL, AND NEVER SHOW HOW THE PAST HAS AFFECTED YOU...
BUT THE SCARS ARE STILL THERE, AFTER ALL...
UM...

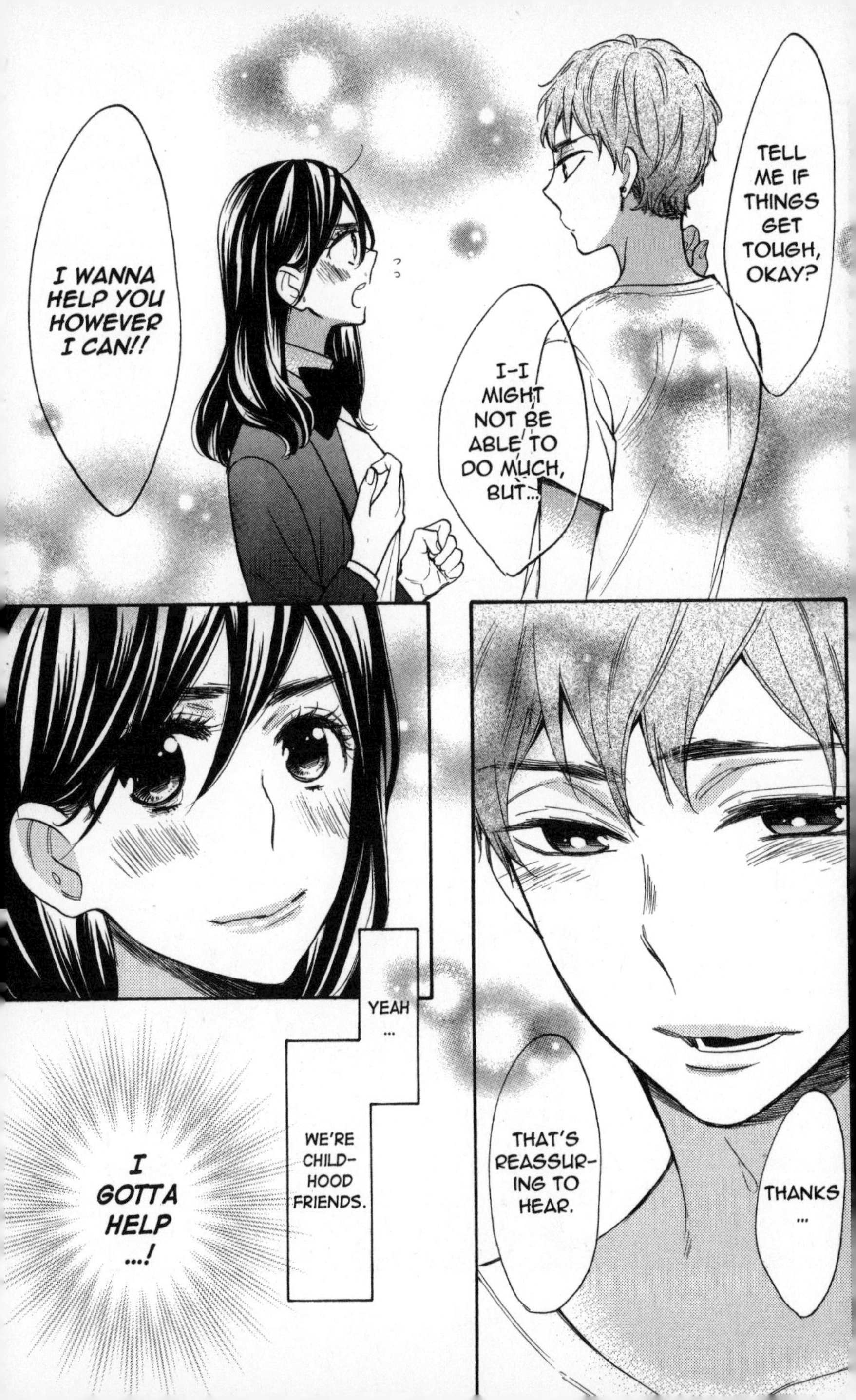
TELL ME IF THINGS GET TOUGH, OKAY?
I-I MIGHT NOT BE ABLE TO DO MUCH, BUT...
I WANNA HELP YOU HOWEVER I CAN!!
THANKS...
THAT'S REASSURING TO HEAR.
YEAH...
WE'RE CHILDHOOD FRIENDS.
I GOTTA HELP...!

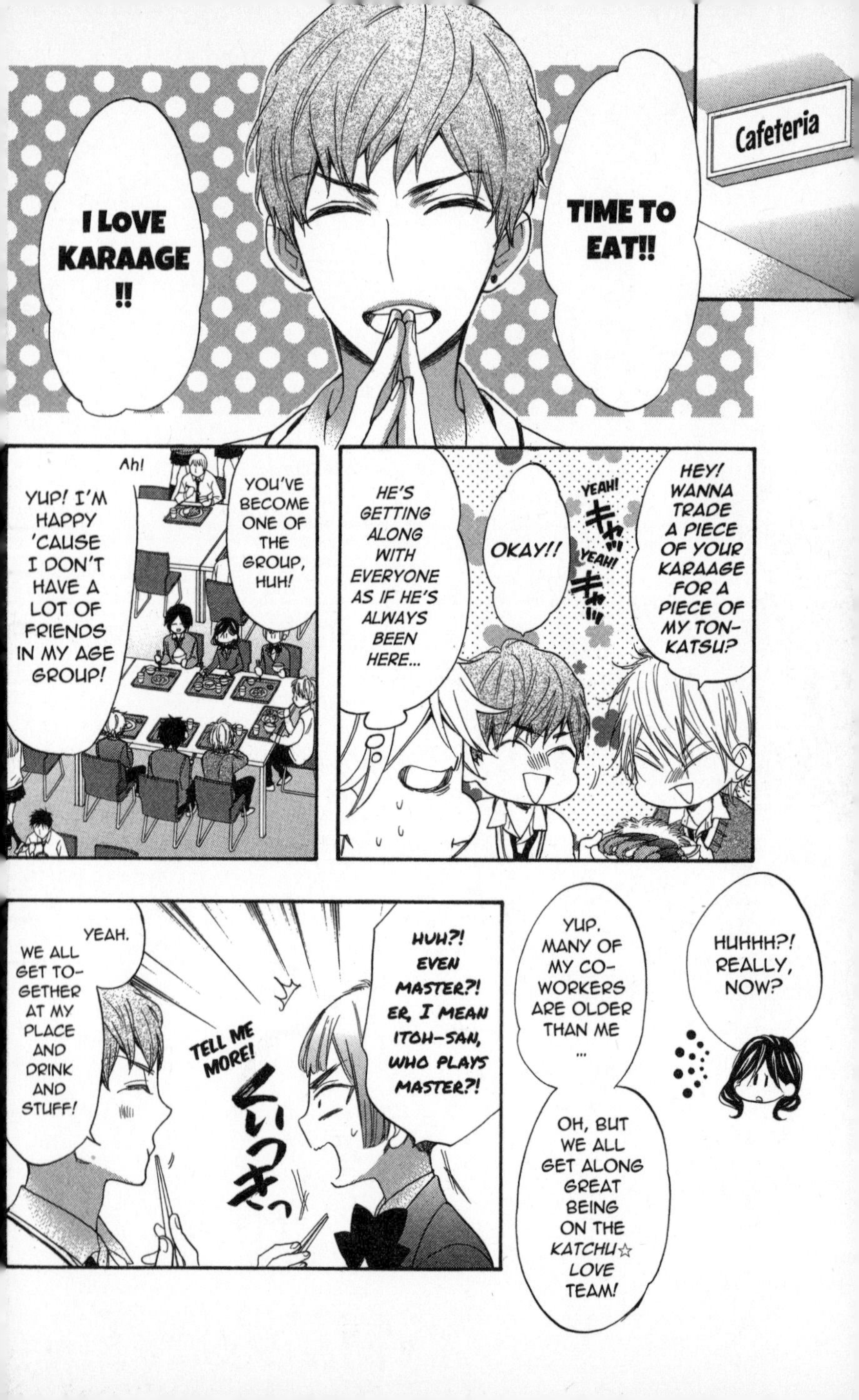
Cafeteria
TIME TO EAT!!
I LOVE KARAAGE!!
HEY! WANNA TRADE A PIECE OF YOUR KARAAGE FOR A PIECE OF MY TON-KATSU?
YEAH! キャッ
YEAH! キャッ
OKAY!!
HE'S GETTING ALONG WITH EVERYONE AS IF HE'S ALWAYS BEEN HERE...
Ah!
YOU'VE BECOME ONE OF THE GROUP, HUH!
YUP! I'M HAPPY 'CAUSE I DON'T HAVE A LOT OF FRIENDS IN MY AGE GROUP!
HUHHH?! REALLY, NOW?
YUP. MANY OF MY CO-WORKERS ARE OLDER THAN ME ...
OH, BUT WE ALL GET ALONG GREAT BEING ON THE KATCHU☆LOVE TEAM!
HUH?! EVEN MASTER?! ER, I MEAN ITOH-SAN, WHO PLAYS MASTER?!
TELL ME MORE!
くいつきっ
YEAH. WE ALL GET TO-GETHER AT MY PLACE AND DRINK AND STUFF!

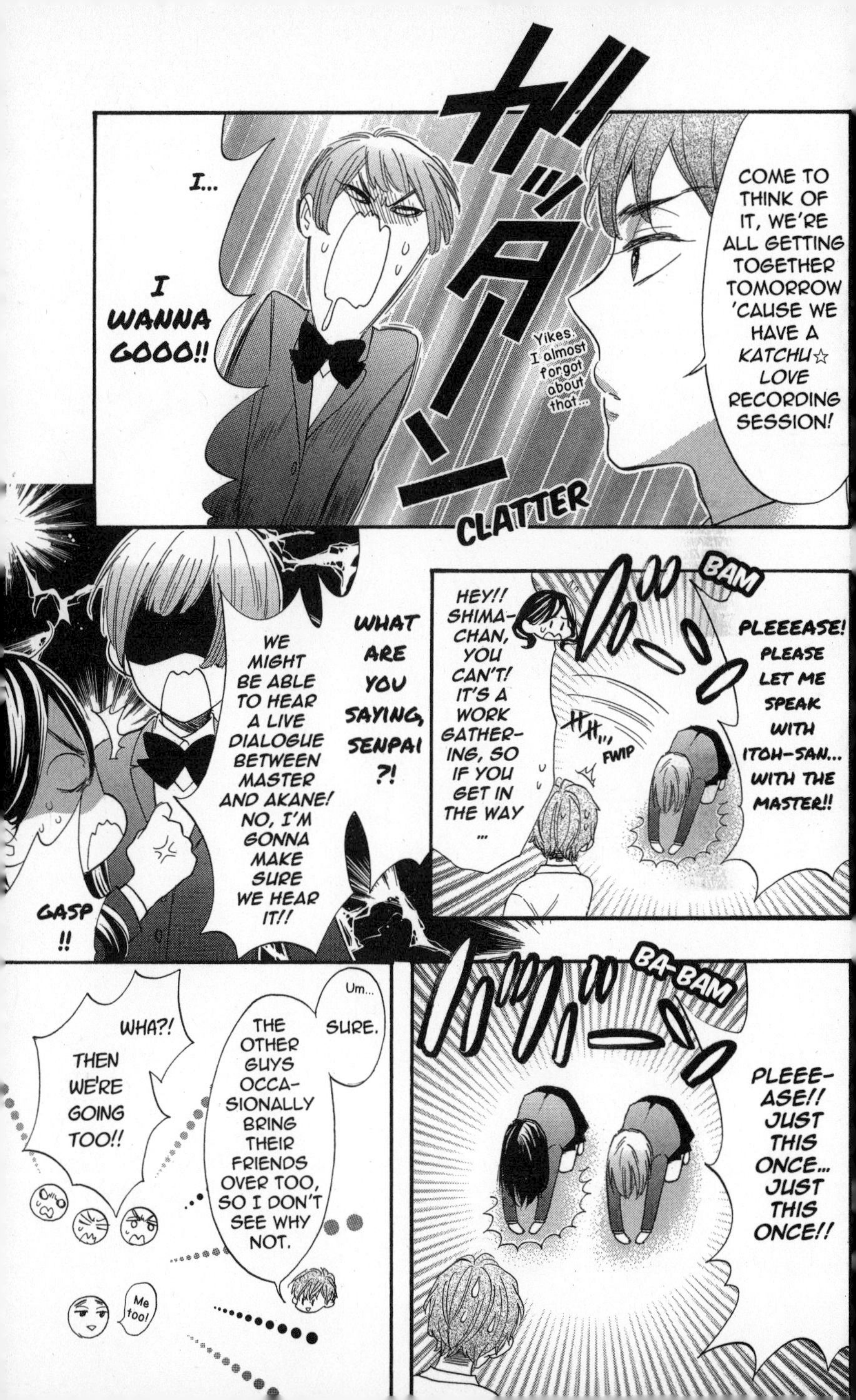

COME TO THINK OF IT, WE'RE ALL GETTING TOGETHER TOMORROW 'CAUSE WE HAVE A KATCHU☆ LOVE RECORDING SESSION!
Yikes, I almost forgot about that...
ガッターン
CLATTER
I...
I WANNA GOOO!!
BAM
PLEEEASE! PLEASE LET ME SPEAK WITH ITOH-SAN... WITH THE MASTER!!
FWIP
HEY!! SHIMA-CHAN, YOU CAN'T! IT'S A WORK GATHERING, SO IF YOU GET IN THE WAY...
WHAT ARE YOU SAYING, SENPAI?!
WE MIGHT BE ABLE TO HEAR A LIVE DIALOGUE BETWEEN MASTER AND AKANE! NO, I'M GONNA MAKE SURE WE HEAR IT!!
GASP!!
BA-BAM
PLEEEASE!! JUST THIS ONCE... JUST THIS ONCE!!
Um... SURE.
THE OTHER GUYS OCCASIONALLY BRING THEIR FRIENDS OVER TOO, SO I DON'T SEE WHY NOT.
WHA?! THEN WE'RE GOING TOO!!
Me too!

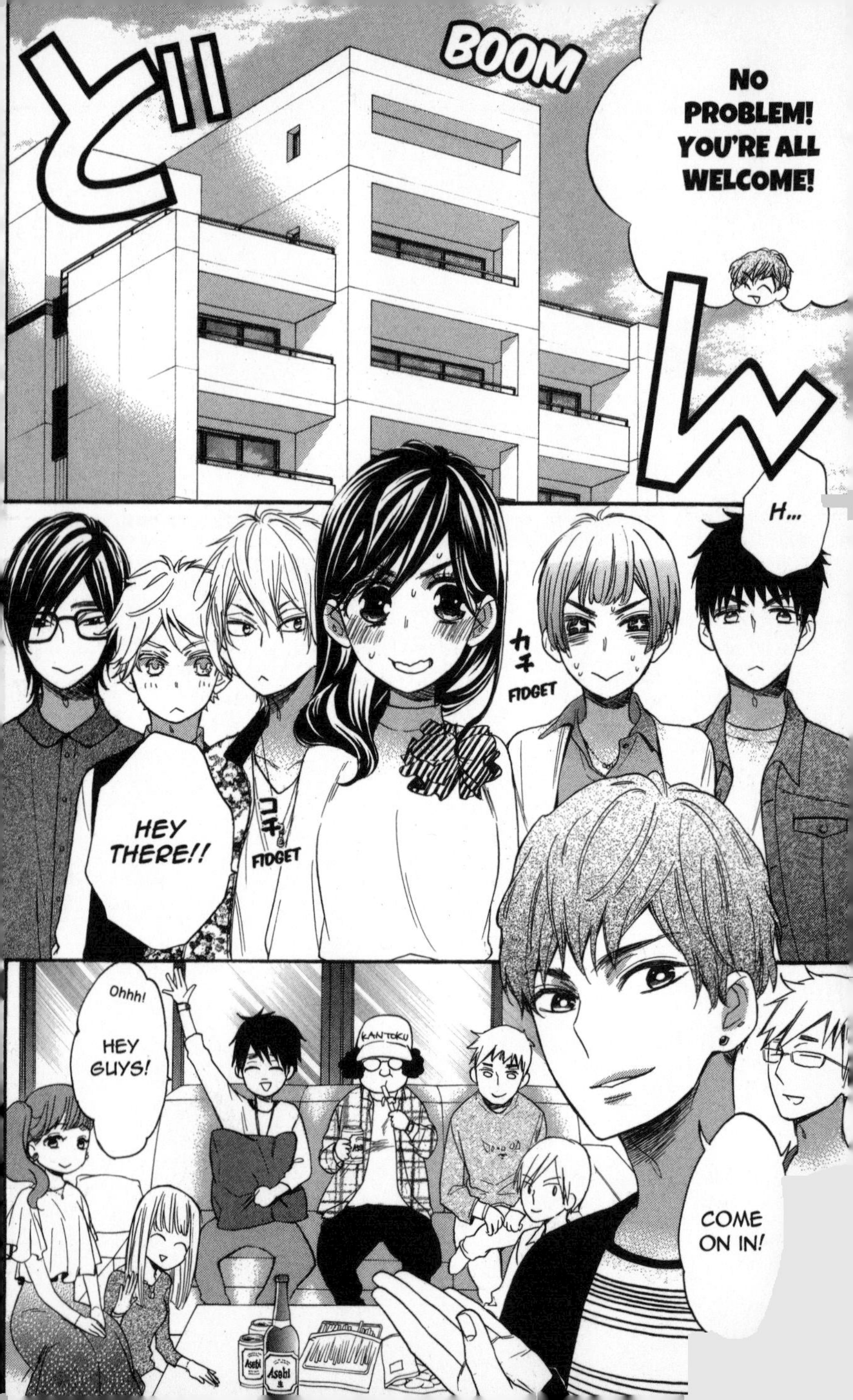
NO PROBLEM! YOU'RE ALL WELCOME!
ん
BOOM
ど
H...
カチ
FIDGET
コチ
FIDGET
HEY THERE!!
COME ON IN!
Ohhh!
HEY GUYS!
KANTOKU
Asahi

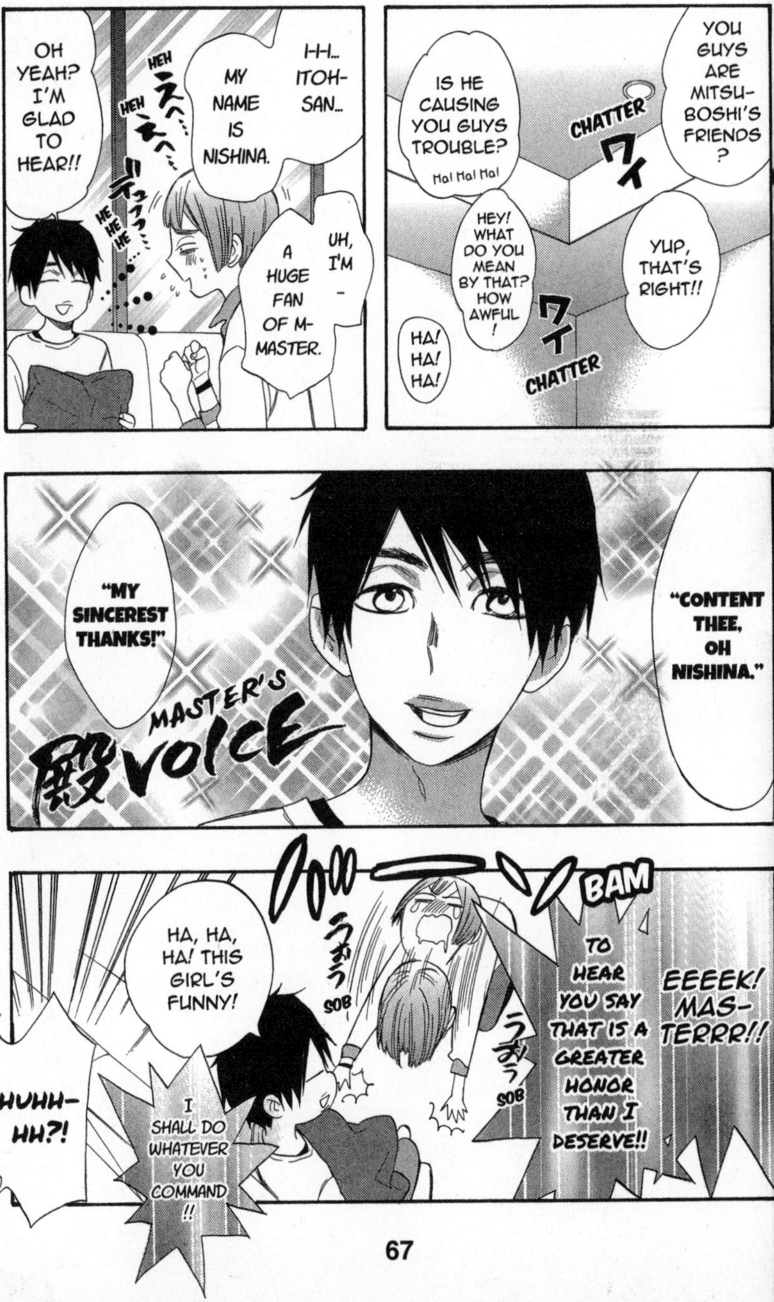
YOU GUYS ARE MITSU-BOSHI'S FRIENDS?
CHATTER
IS HE CAUSING YOU GUYS TROUBLE?
Ha! Ha! Ha!
YUP, THAT'S RIGHT!!
HEY! WHAT DO YOU MEAN BY THAT? HOW AWFUL!
CHATTER
HA! HA! HA!
I-I-I... ITOH-SAN...
MY NAME IS NISHINA.
HEH HEH
OH YEAH? I'M GLAD TO HEAR!!
UH, I'M ...
A HUGE FAN OF M-MASTER.
HE HE HE
"CONTENT THEE, OH NISHINA."
"MY SINCEREST THANKS!"
MASTER'S VOICE
BAM
EEEEK! MAS-TERRR!!
TO HEAR YOU SAY THAT IS A GREATER HONOR THAN I DESERVE!!
SOB
SOB
HA, HA, HA! THIS GIRL'S FUNNY!
I SHALL DO WHATEVER YOU COMMAND!!
HUHH-HH?!

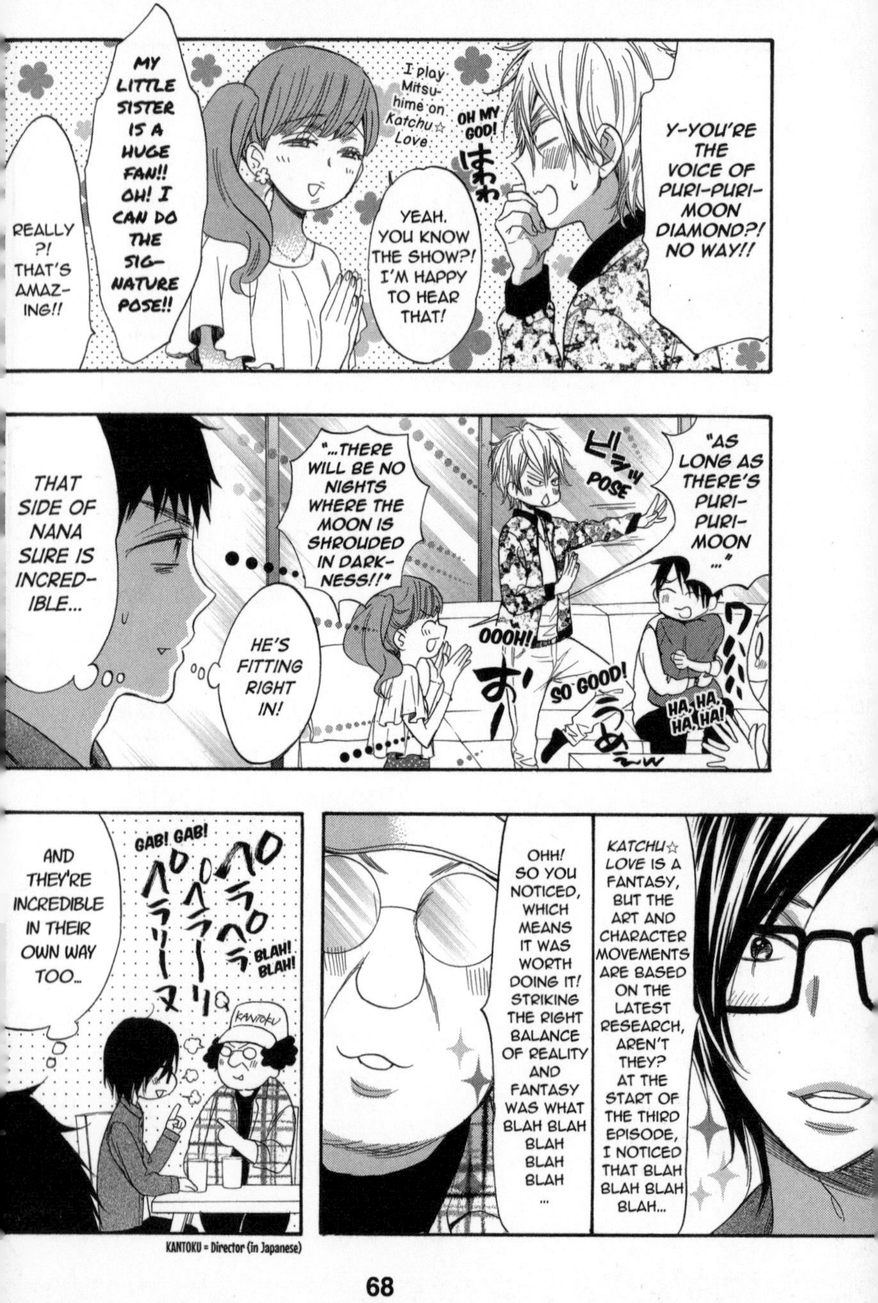
Y-YOU'RE THE VOICE OF PURI-PURI-MOON DIAMOND?! NO WAY!!
OH MY GOD!
はわわ
I play Mitsu-hime on Katchu☆Love
YEAH. YOU KNOW THE SHOW?! I'M HAPPY TO HEAR THAT!
MY LITTLE SISTER IS A HUGE FAN!! OH! I CAN DO THE SIG-NATURE POSE!!
REALLY?! THAT'S AMAZ-ING!!
"AS LONG AS THERE'S PURI-PURI-MOON..."
POSE
"...THERE WILL BE NO NIGHTS WHERE THE MOON IS SHROUDED IN DARK-NESS!!"
HA, HA, HA, HA!
SO GOOD!
OOOH!
HE'S FITTING RIGHT IN!
.....
THAT SIDE OF NANA SURE IS INCRED-IBLE...
KATCHU☆LOVE IS A FANTASY, BUT THE ART AND CHARACTER MOVEMENTS ARE BASED ON THE LATEST RESEARCH, AREN'T THEY? AT THE START OF THE THIRD EPISODE, I NOTICED THAT BLAH BLAH BLAH BLAH...
OHH! SO YOU NOTICED, WHICH MEANS IT WAS WORTH DOING IT! STRIKING THE RIGHT BALANCE OF REALITY AND FANTASY WAS WHAT BLAH BLAH BLAH BLAH BLAH...
GAB! GAB!
BLAH! BLAH!
KANTOKU
AND THEY'RE INCREDIBLE IN THEIR OWN WAY TOO...

KANTOKU = Director (in Japanese)

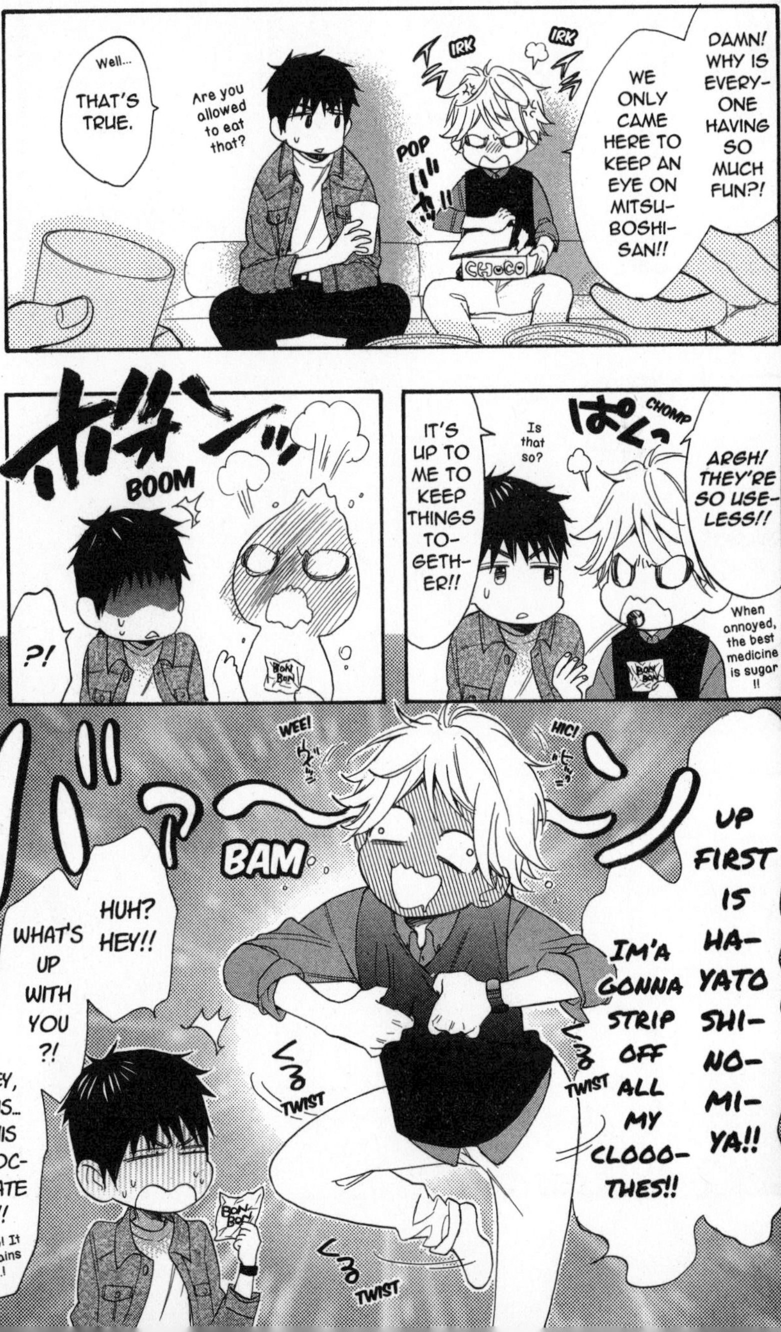
DAMN! WHY IS EVERY-ONE HAVING SO MUCH FUN?!
WE ONLY CAME HERE TO KEEP AN EYE ON MITSU-BOSHI-SAN!!
IRK
IRK
POP
Are you allowed to eat that?
Well...
THAT'S TRUE.
ARGH! THEY'RE SO USE-LESS!!
CHOMP
Is that so?
IT'S UP TO ME TO KEEP THINGS TO-GETH-ER!!
When annoyed, the best medicine is sugar !!
BON BON
CHOCO
BOOM
?!
BON BON
UP FIRST IS HA-YATO SHI-NO-MI-YA!!
IM'A GONNA STRIP OFF ALL MY CLOOO-THES!!
HIC!
WEE!
BAM
HUH? HEY!!
WHAT'S UP WITH YOU ?!
TWIST
TWIST
HEY, THIS... THIS CHOC-OLATE ...!!
Oh no! It contains ...!
BON-BON
TWIST

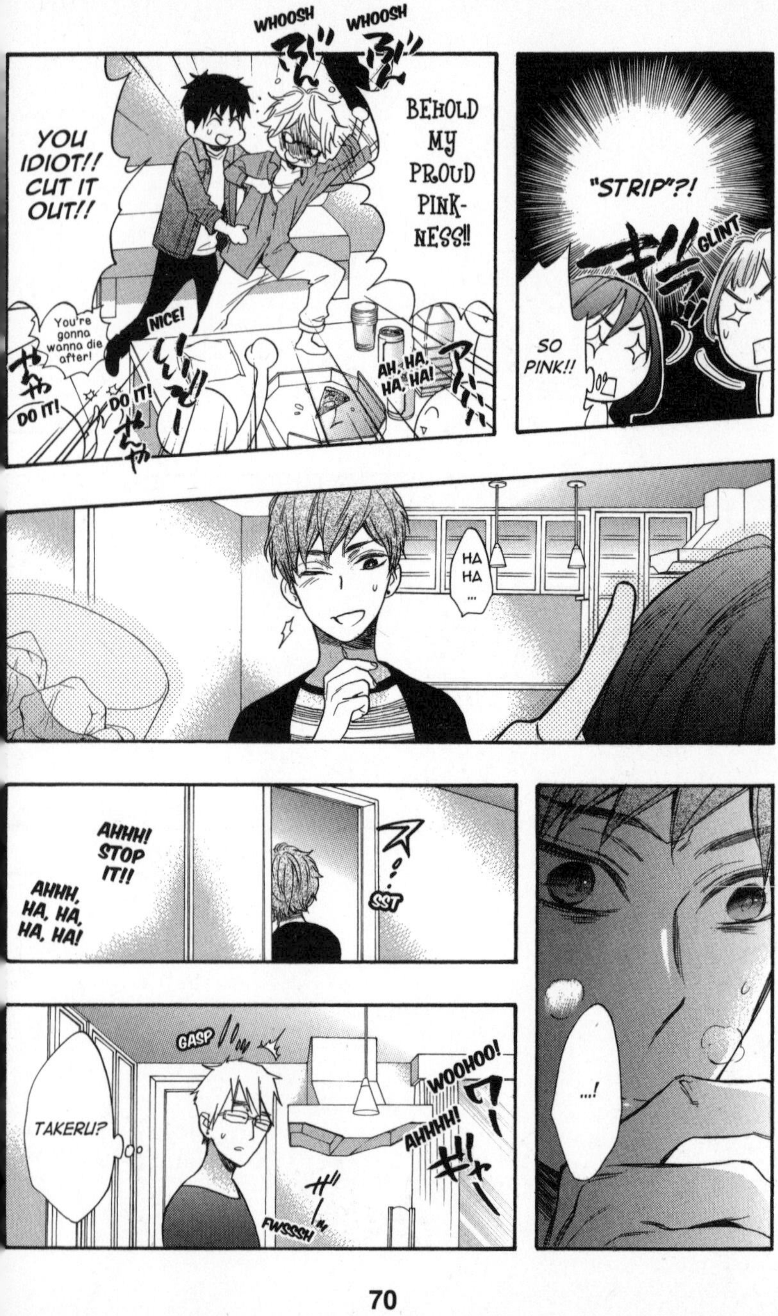
"STRIP"?!
GLINT
SO PINK!!
WHOOSH
WHOOSH
BEHOLD MY PROUD PINK-NESS!!
YOU IDIOT!! CUT IT OUT!!
AH, HA, HA, HA!
NICE!
You're gonna wanna die after!
DO IT!
DO IT!
HA HA ...
...!
SST
AHHH! STOP IT!!
AHHH, HA, HA, HA, HA!
WOOHOO!
AHHHH!
GASP
FWSSSH
TAKERU?

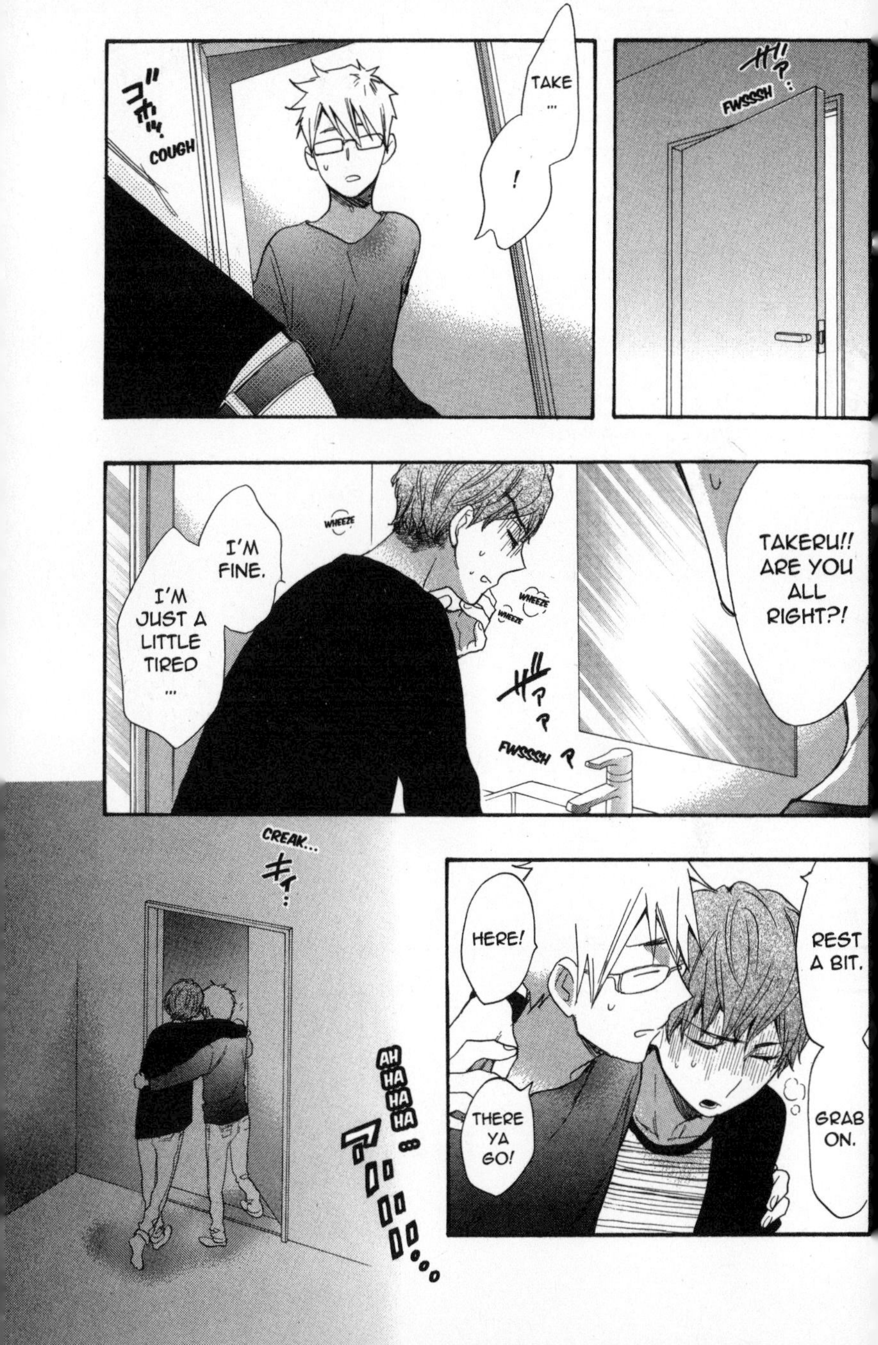
ザァ..
FWSSSH
ゴホッ
COUGH
TAKE ...
!
TAKERU!! ARE YOU ALL RIGHT?!
ザァァァ
FWSSSH
WHEEZE
WHEEZE
WHEEZE
I'M FINE.
I'M JUST A LITTLE TIRED ...
REST A BIT.
GRAB ON.
HERE!
THERE YA GO!
CREAK...
キィ..
AH HA HA HA...

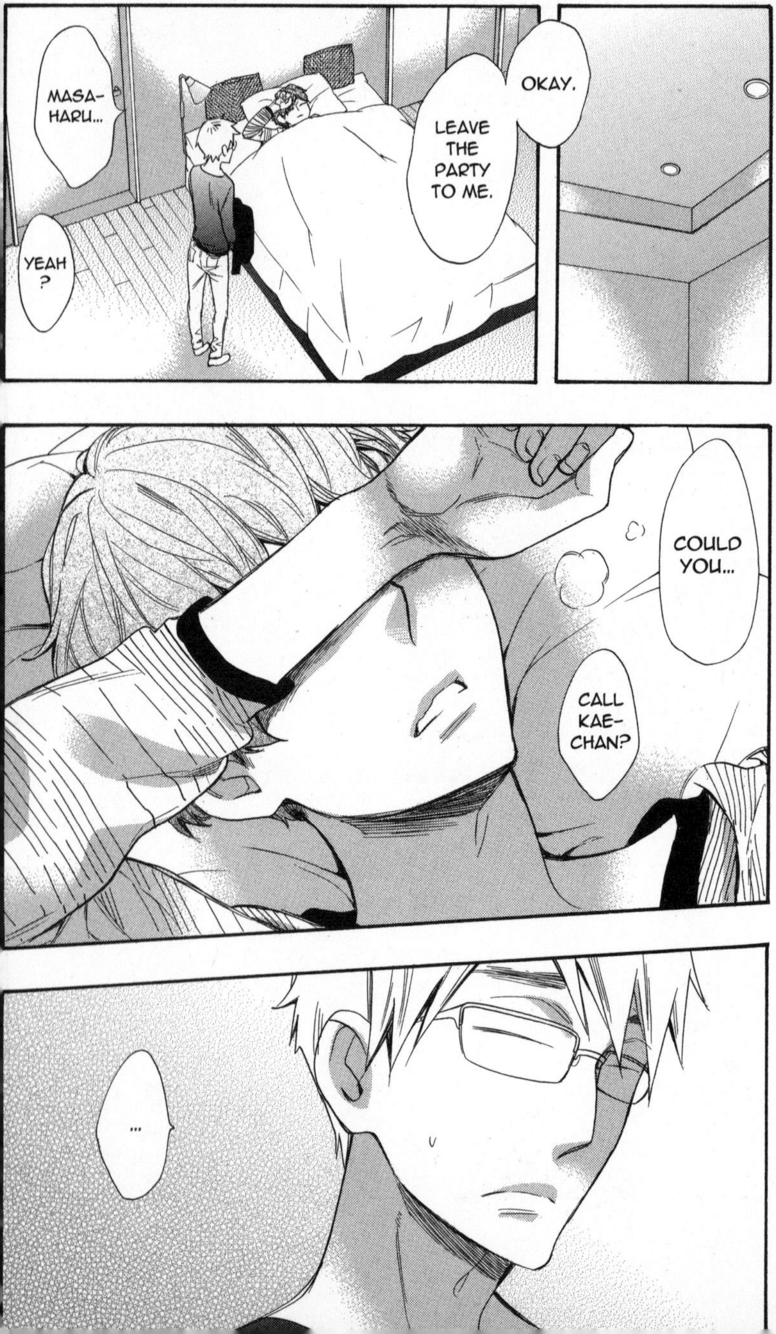
OKAY.
LEAVE THE PARTY TO ME.
MASA-HARU...
YEAH?
COULD YOU...
CALL KAE-CHAN?
...

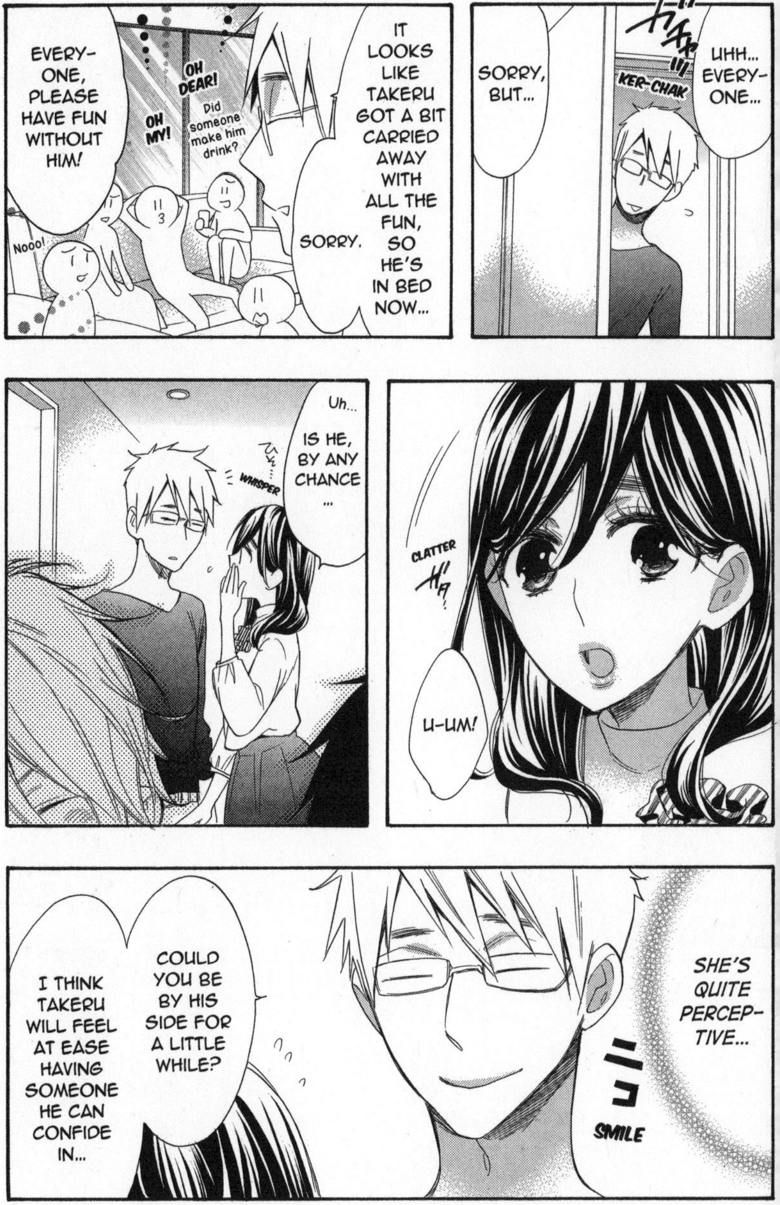
UHH... EVERY-ONE...
KER-CHAK
SORRY, BUT...
IT LOOKS LIKE TAKERU GOT A BIT CARRIED AWAY WITH ALL THE FUN, SO HE'S IN BED NOW...
SORRY.
OH DEAR!
Did someone make him drink?
OH MY!
EVERY-ONE, PLEASE HAVE FUN WITHOUT HIM!
Nooo!
CLATTER
U-UM!
Uh...
IS HE, BY ANY CHANCE ...
WHISPER
SHE'S QUITE PERCEP-TIVE...
SMILE
COULD YOU BE BY HIS SIDE FOR A LITTLE WHILE?
I THINK TAKERU WILL FEEL AT EASE HAVING SOMEONE HE CAN CONFIDE IN...

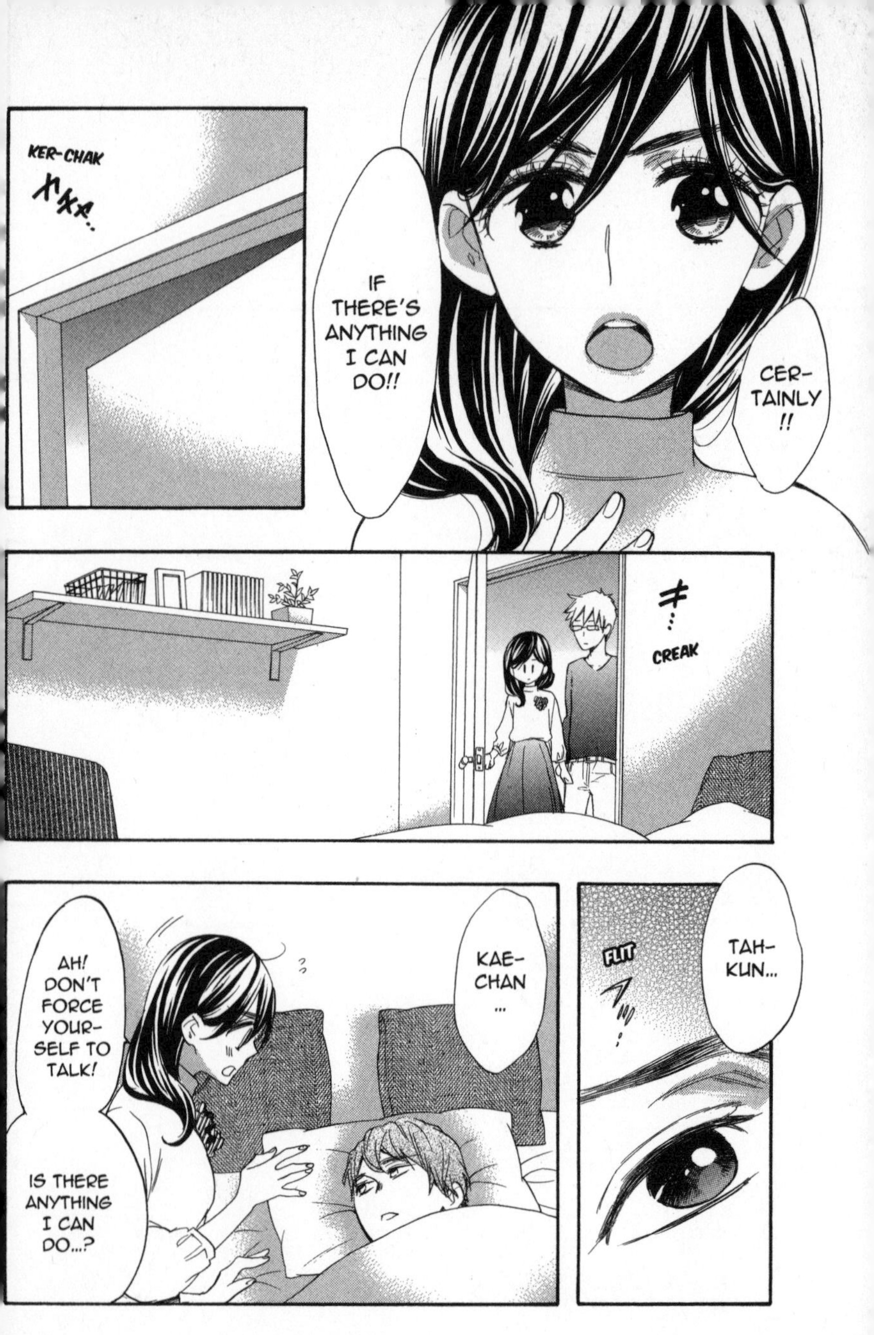
IF THERE'S ANYTHING I CAN DO!!
CER-TAINLY!!
KER-CHAK
CREAK
TAH-KUN...
FLIT
KAE-CHAN...
AH! DON'T FORCE YOUR-SELF TO TALK!
IS THERE ANYTHING I CAN DO...?

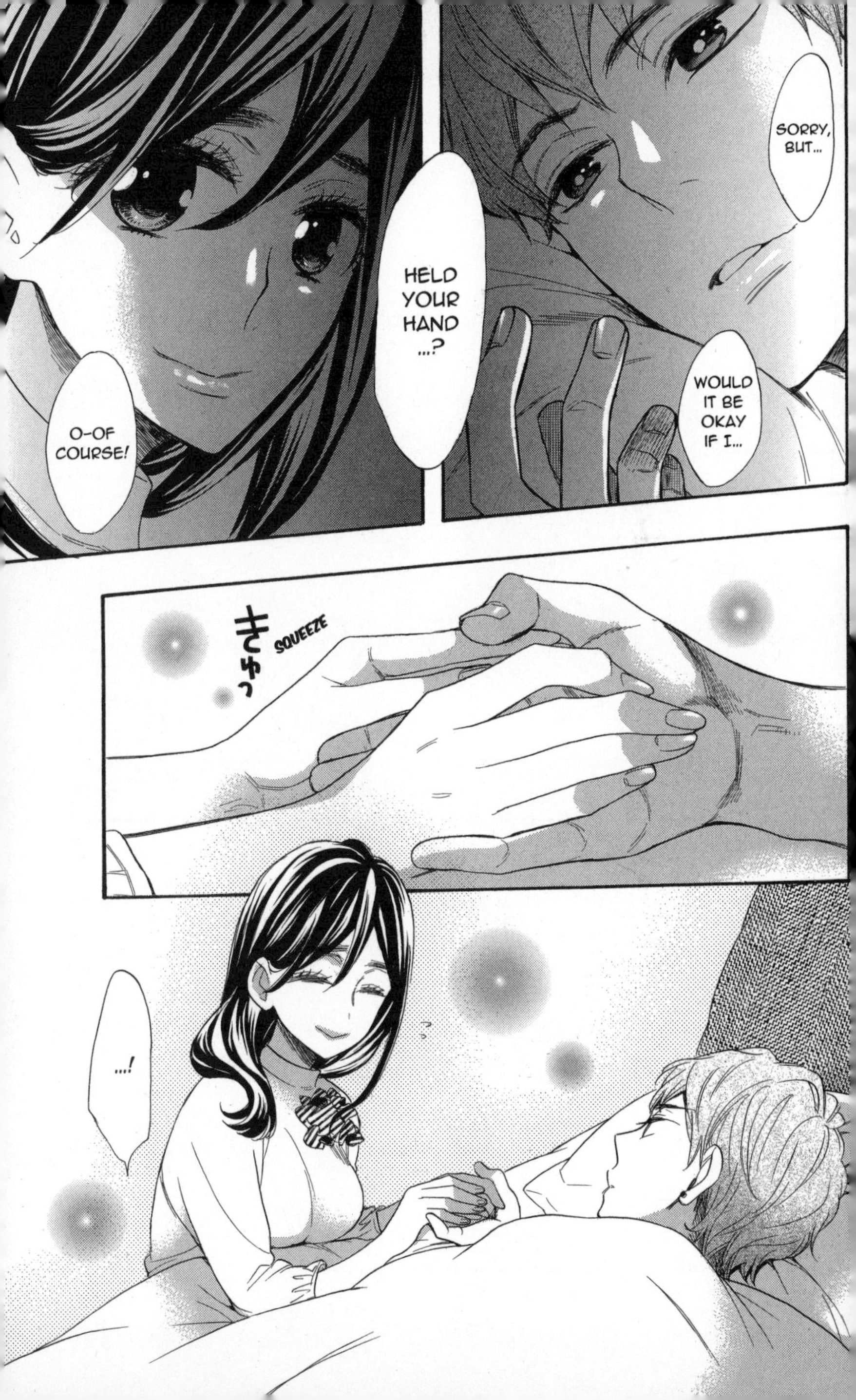
SORRY, BUT...
WOULD IT BE OKAY IF I...
HELD YOUR HAND ...?
O-OF COURSE!
きゅっ
SQUEEZE
...!

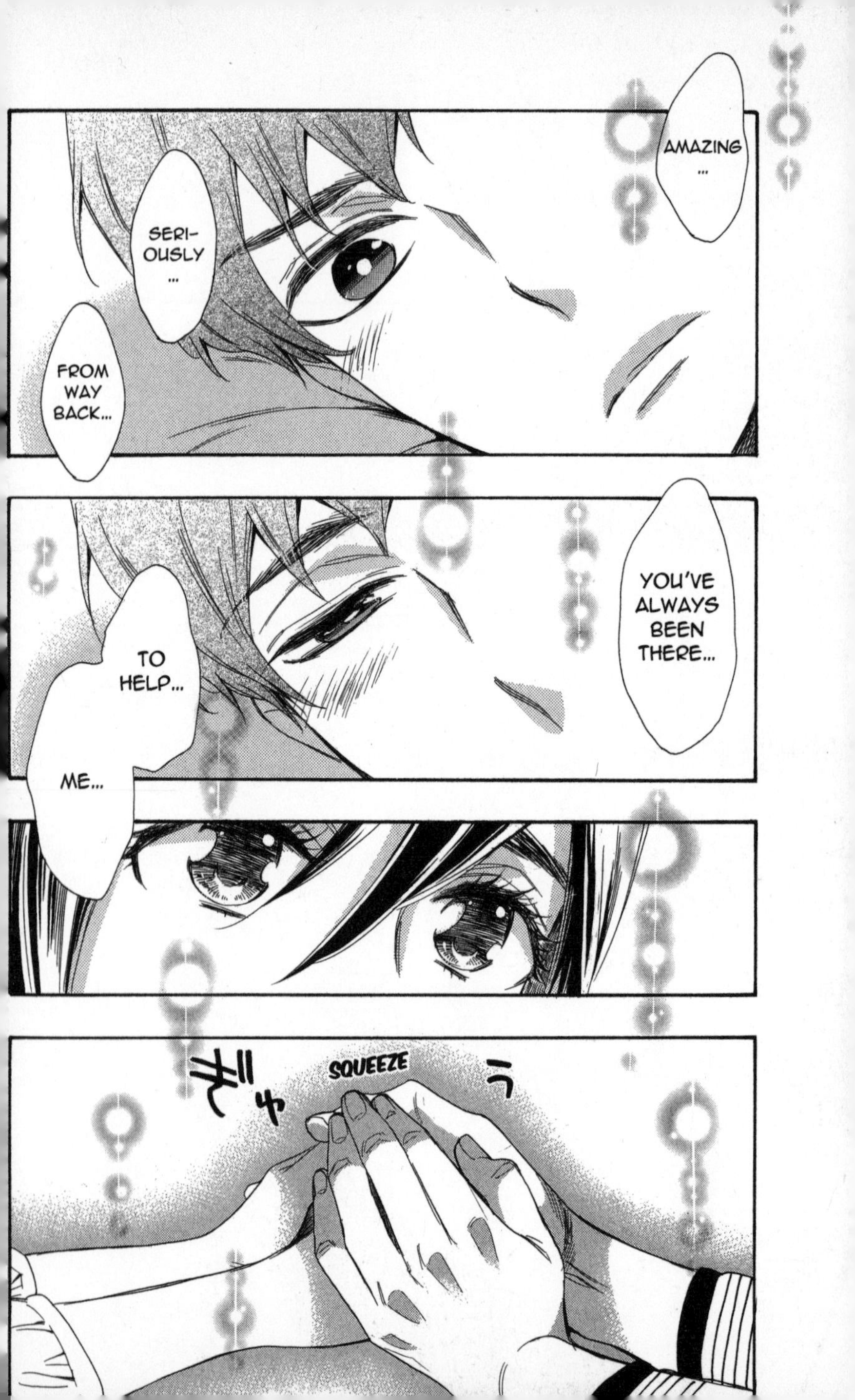
AMAZING...
SERI-OUSLY...
FROM WAY BACK...
YOU'VE ALWAYS BEEN THERE...
TO HELP...
ME...
ぎゅう
SQUEEZE

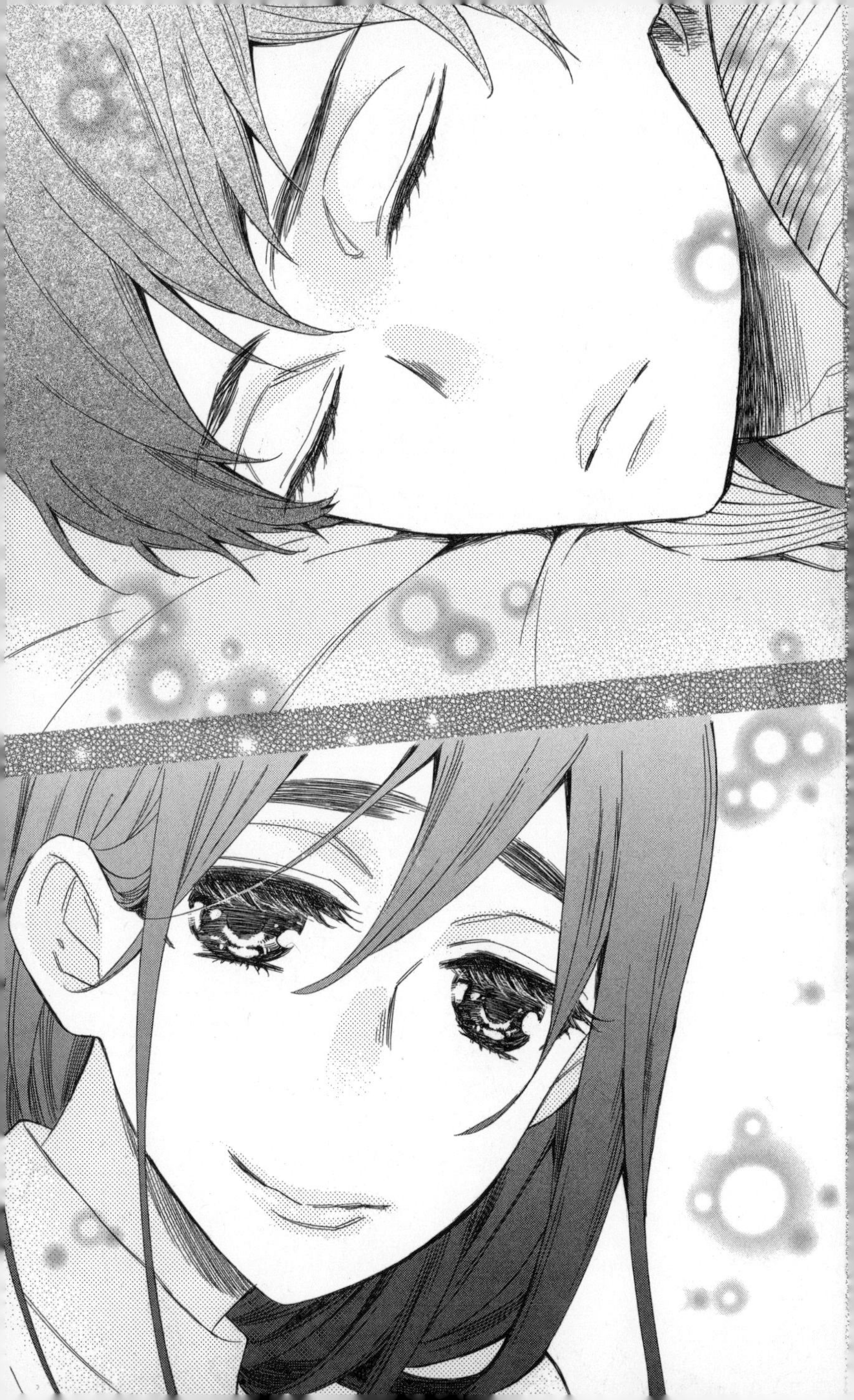

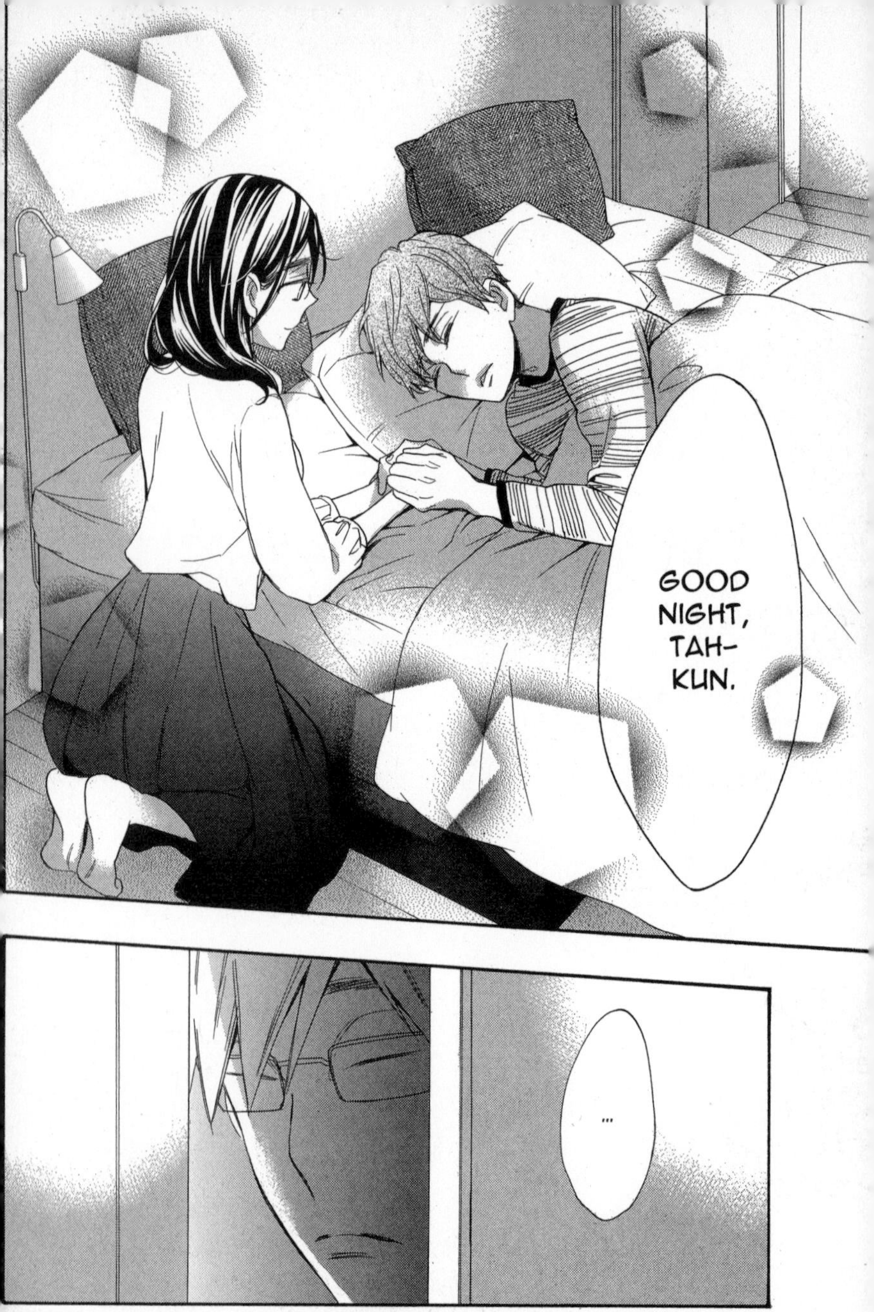
GOOD NIGHT, TAH-KUN.
...

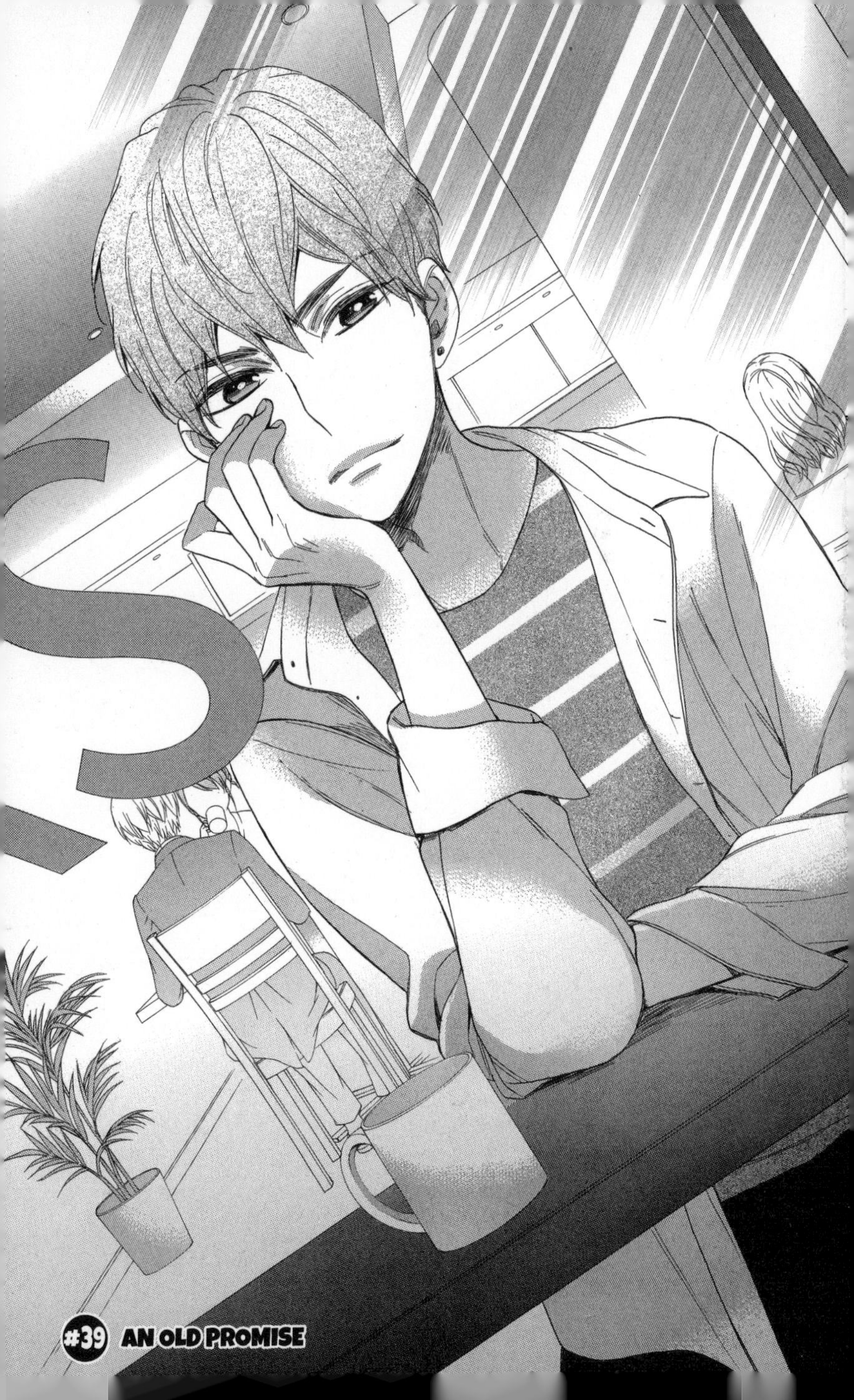
#39 AN OLD PROMISE

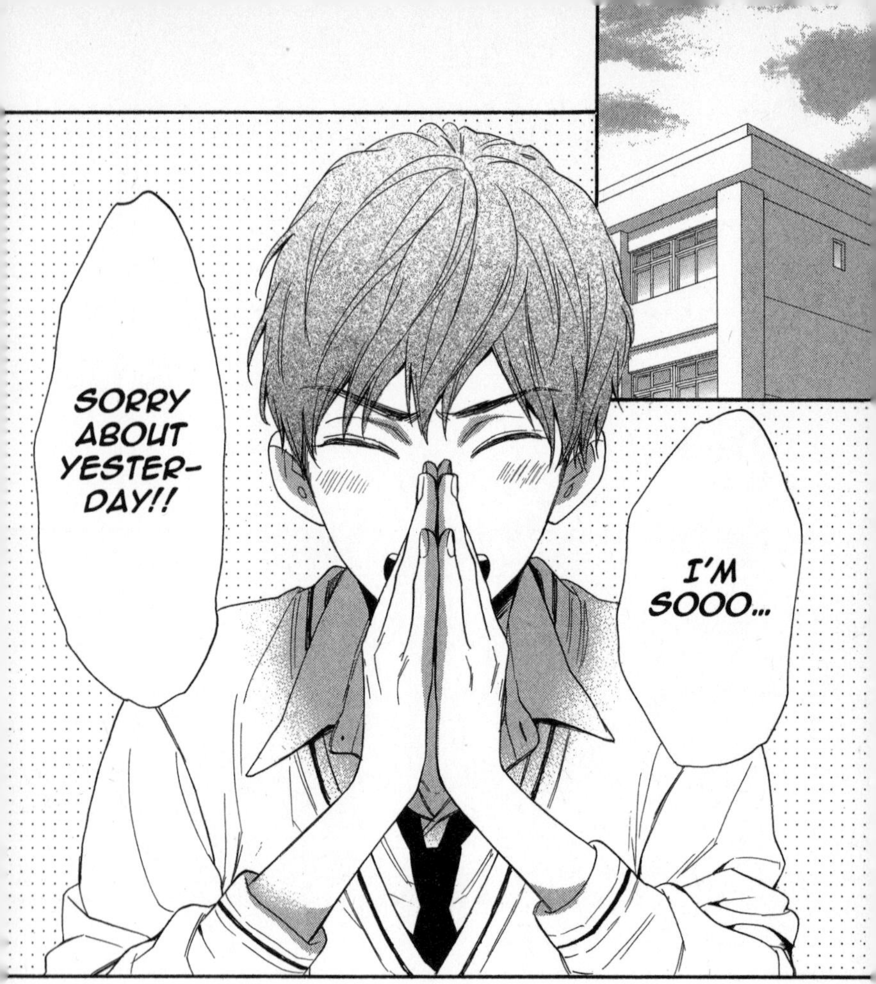
I'M SOOO...
SORRY ABOUT YESTER-DAY!!

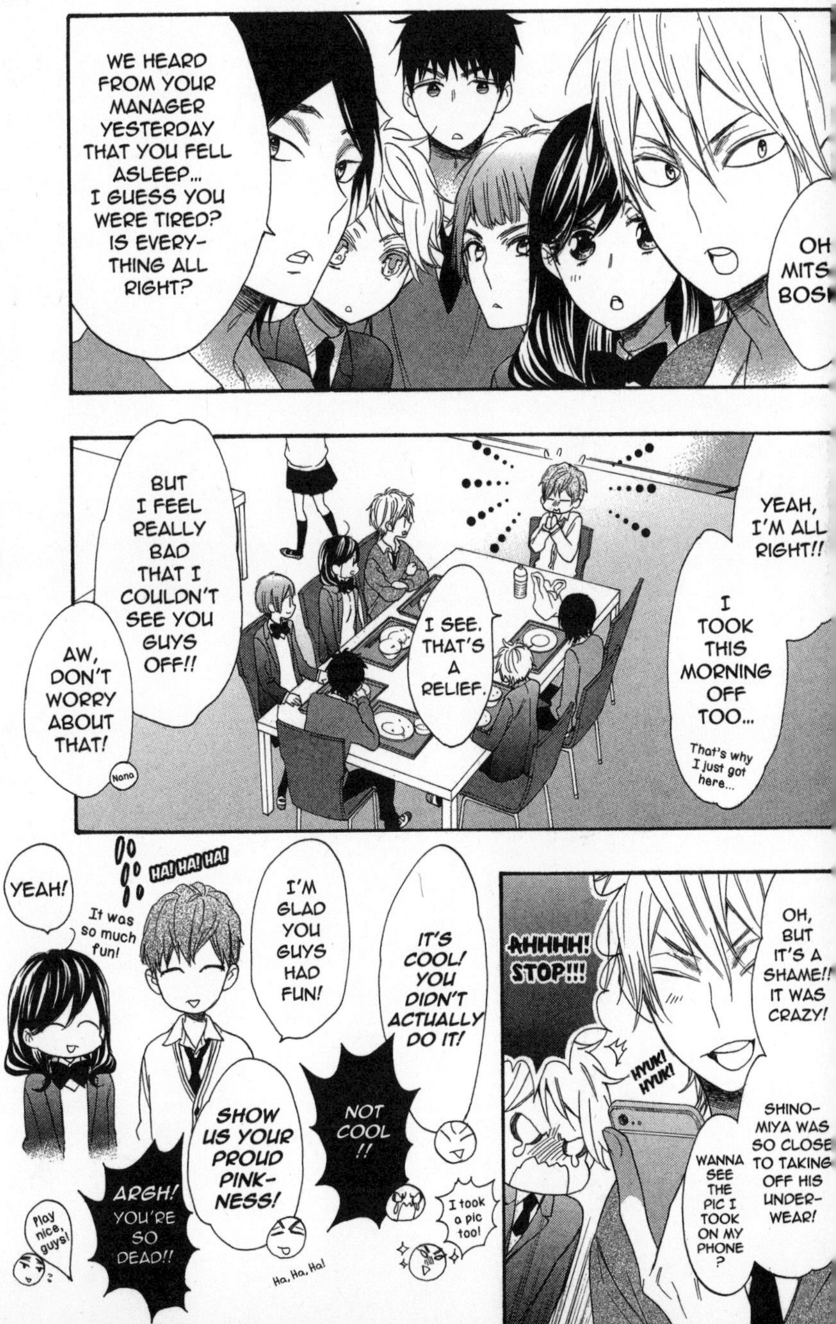
OH MITS BOS
WE HEARD FROM YOUR MANAGER YESTERDAY THAT YOU FELL ASLEEP... I GUESS YOU WERE TIRED? IS EVERYTHING ALL RIGHT?
YEAH, I'M ALL RIGHT!!
I TOOK THIS MORNING OFF TOO...
That's why I just got here...
I SEE. THAT'S A RELIEF.
BUT I FEEL REALLY BAD THAT I COULDN'T SEE YOU GUYS OFF!!
AW, DON'T WORRY ABOUT THAT!
Nana
OH, BUT IT'S A SHAME!! IT WAS CRAZY!
AHHHH! STOP!!!
SHINOMIYA WAS SO CLOSE TO TAKING OFF HIS UNDERWEAR!
WANNA SEE THE PIC I TOOK ON MY PHONE?
HYUK! HYUK!
IT'S COOL! YOU DIDN'T ACTUALLY DO IT!
I'M GLAD YOU GUYS HAD FUN!
HA! HA! HA!
YEAH!
It was so much fun!
NOT COOL!!
I took a pic too!
SHOW US YOUR PROUD PINKNESS!
Ha, Ha, Ha!
ARGH! YOU'RE SO DEAD!!
Play nice, guys!

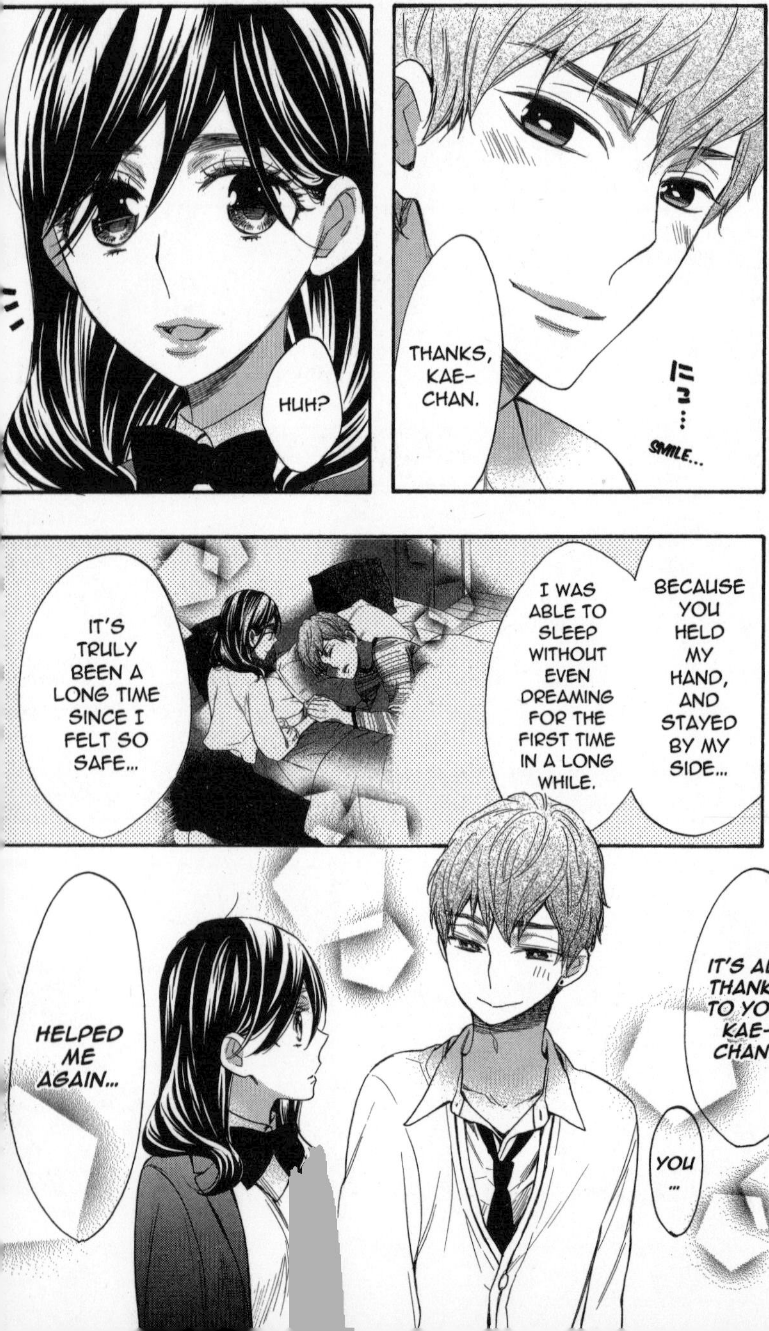
THANKS, KAE-CHAN.
にこ…
SMILE...
HUH?
BECAUSE YOU HELD MY HAND, AND STAYED BY MY SIDE...
I WAS ABLE TO SLEEP WITHOUT EVEN DREAMING FOR THE FIRST TIME IN A LONG WHILE.
IT'S TRULY BEEN A LONG TIME SINCE I FELT SO SAFE...
IT'S ALL THANKS TO YOU, KAE-CHAN...
YOU...
HELPED ME AGAIN...

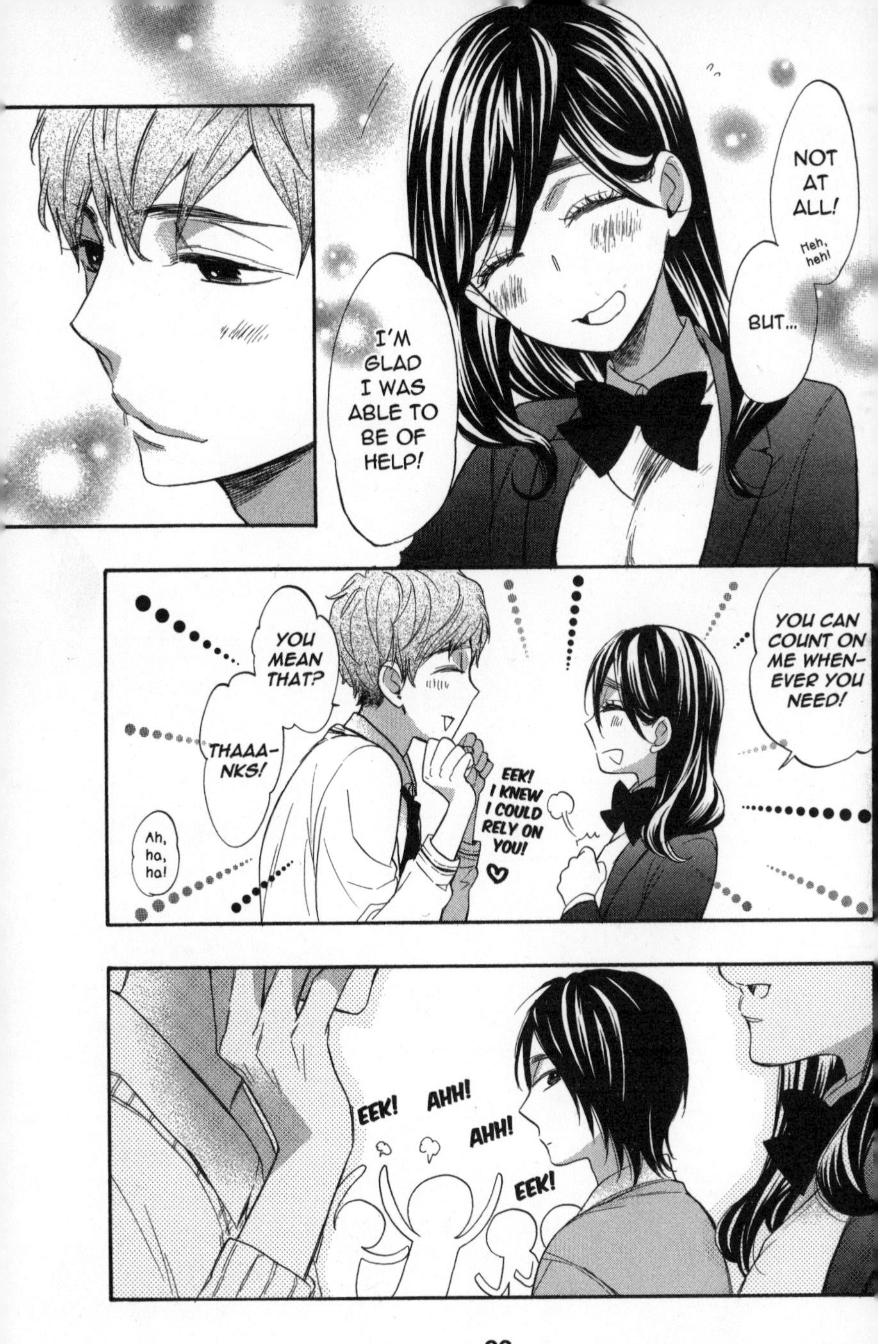
NOT AT ALL!
Heh, heh!
BUT...
I'M GLAD I WAS ABLE TO BE OF HELP!
YOU CAN COUNT ON ME WHEN-EVER YOU NEED!
EEK! I KNEW I COULD RELY ON YOU!
YOU MEAN THAT?
THAAA-NKS!
Ah, ha, ha!
EEK!
AHH!
AHH!
EEK!

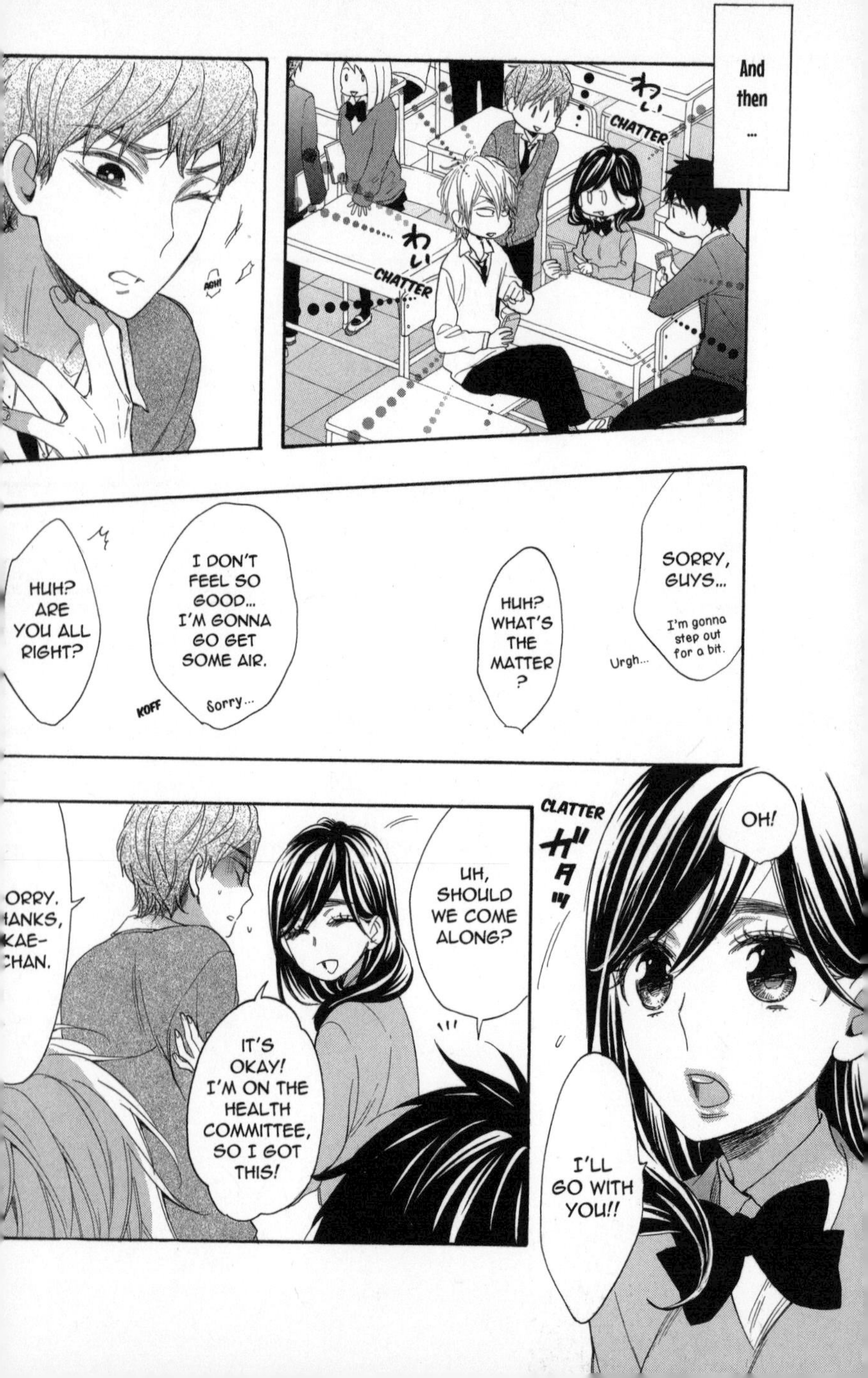
And then ...
わい
CHATTER
わい
CHATTER
AGH!
SORRY, GUYS...
I'm gonna step out for a bit.
Urgh...
HUH? WHAT'S THE MATTER?
I DON'T FEEL SO GOOD... I'M GONNA GO GET SOME AIR.
Sorry...
KOFF
HUH? ARE YOU ALL RIGHT?
CLATTER
ガタッ
OH!
I'LL GO WITH YOU!!
UH, SHOULD WE COME ALONG?
IT'S OKAY! I'M ON THE HEALTH COMMITTEE, SO I GOT THIS!
ORRY. HANKS, KAE- CHAN.

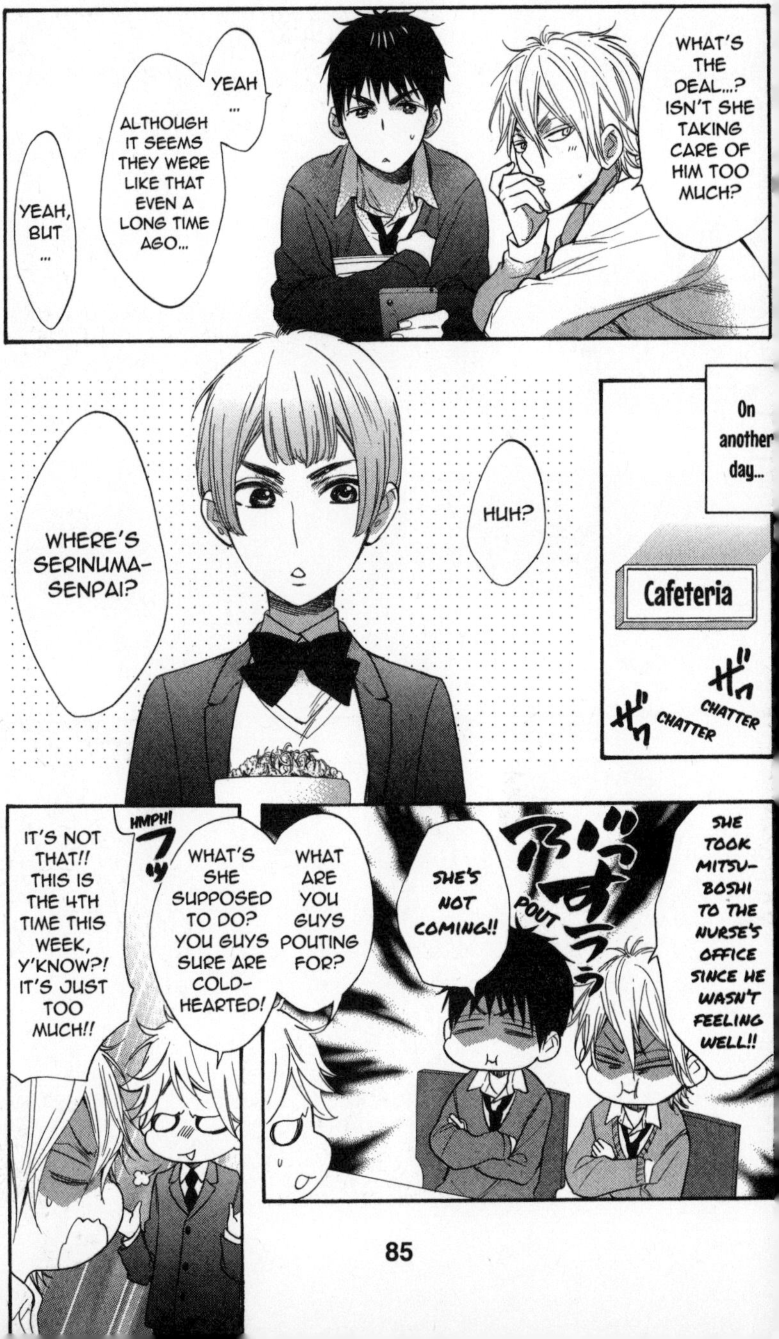
WHAT'S THE DEAL...? ISN'T SHE TAKING CARE OF HIM TOO MUCH?
YEAH ...
ALTHOUGH IT SEEMS THEY WERE LIKE THAT EVEN A LONG TIME AGO...
YEAH, BUT ...
On another day...
Cafeteria
CHATTER
CHATTER
HUH?
WHERE'S SERINUMA-SENPAI?
SHE TOOK MITSU-BOSHI TO THE NURSE'S OFFICE SINCE HE WASN'T FEELING WELL!!
SHE'S NOT COMING!!
POUT
WHAT ARE YOU GUYS POUTING FOR?
WHAT'S SHE SUPPOSED TO DO? YOU GUYS SURE ARE COLD-HEARTED!
HMPH!
IT'S NOT THAT!! THIS IS THE 4TH TIME THIS WEEK, Y'KNOW?! IT'S JUST TOO MUCH!!

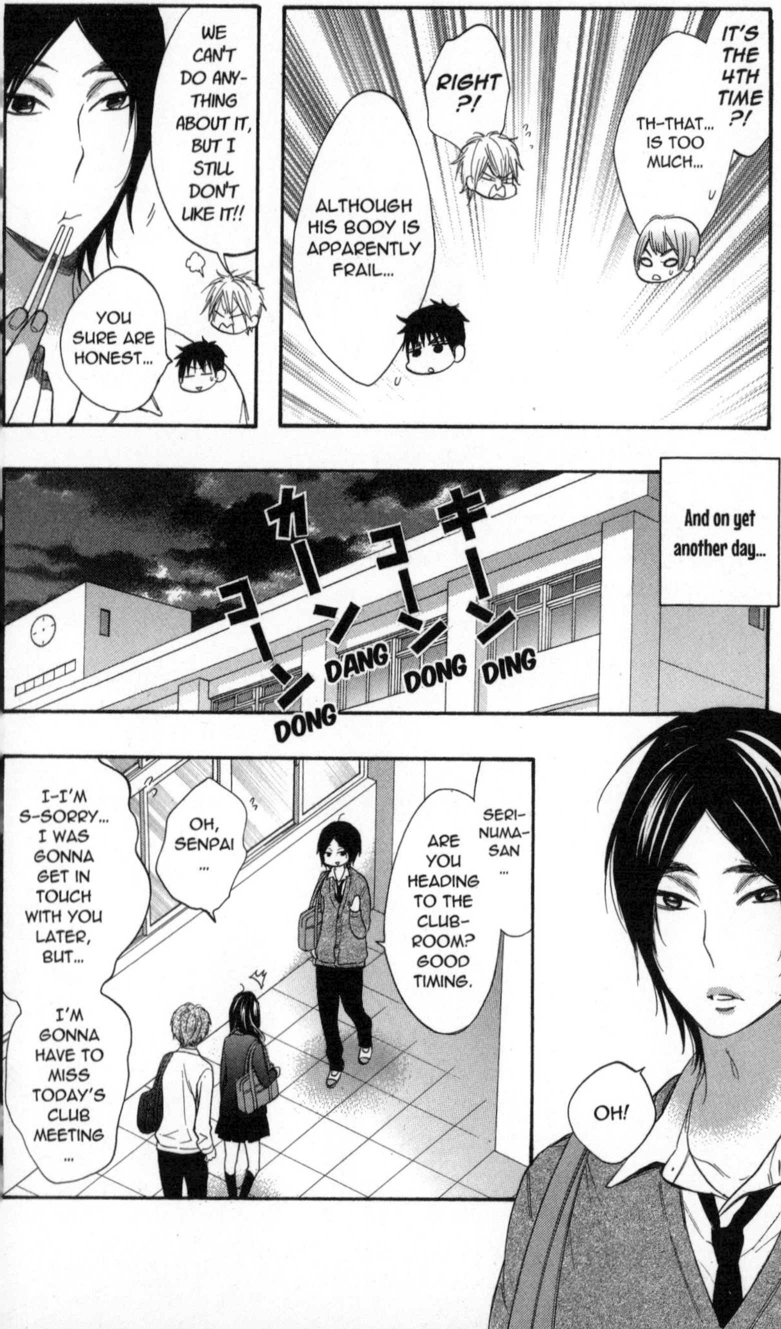
IT'S THE 4TH TIME ?!
RIGHT ?!
TH-THAT... IS TOO MUCH...
ALTHOUGH HIS BODY IS APPARENTLY FRAIL...
WE CAN'T DO ANY-THING ABOUT IT, BUT I STILL DON'T LIKE IT!!
YOU SURE ARE HONEST...
And on yet another day...
キーン
DING
コーン
DONG
カーン
DANG
コーン
DONG
OH!
SERI-NUMA-SAN ...
ARE YOU HEADING TO THE CLUB-ROOM? GOOD TIMING.
OH, SENPAI ...
I-I'M S-SORRY... I WAS GONNA GET IN TOUCH WITH YOU LATER, BUT...
I'M GONNA HAVE TO MISS TODAY'S CLUB MEETING ...

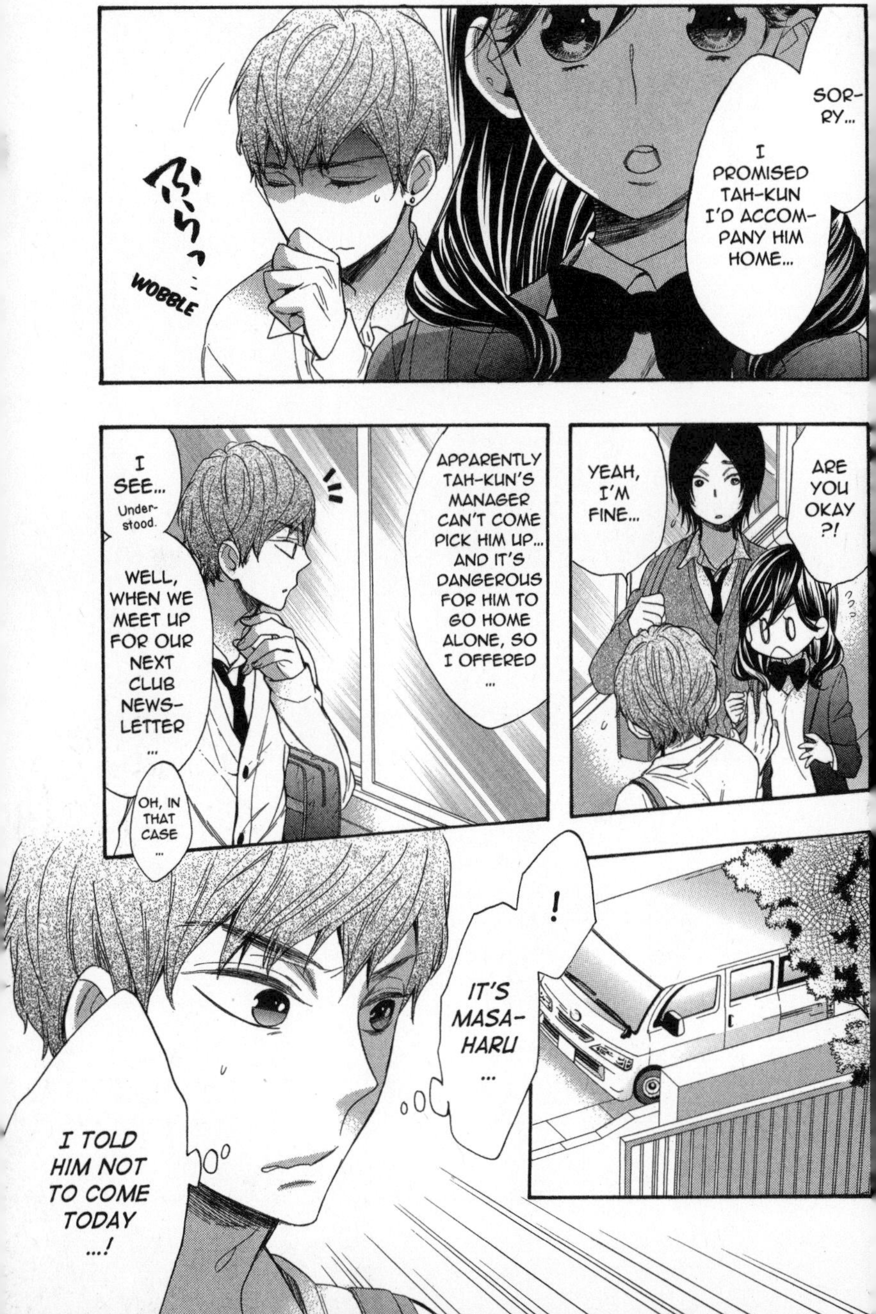
SORRY... I PROMISED TAH-KUN I'D ACCOMPANY HIM HOME...
ふらっ
WOBBLE
ARE YOU OKAY?!
YEAH, I'M FINE...
APPARENTLY TAH-KUN'S MANAGER CAN'T COME PICK HIM UP... AND IT'S DANGEROUS FOR HIM TO GO HOME ALONE, SO I OFFERED...
I SEE...
Understood.
WELL, WHEN WE MEET UP FOR OUR NEXT CLUB NEWSLETTER...
OH, IN THAT CASE...
!
IT'S MASAHARU...
I TOLD HIM NOT TO COME TODAY...!

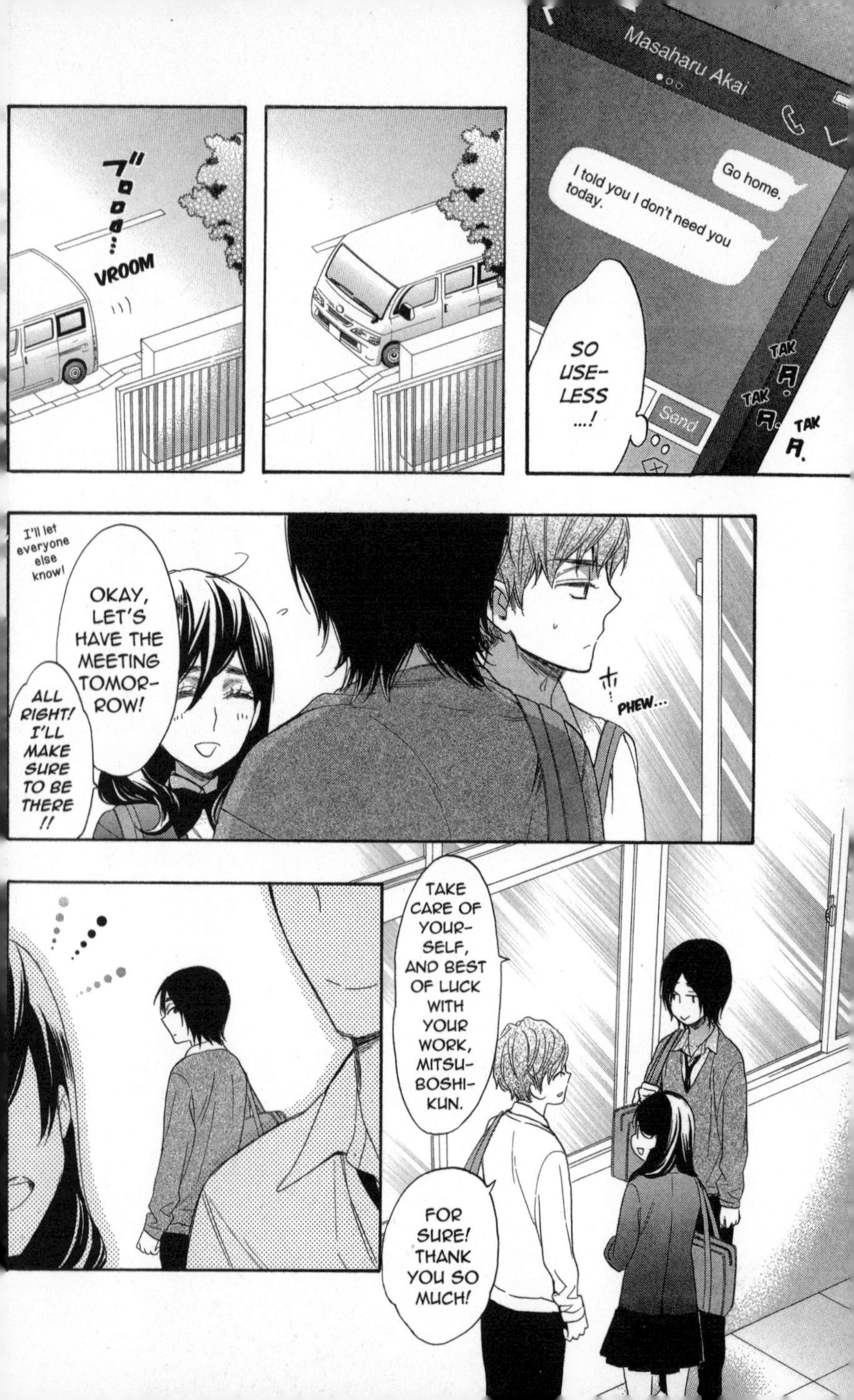
Masaharu Akai
Go home.
I told you I don't need you today.
SO USELESS ...!
Send
TAK
TAK
TAK
VROOM
PHEW...
OKAY, LET'S HAVE THE MEETING TOMORROW!
I'll let everyone else know!
ALL RIGHT! I'LL MAKE SURE TO BE THERE !!
TAKE CARE OF YOURSELF, AND BEST OF LUCK WITH YOUR WORK, MITSUBOSHI-KUN.
FOR SURE! THANK YOU SO MUCH!

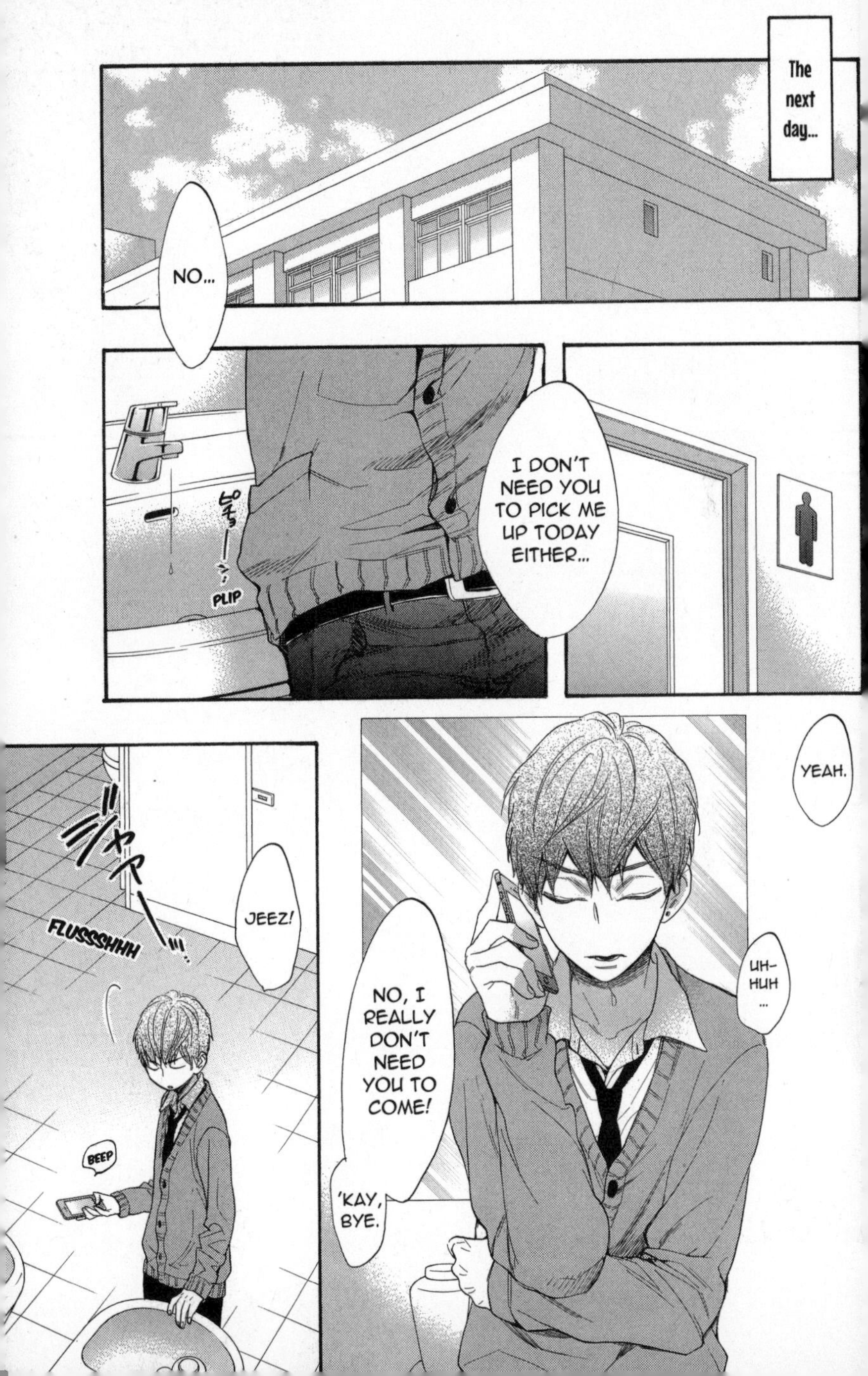
The next day...
NO...
I DON'T NEED YOU TO PICK ME UP TODAY EITHER...
PLIP
YEAH.
UH-HUH...
NO, I REALLY DON'T NEED YOU TO COME!
'KAY, BYE.
JEEZ!
FLUSSSHHH
BEEP

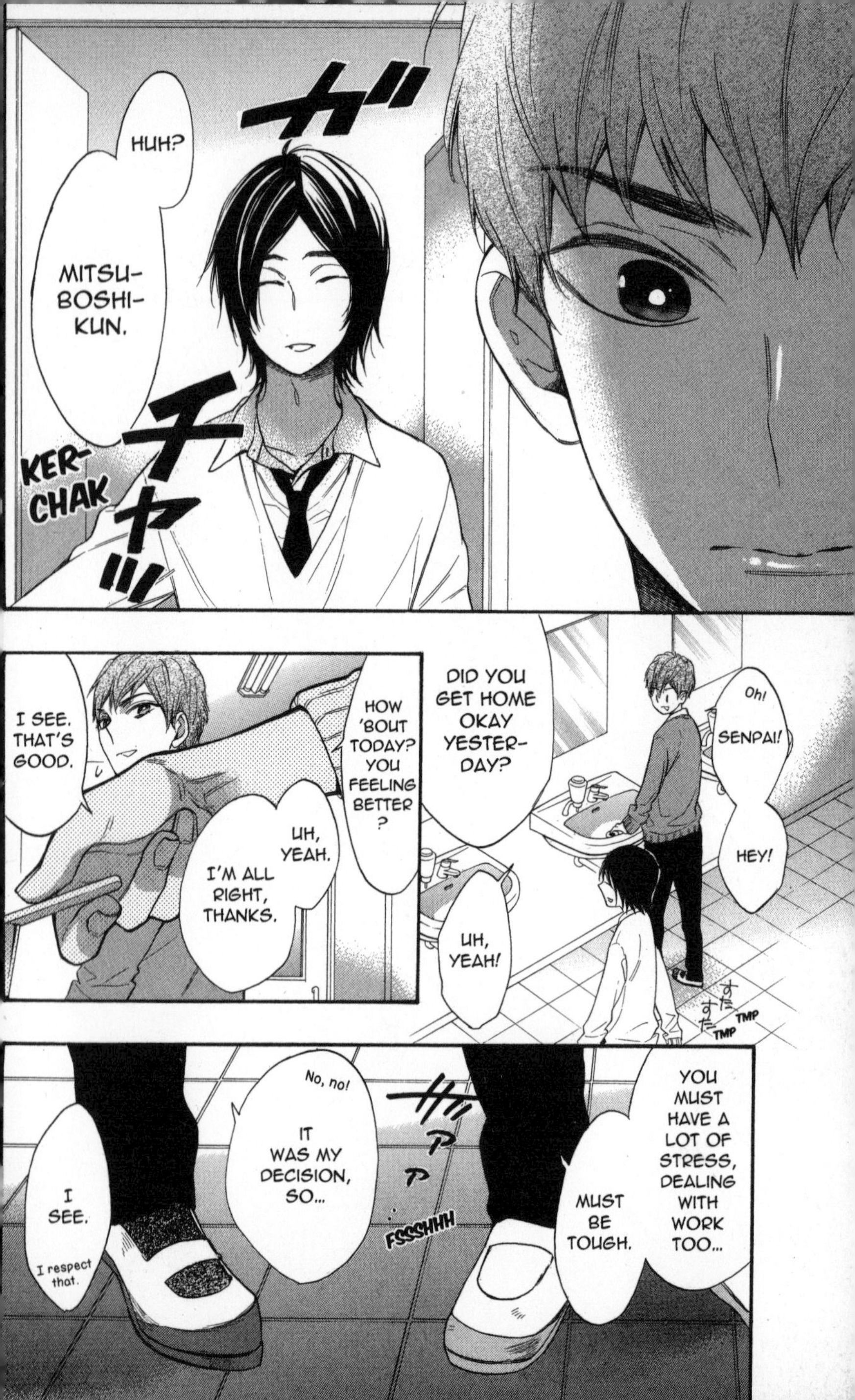
ガチャ!!
KER-CHAK
HUH?
MITSU-BOSHI-KUN.
Oh! SENPAI!
HEY!
DID YOU GET HOME OKAY YESTER-DAY?
UH, YEAH!
すたすた
TMP TMP
HOW 'BOUT TODAY? YOU FEELING BETTER?
UH, YEAH.
I'M ALL RIGHT, THANKS.
I SEE. THAT'S GOOD.
YOU MUST HAVE A LOT OF STRESS, DEALING WITH WORK TOO...
MUST BE TOUGH.
ザァァ
FSSSHHH
No, no!
IT WAS MY DECISION, SO...
I SEE.
I respect that.

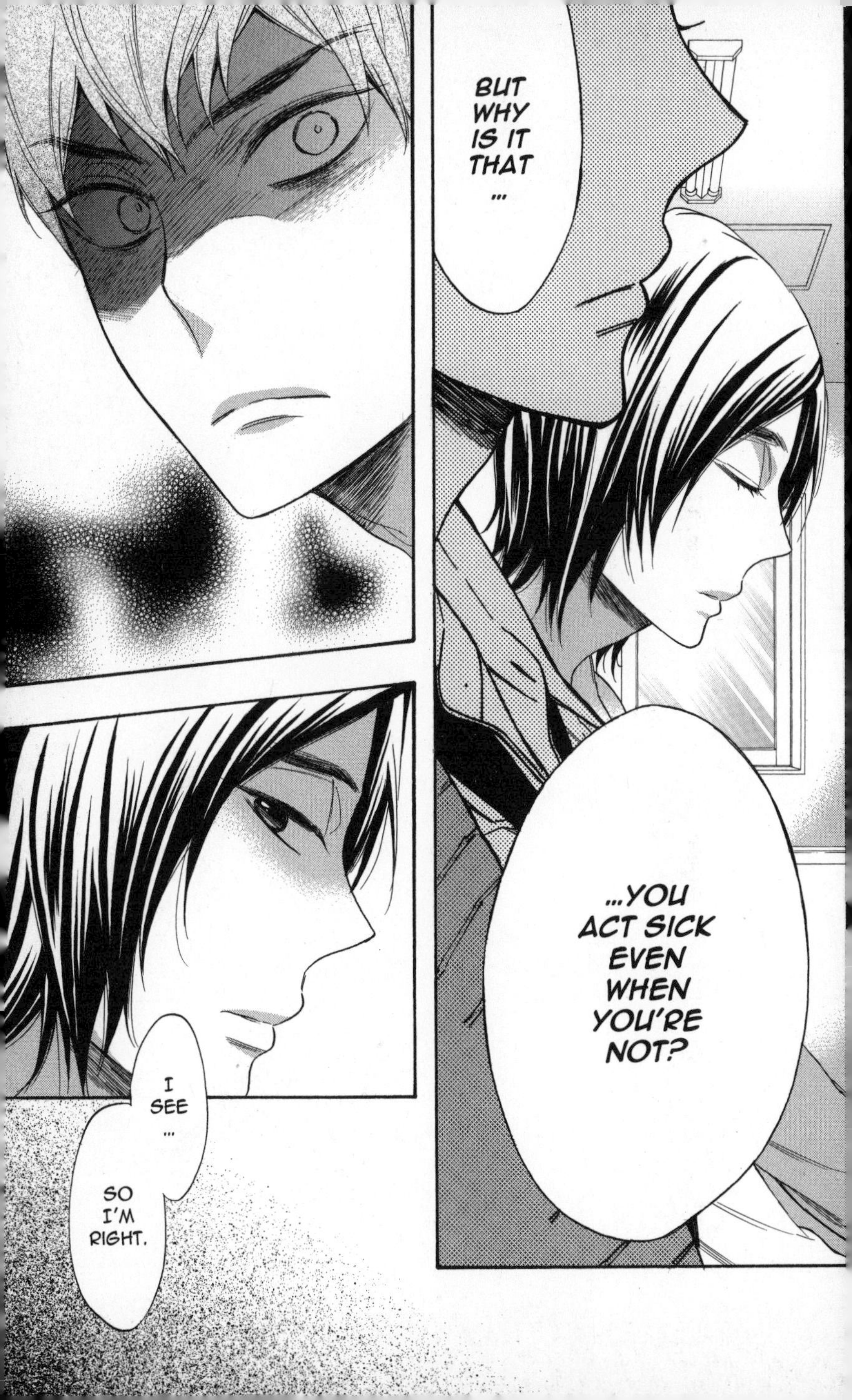
BUT WHY IS IT THAT ...
...YOU ACT SICK EVEN WHEN YOU'RE NOT?
I SEE ...
SO I'M RIGHT.

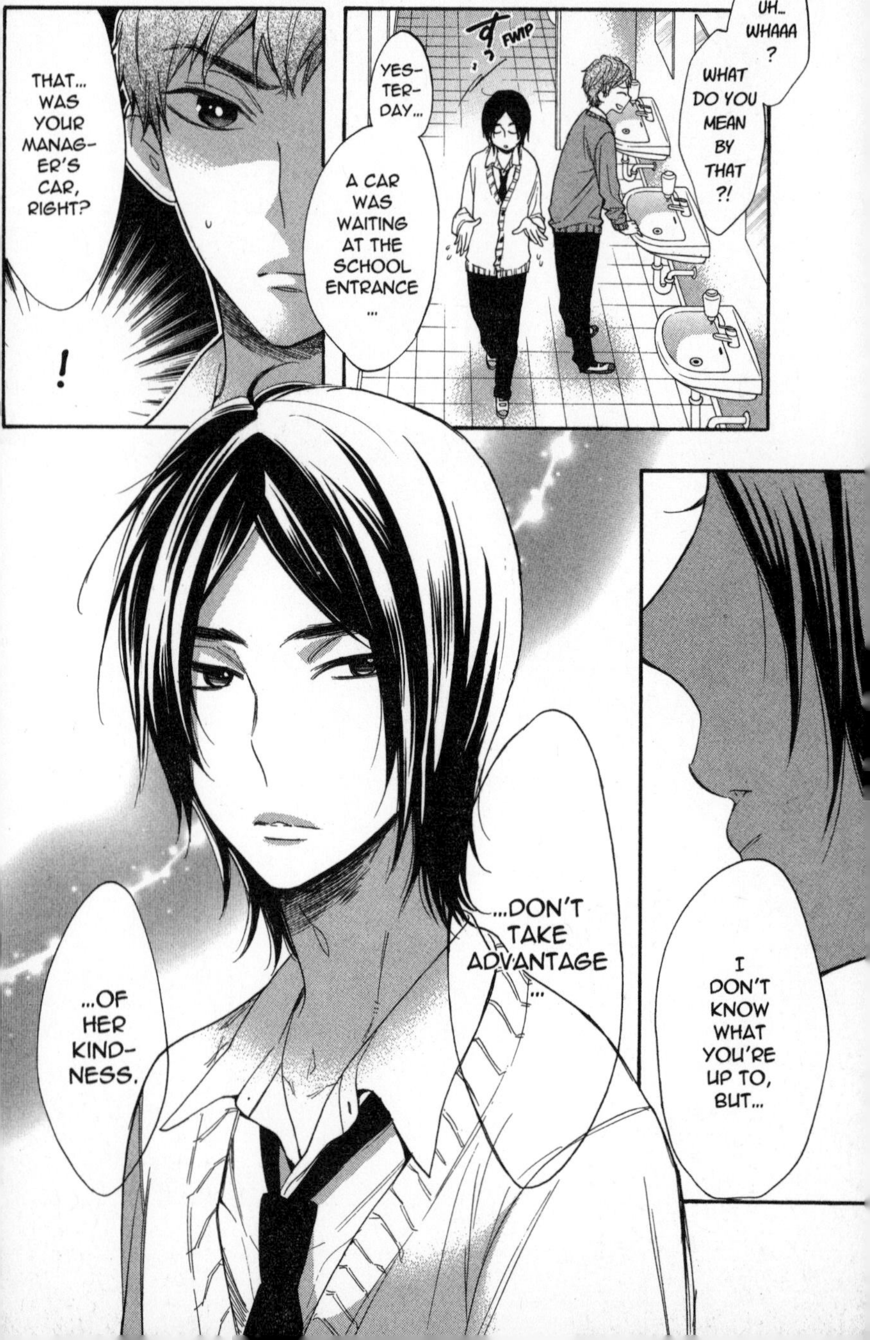
UH... WHAAA? WHAT DO YOU MEAN BY THAT?!
す FWIP
YES-TERDAY...
A CAR WAS WAITING AT THE SCHOOL ENTRANCE...
THAT... WAS YOUR MANAGER'S CAR, RIGHT?
!
I DON'T KNOW WHAT YOU'RE UP TO, BUT...
...DON'T TAKE ADVANTAGE...
...OF HER KINDNESS.

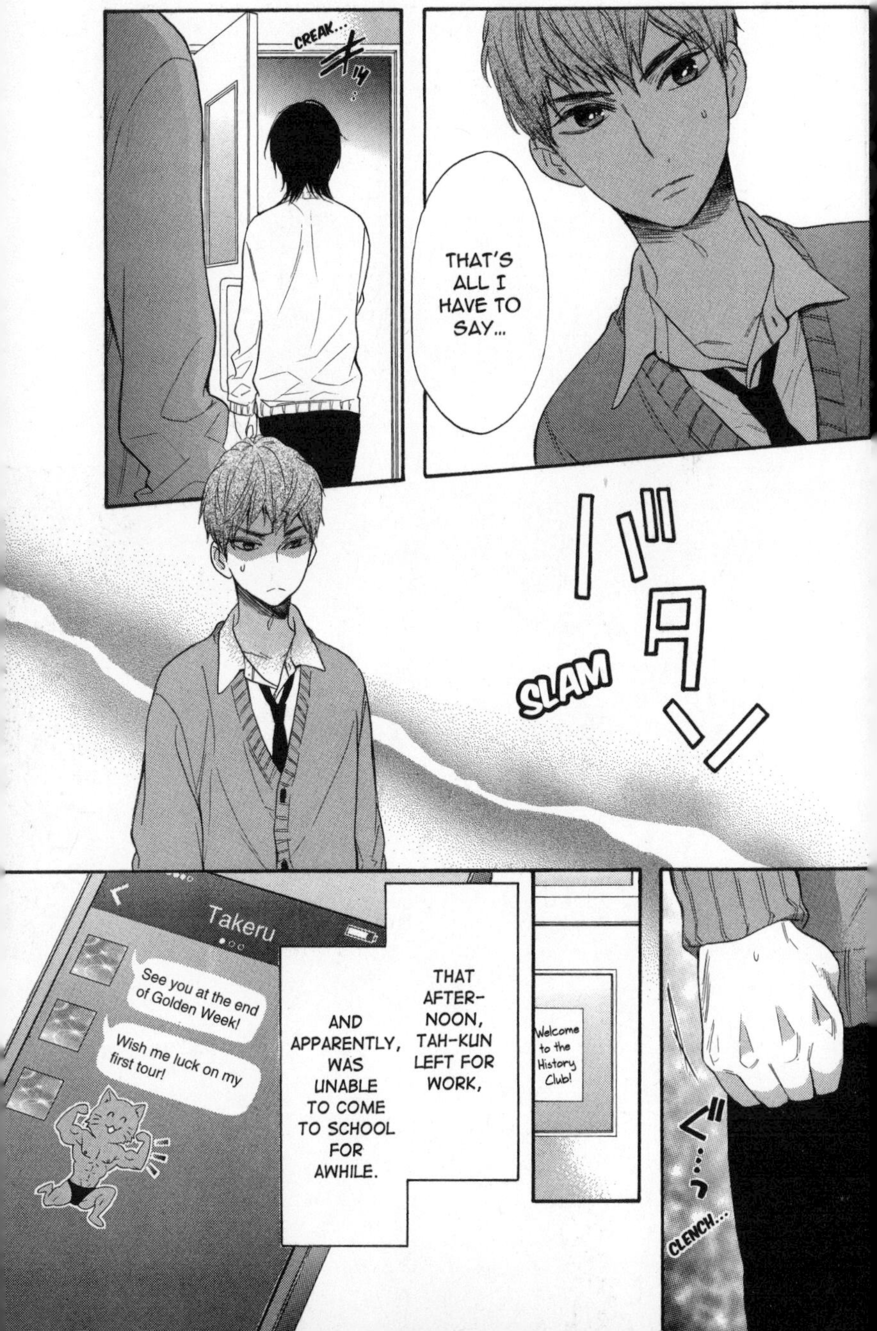
THAT'S ALL I HAVE TO SAY...
CREAK...
バタン
SLAM
CLENCH...
Welcome to the History Club!
THAT AFTERNOON, TAH-KUN LEFT FOR WORK,
AND APPARENTLY, WAS UNABLE TO COME TO SCHOOL FOR AWHILE.
Takeru
See you at the end of Golden Week!
Wish me luck on my first tour!

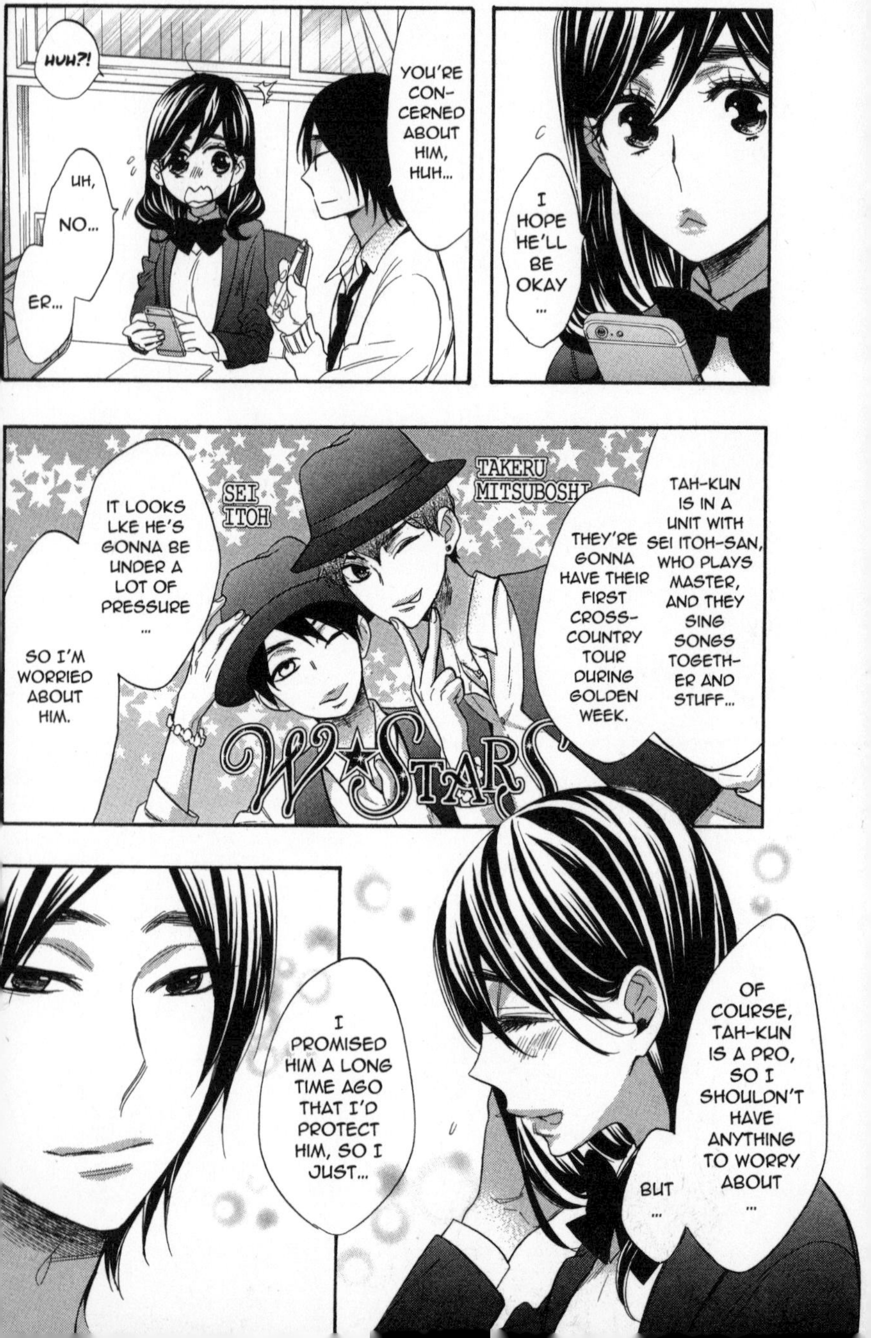
I HOPE HE'LL BE OKAY ...
YOU'RE CON-CERNED ABOUT HIM, HUH...
HUH?!
UH, NO... ER...
TAH-KUN IS IN A UNIT WITH SEI ITOH-SAN, WHO PLAYS MASTER, AND THEY SING SONGS TOGETH-ER AND STUFF...
THEY'RE GONNA HAVE THEIR FIRST CROSS-COUNTRY TOUR DURING GOLDEN WEEK.
TAKERU MITSUBOSHI
SEI ITOH
W☆STARS
IT LOOKS LKE HE'S GONNA BE UNDER A LOT OF PRESSURE ...
SO I'M WORRIED ABOUT HIM.
OF COURSE, TAH-KUN IS A PRO, SO I SHOULDN'T HAVE ANYTHING TO WORRY ABOUT ...
BUT ...
I PROMISED HIM A LONG TIME AGO THAT I'D PROTECT HIM, SO I JUST...

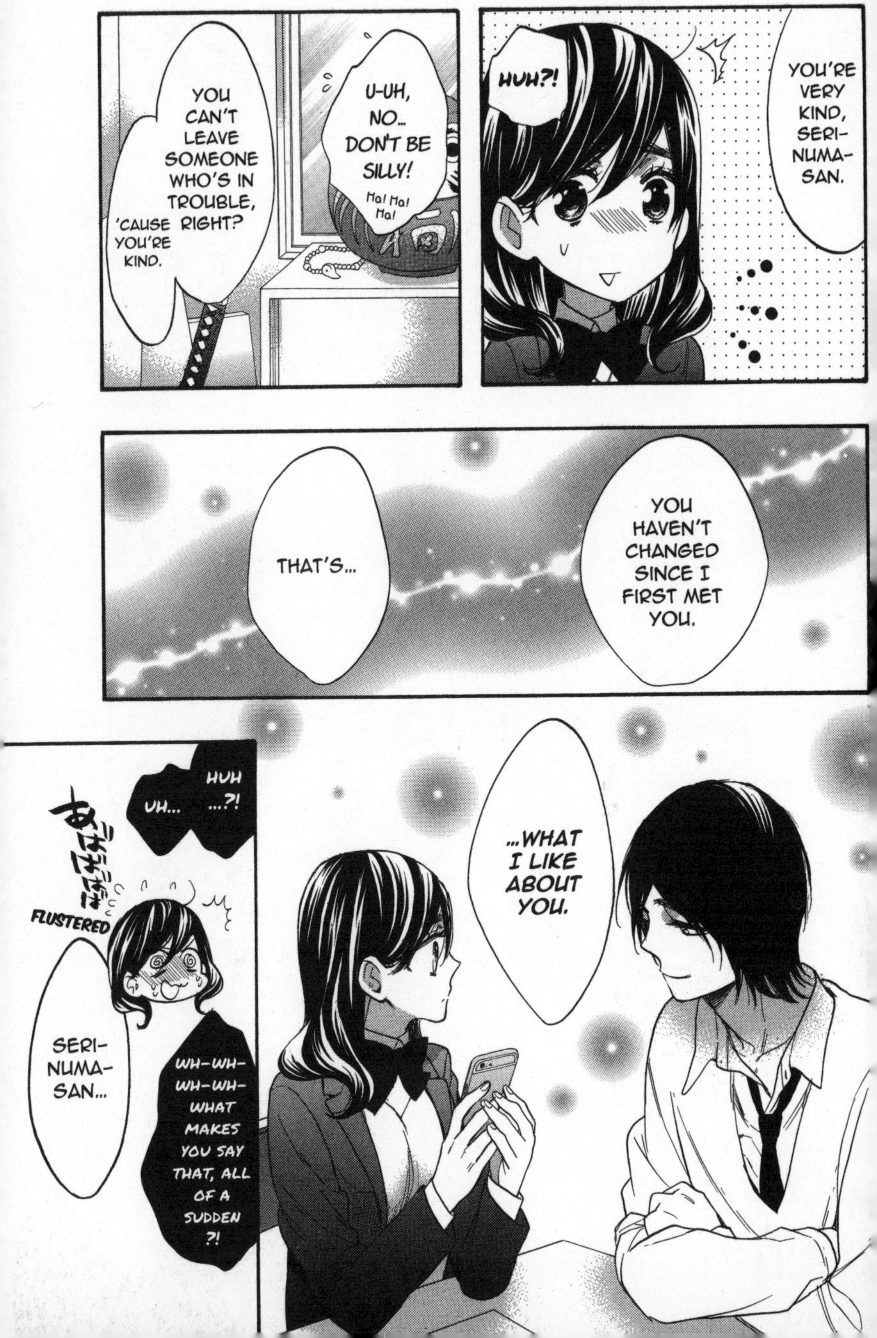
YOU'RE VERY KIND, SERI-NUMA-SAN.
HUH?!
U-UH, NO... DON'T BE SILLY!
Ha! Ha! Ha!
YOU CAN'T LEAVE SOMEONE WHO'S IN TROUBLE, RIGHT?
'CAUSE YOU'RE KIND.
YOU HAVEN'T CHANGED SINCE I FIRST MET YOU.
THAT'S...
...WHAT I LIKE ABOUT YOU.
HUH ...?!
UH...
FLUSTERED
WH-WH-WH-WH-WHAT MAKES YOU SAY THAT, ALL OF A SUDDEN ?!
SERI-NUMA-SAN...

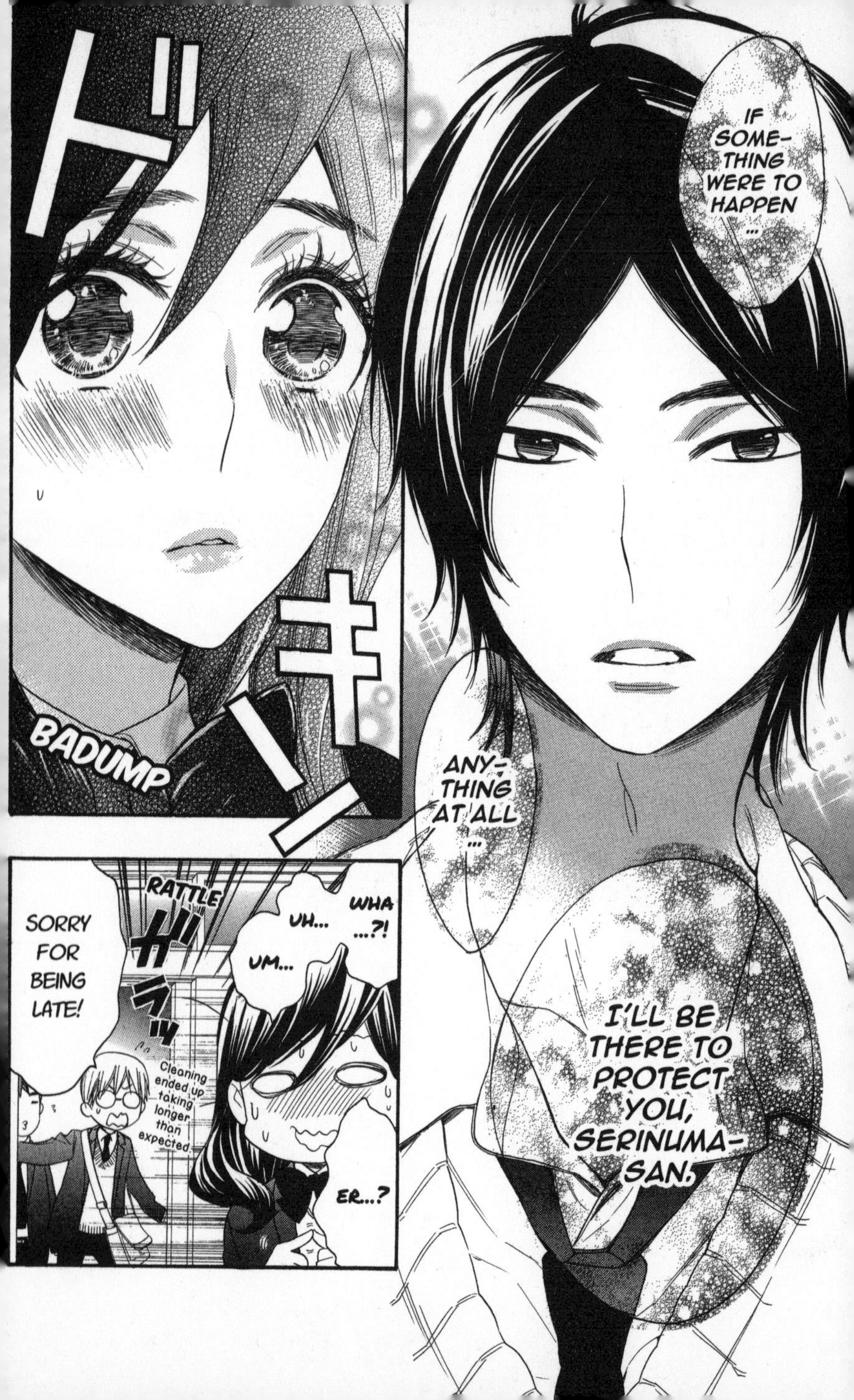
IF SOMETHING WERE TO HAPPEN...
ANYTHING AT ALL...
I'LL BE THERE TO PROTECT YOU, SERINUMA-SAN.
BADUMP
WHA ...?!
UH...
RATTLE
UM...
SORRY FOR BEING LATE!
Cleaning ended up taking longer than expected.
ER...?

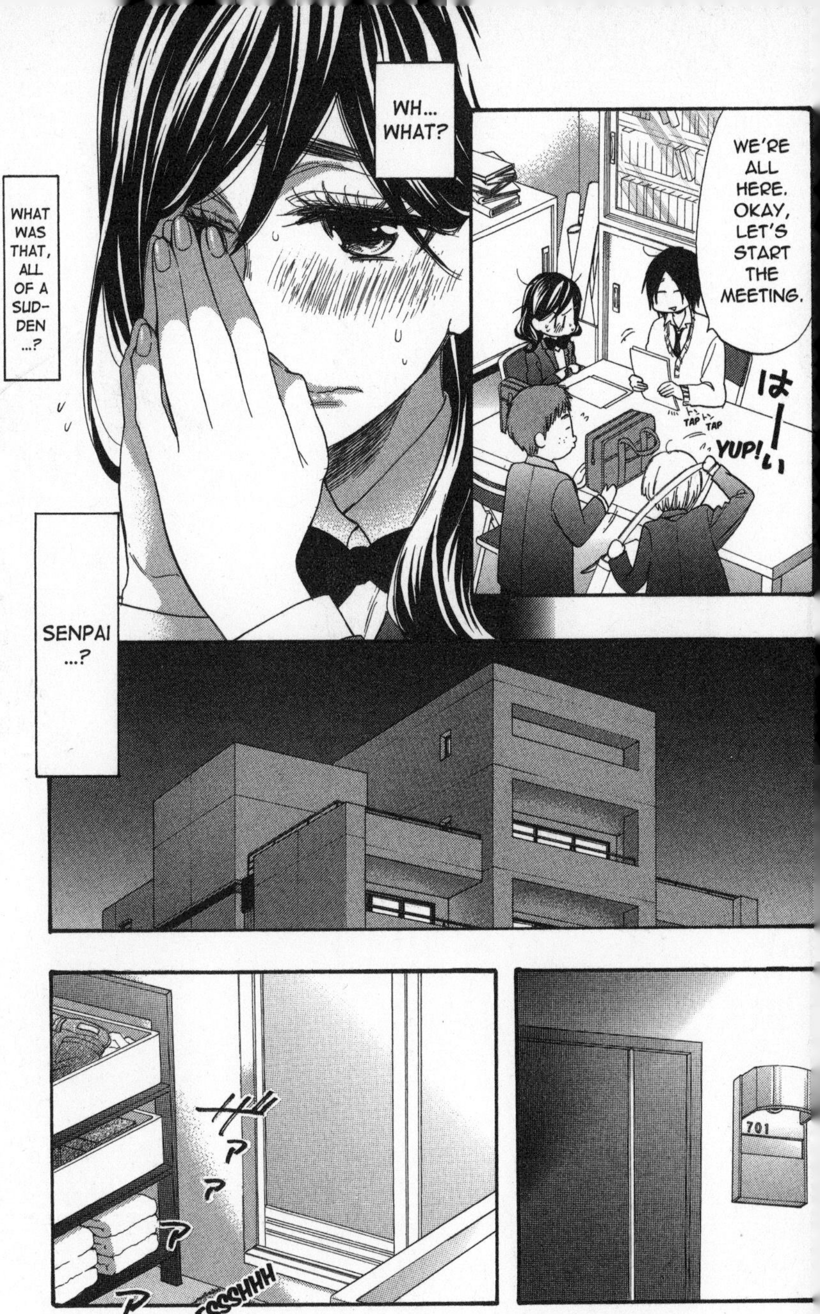
WE'RE ALL HERE. OKAY, LET'S START THE MEETING.
TAP TAP
はーい
YUP!
WH... WHAT?
WHAT WAS THAT, ALL OF A SUDDEN...?
SENPAI...?
701
ザァァァァ
FSSSHHH

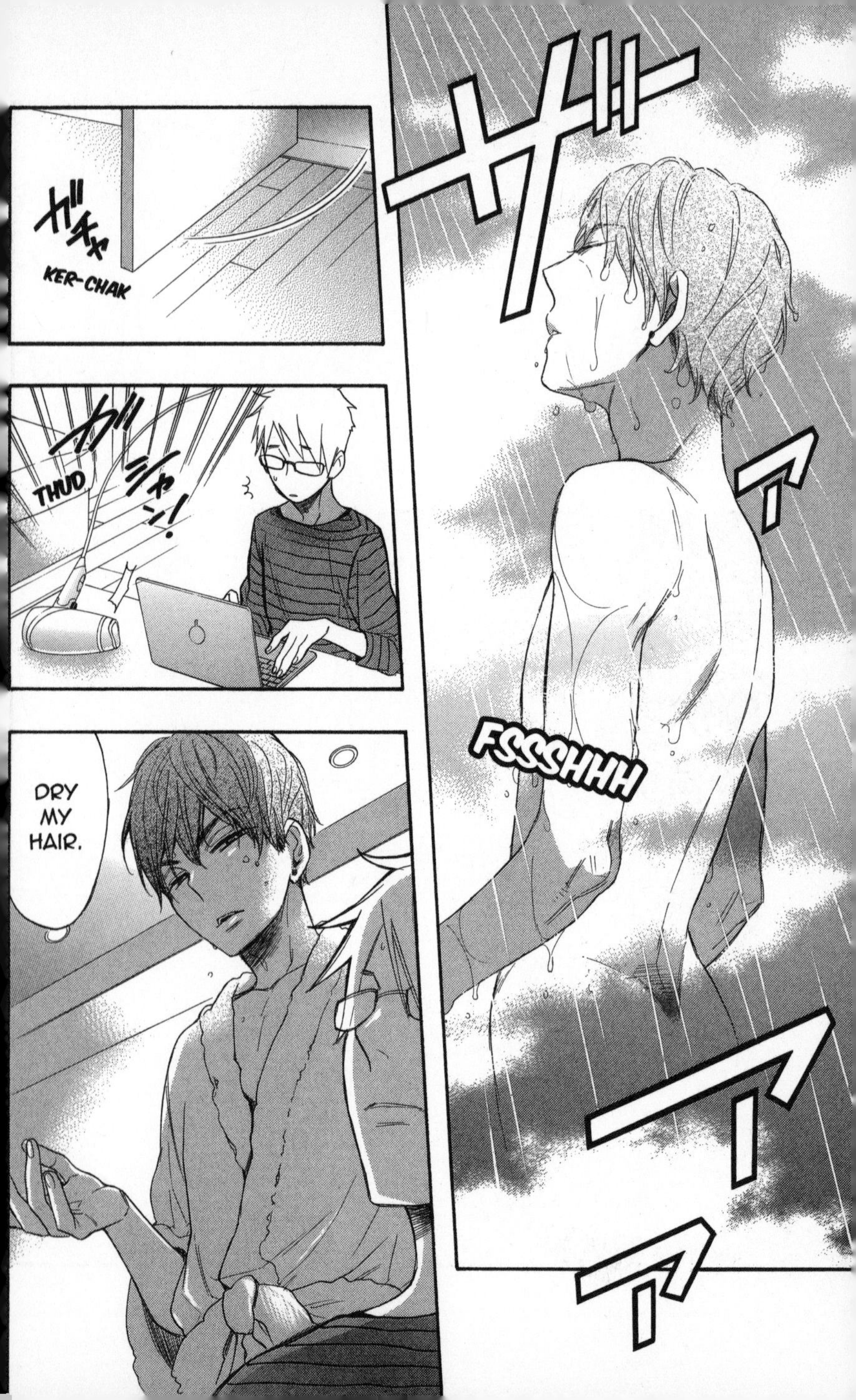

ザァァァ
FSSSHHH
ガチャ
KER-CHAK
ガシャン!
THUD
DRY MY HAIR.

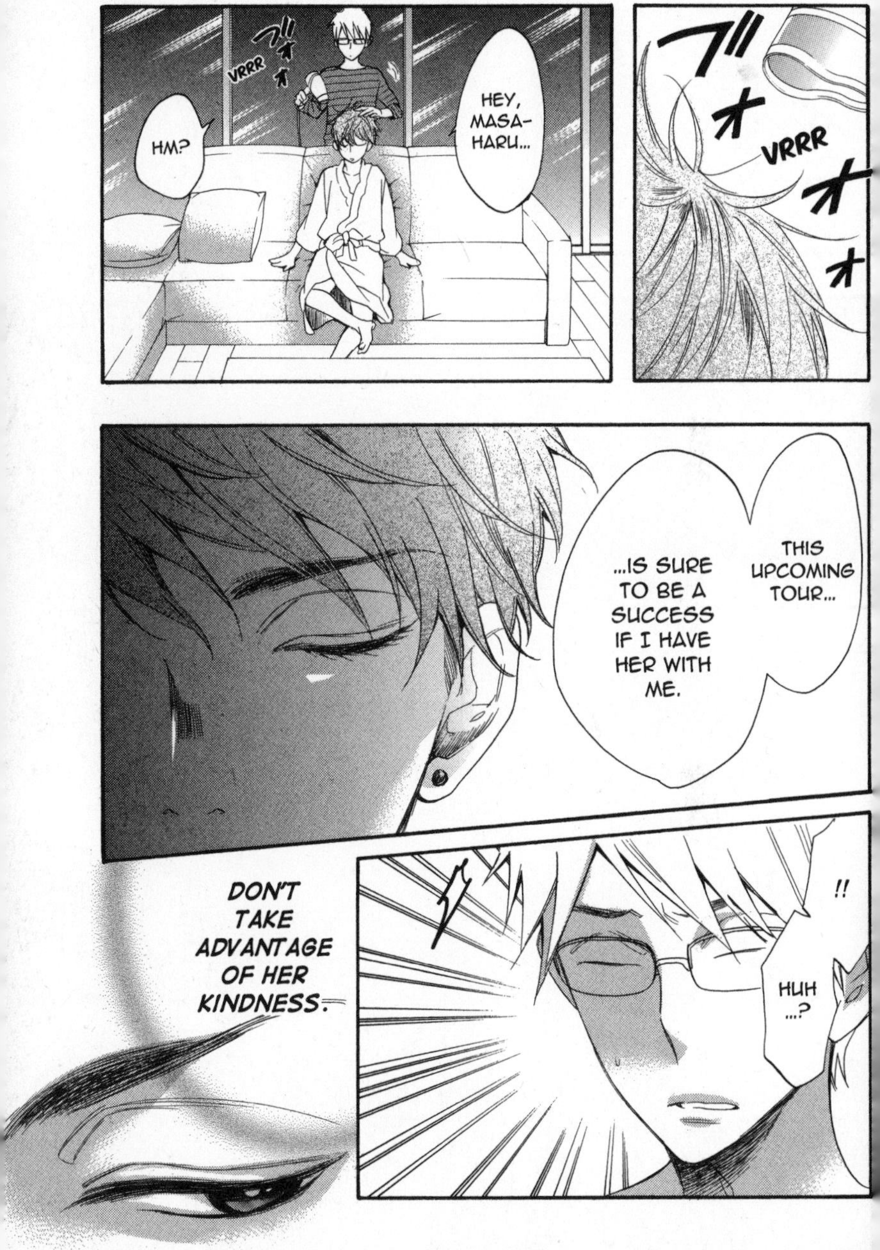
ブオオオ
VRRR
HEY, MASA-HARU...
ブオオ
VRRR
HM?
THIS UPCOMING TOUR...
...IS SURE TO BE A SUCCESS IF I HAVE HER WITH ME.
!!
HUH ...?
DON'T TAKE ADVANTAGE OF HER KINDNESS.

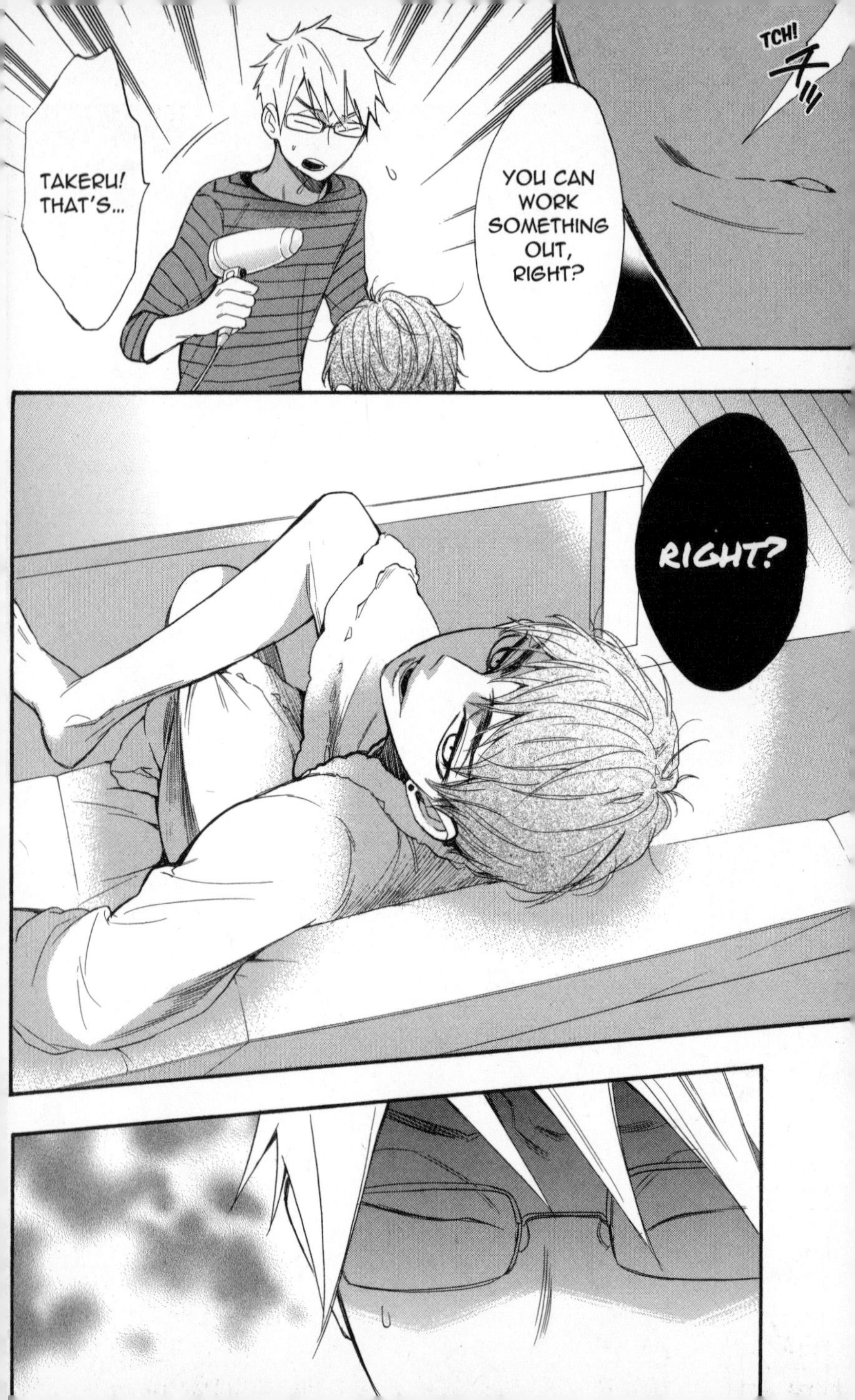
TCH!
チッ
YOU CAN WORK SOMETHING OUT, RIGHT?
TAKERU! THAT'S...
RIGHT?

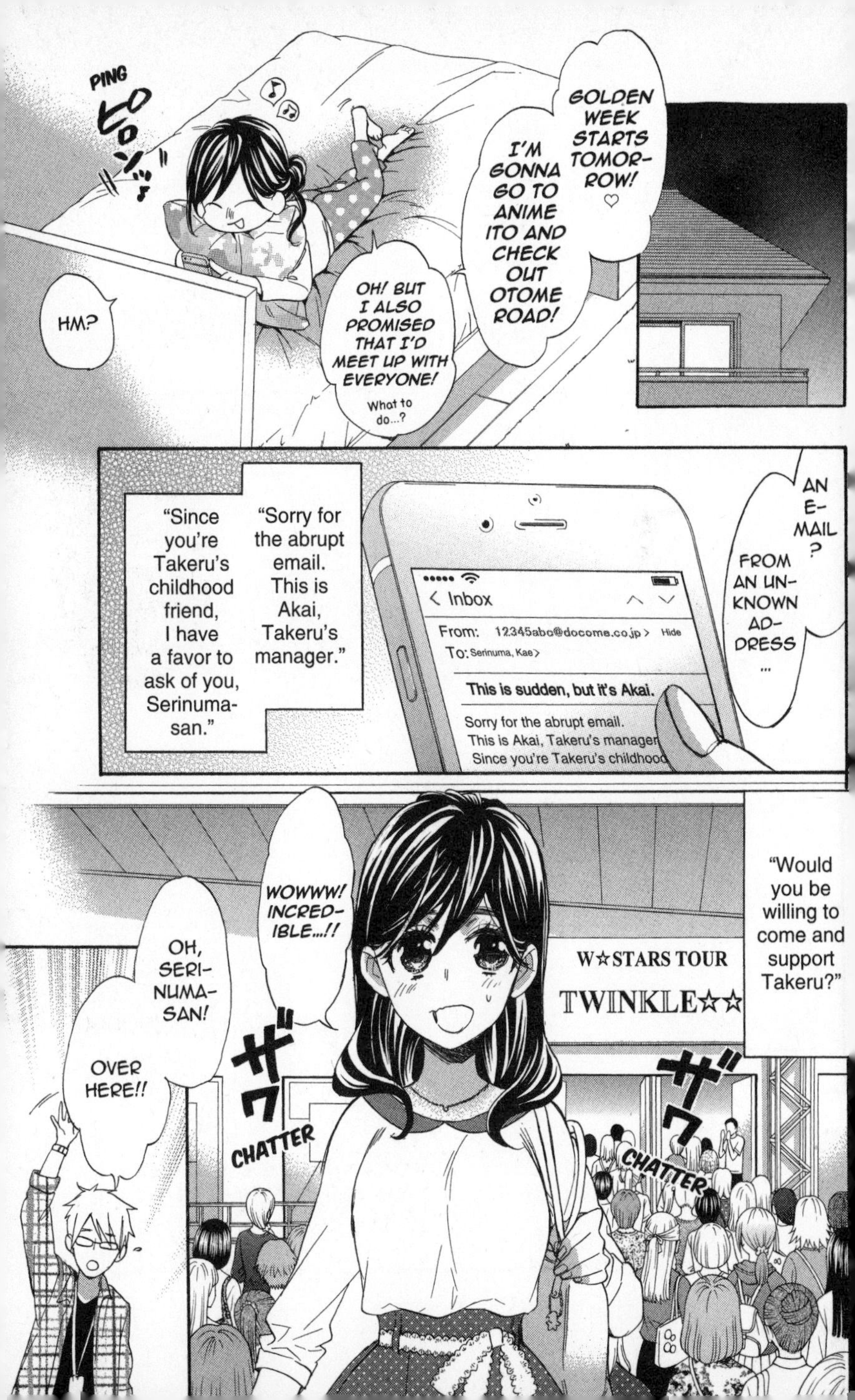
GOLDEN WEEK STARTS TOMORROW! ♡
I'M GONNA GO TO ANIME ITO AND CHECK OUT OTOME ROAD!
OH! BUT I ALSO PROMISED THAT I'D MEET UP WITH EVERYONE!
What to do...?
PING
HM?
AN E-MAIL?
FROM AN UNKNOWN ADDRESS...
< Inbox
From: 12345abc@docome.co.jp > Hide
To: Serinuma, Kae >
This is sudden, but it's Akai.
Sorry for the abrupt email.
This is Akai, Takeru's manager
Since you're Takeru's childhood
"Sorry for the abrupt email. This is Akai, Takeru's manager."
"Since you're Takeru's childhood friend, I have a favor to ask of you, Serinuma-san."
"Would you be willing to come and support Takeru?"
W☆STARS TOUR
TWINKLE☆☆
CHATTER
WOWWW! INCREDIBLE...!!
CHATTER
OH, SERINUMA-SAN!
OVER HERE!!

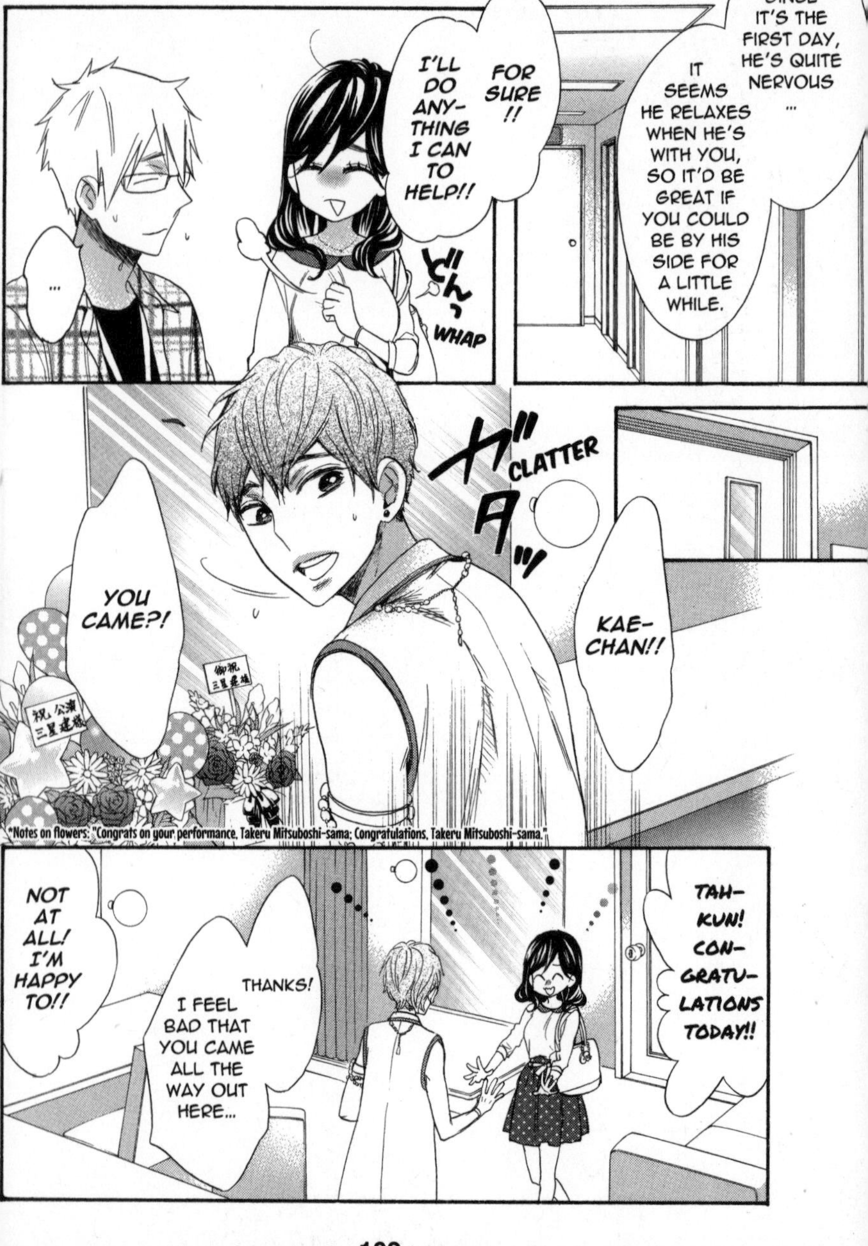
SINCE IT'S THE FIRST DAY, HE'S QUITE NERVOUS ...
IT SEEMS HE RELAXES WHEN HE'S WITH YOU, SO IT'D BE GREAT IF YOU COULD BE BY HIS SIDE FOR A LITTLE WHILE.
FOR SURE !!
I'LL DO ANYTHING I CAN TO HELP!!
WHAP
...
KAE-CHAN!!
CLATTER
YOU CAME?!
TAH-KUN! CONGRATULATIONS TODAY!!
THANKS! I FEEL BAD THAT YOU CAME ALL THE WAY OUT HERE...
NOT AT ALL! I'M HAPPY TO!!
*Notes on flowers: "Congrats on your performance, Takeru Mitsuboshi-sama; Congratulations, Takeru Mitsuboshi-sama."

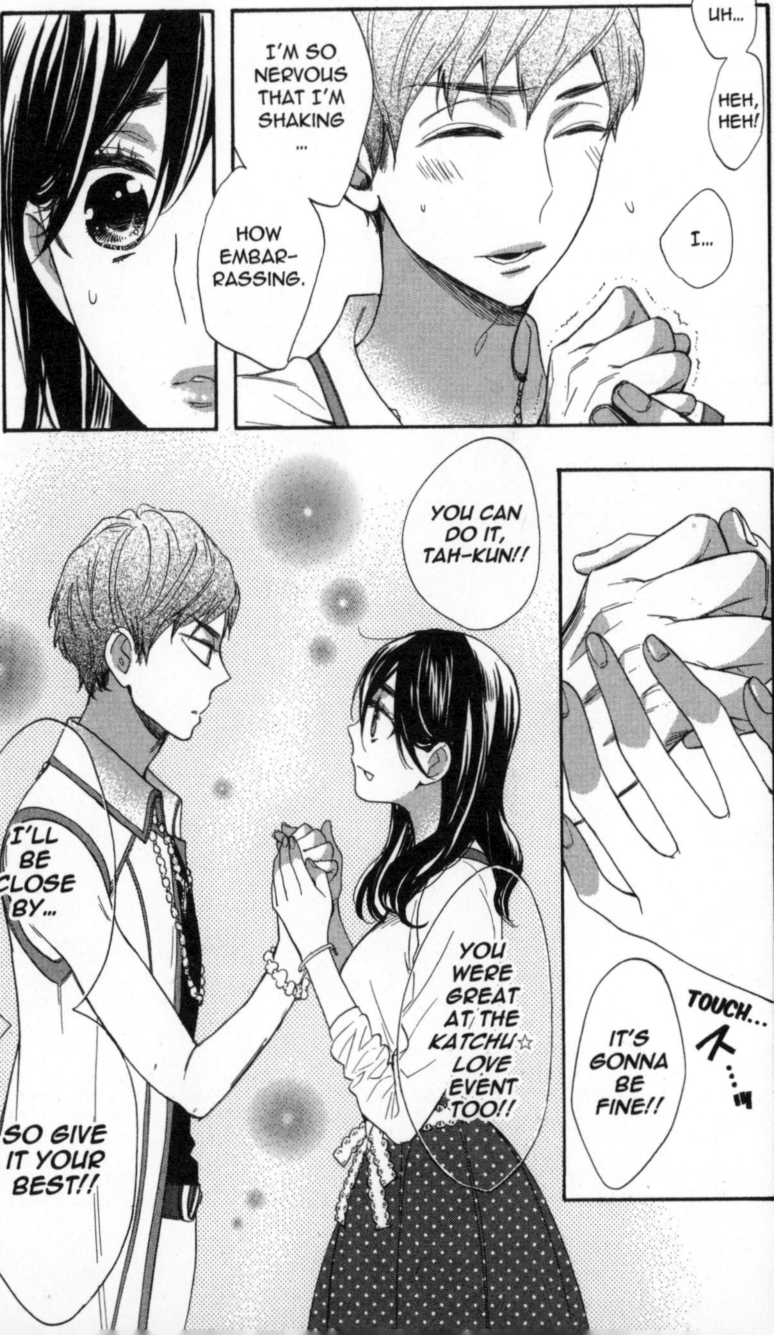
UH...
HEH, HEH!
I...
I'M SO NERVOUS THAT I'M SHAKING...
HOW EMBARRASSING.
TOUCH...
IT'S GONNA BE FINE!!
YOU CAN DO IT, TAH-KUN!!
YOU WERE GREAT AT THE KATCHU☆LOVE EVENT TOO!!
I'LL BE CLOSE BY...
SO GIVE IT YOUR BEST!!

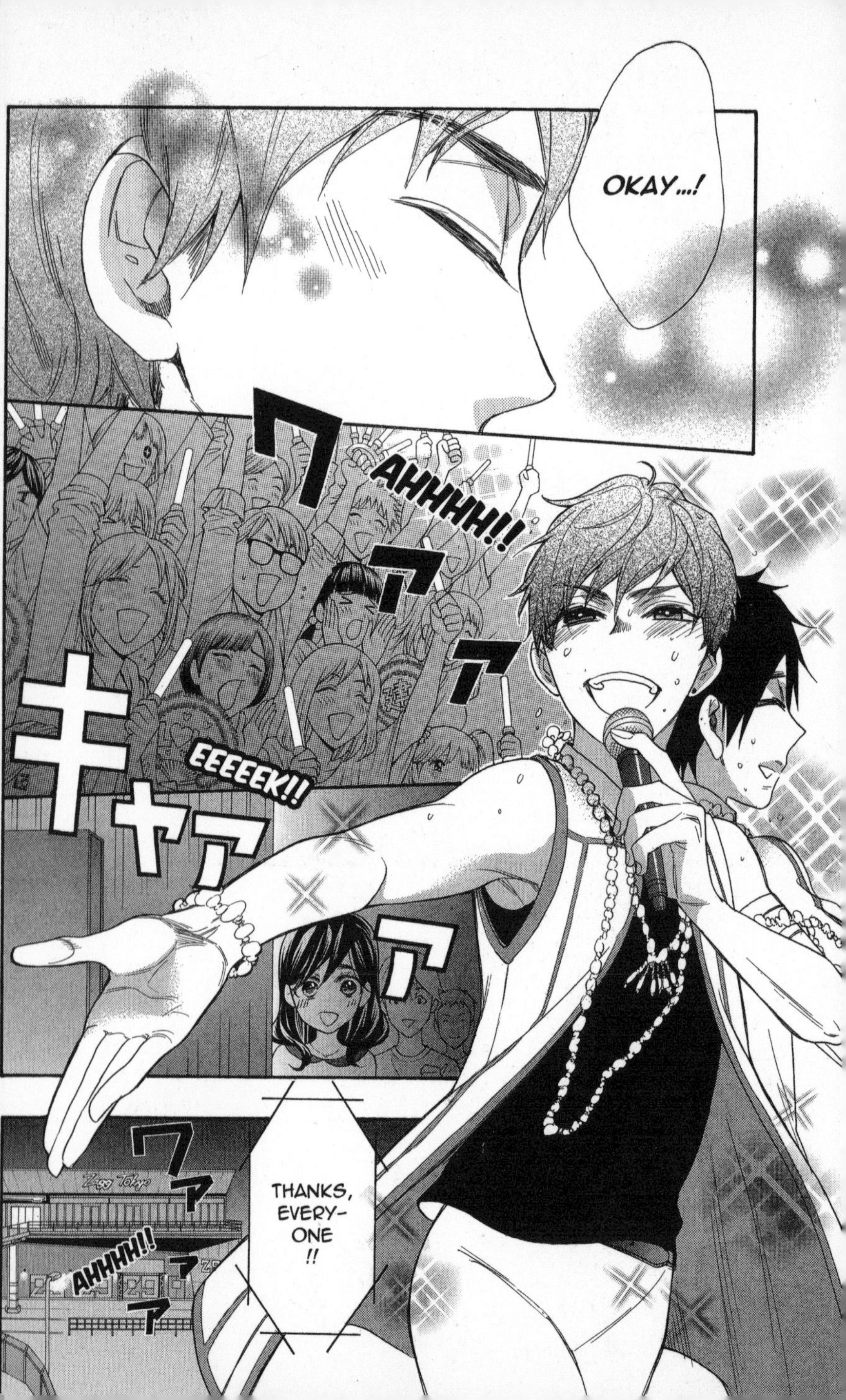

OKAY...!
ワアア
AHHHHH!!
キャアア
EEEEEK!!
THANKS, EVERY-ONE !!
ワアアア
AHHHH!!

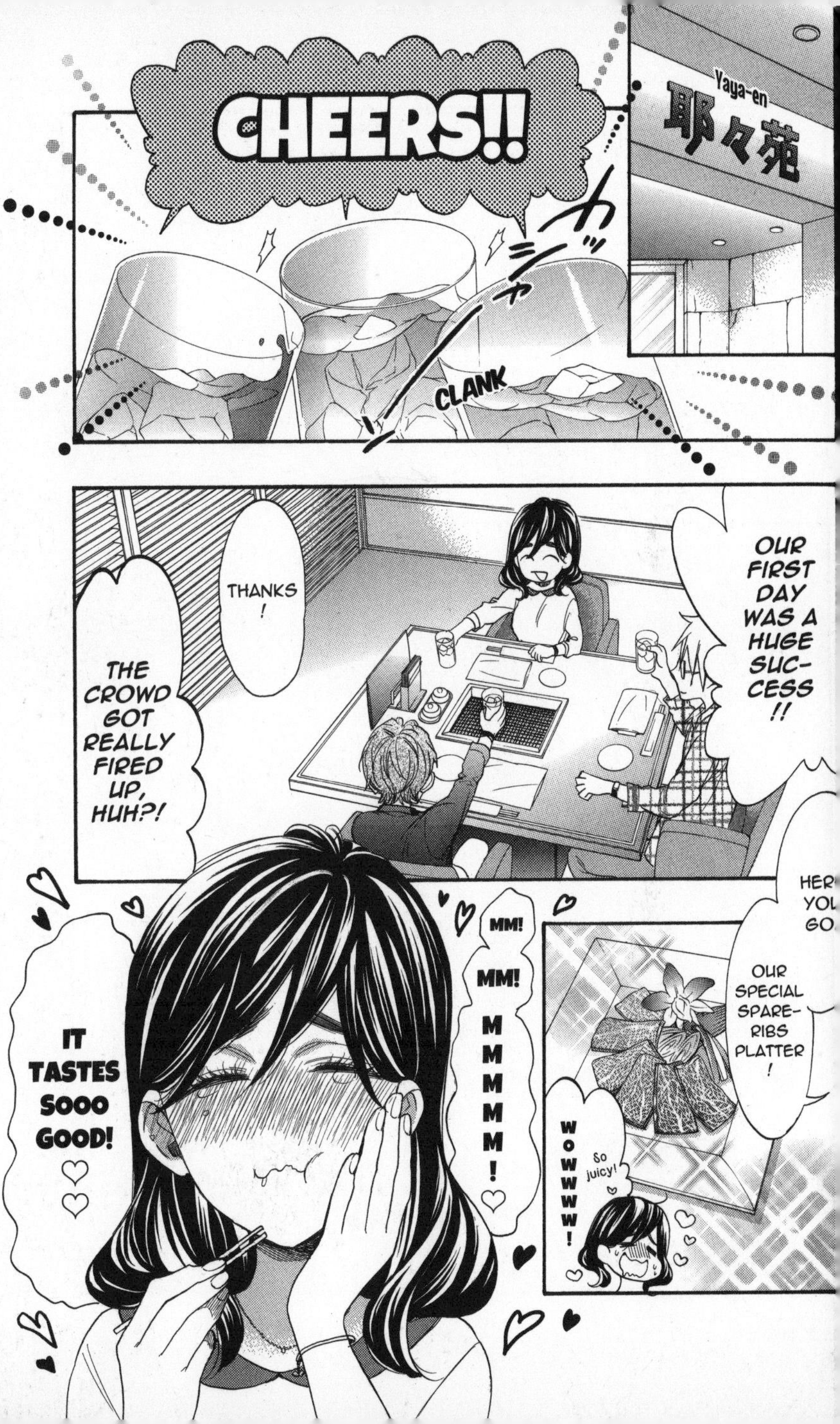
Yaya-en
耶々苑
CHEERS!!
カシャッ
CLANK
OUR FIRST DAY WAS A HUGE SUCCESS!!
THANKS!
THE CROWD GOT REALLY FIRED UP, HUH?!
HER YOU GO
OUR SPECIAL SPARE-RIBS PLATTER!
WOWWWW!
So juicy!
MM!
MM!
MMMMMM!
IT TASTES SOOO GOOD!

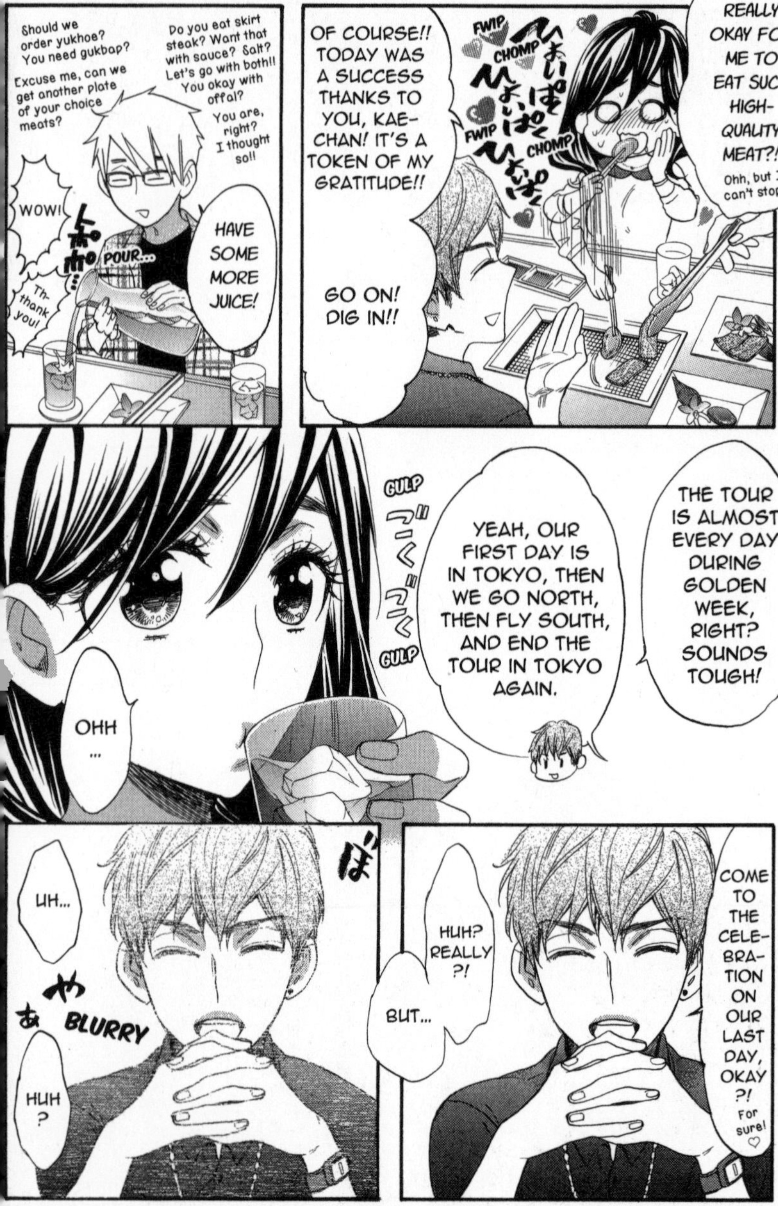
IS IT REALLY OKAY FOR ME TO EAT SUCH HIGH-QUALITY MEAT?!
Ohh, but I can't stop!
FWIP
CHOMP
FWIP
CHOMP
OF COURSE!! TODAY WAS A SUCCESS THANKS TO YOU, KAE-CHAN! IT'S A TOKEN OF MY GRATITUDE!!
GO ON! DIG IN!!
Do you eat skirt steak? Want that with sauce? Salt? Let's go with both!! You okay with offal? You are, right? I thought so!!
Should we order yukhoe? You need gukbap?
Excuse me, can we get another plate of your choice meats?
HAVE SOME MORE JUICE!
POUR...
WOW!
Th-thank you!
THE TOUR IS ALMOST EVERY DAY DURING GOLDEN WEEK, RIGHT? SOUNDS TOUGH!
YEAH, OUR FIRST DAY IS IN TOKYO, THEN WE GO NORTH, THEN FLY SOUTH, AND END THE TOUR IN TOKYO AGAIN.
GULP
GULP
OHH...
COME TO THE CELEBRATION ON OUR LAST DAY, OKAY?!
For sure! ♡
HUH? REALLY?!
BUT...
UH...
BLURRY
HUH?

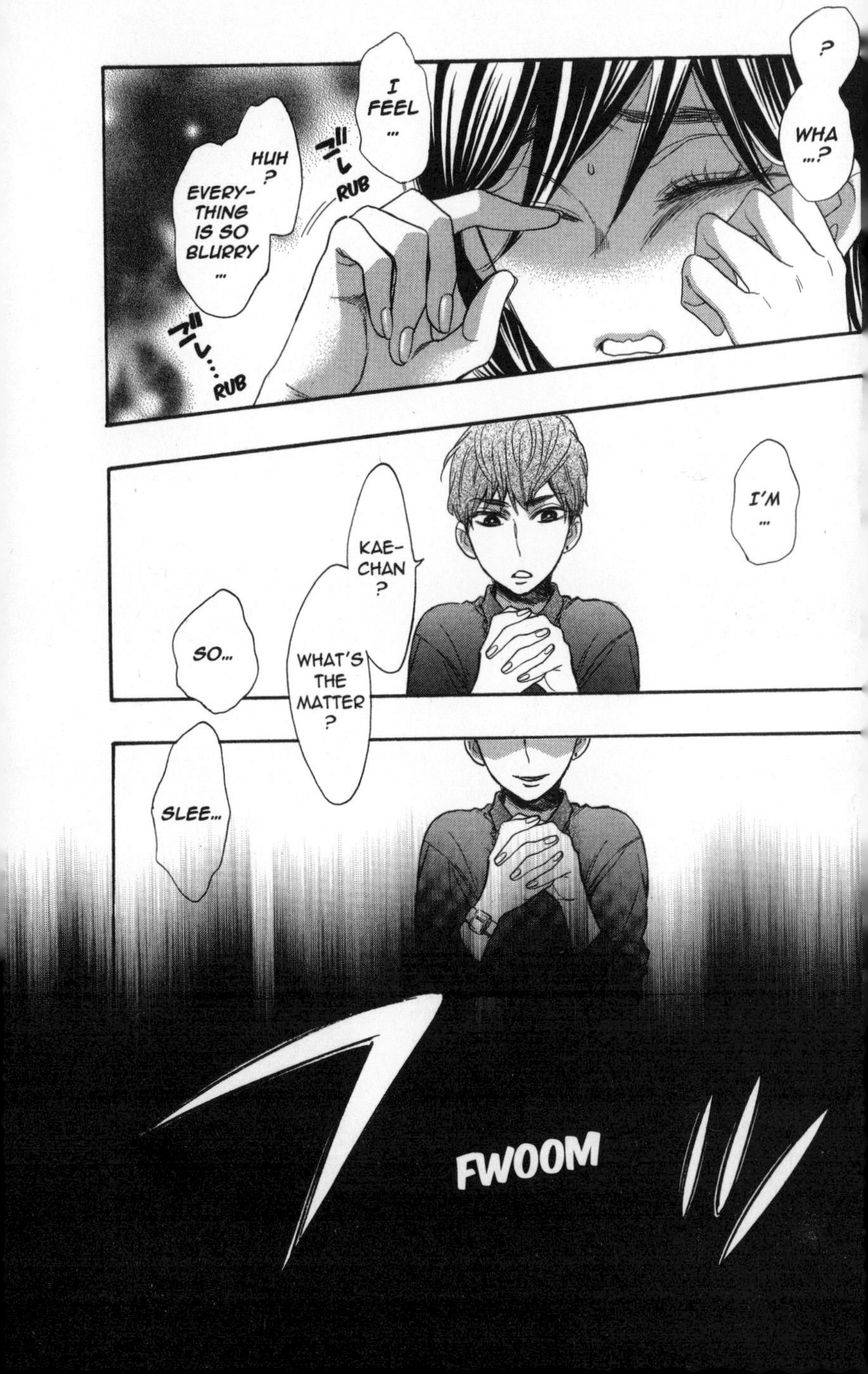
? WHA...?
I FEEL...
HUH? EVERYTHING IS SO BLURRY...
RUB
RUB
I'M...
KAE-CHAN? WHAT'S THE MATTER?
SO...
SLEE...
FWOOM

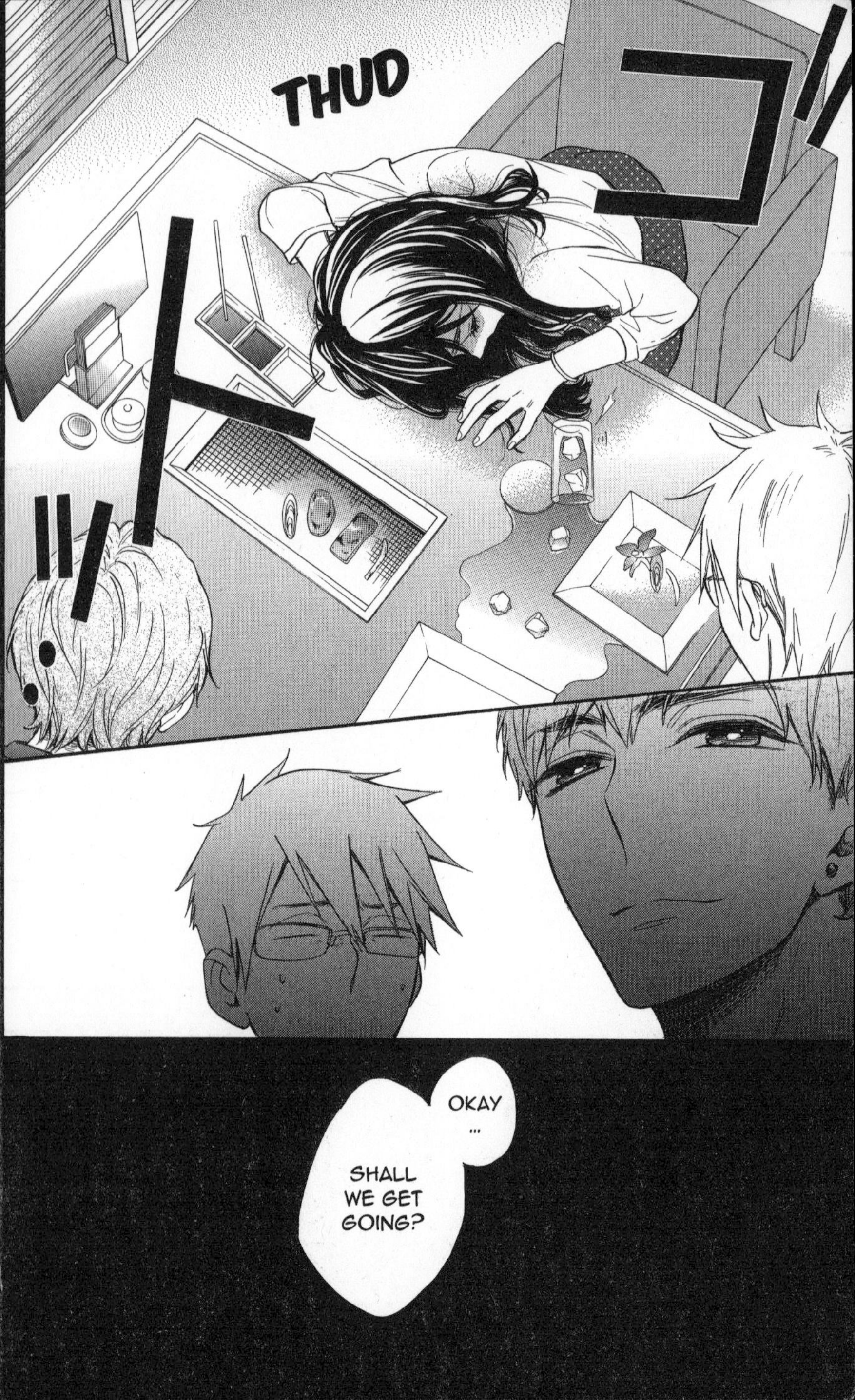
THUD
OKAY ...
SHALL WE GET GOING?

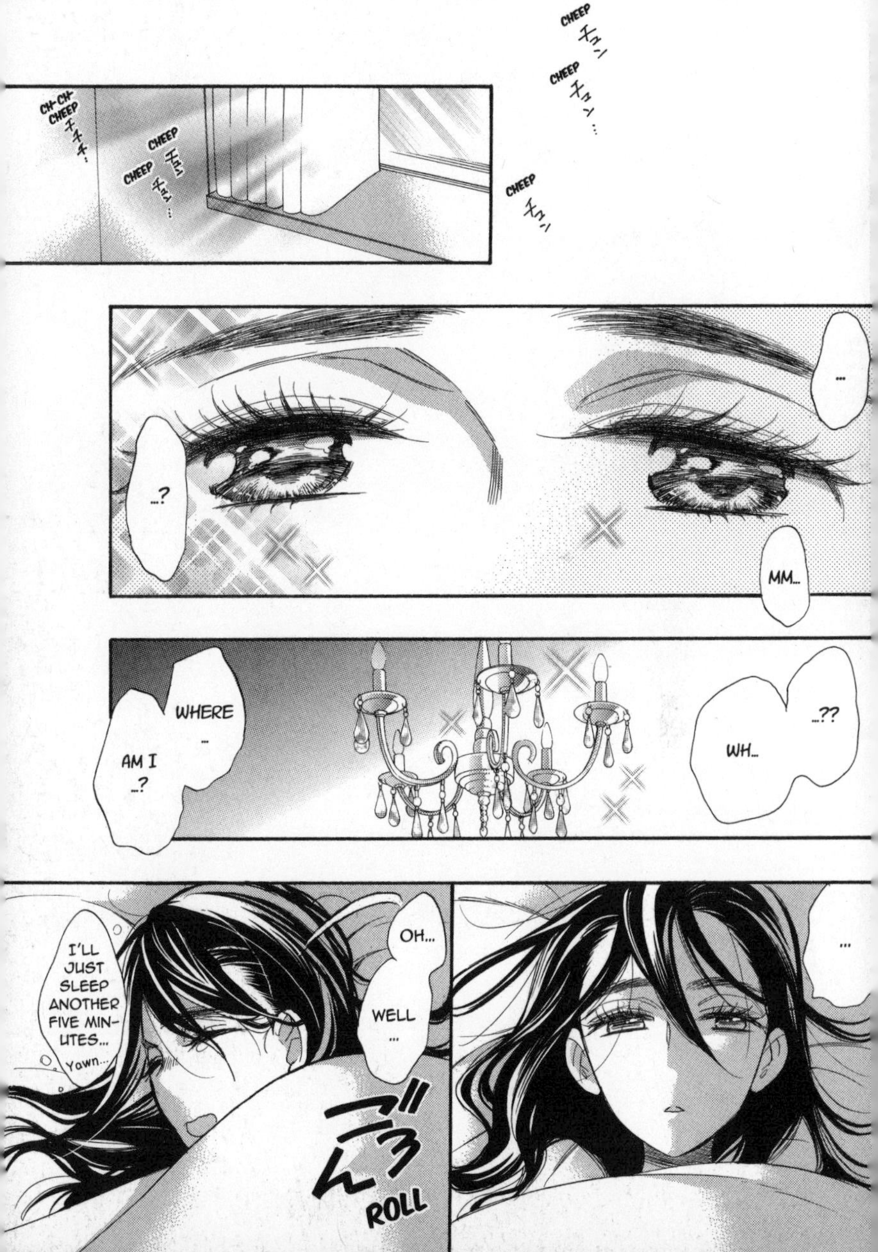
CHEEP チュン
CHEEP チュン…
CHEEP チュン
CH-CH-CHEEP チチチ…
CHEEP チュン
CHEEP チュン…
…
MM…
…?
…??
WH…
WHERE… AM I…?
…
OH… WELL…
ごろん ROLL
I'LL JUST SLEEP ANOTHER FIVE MIN-UTES…
Yawn…

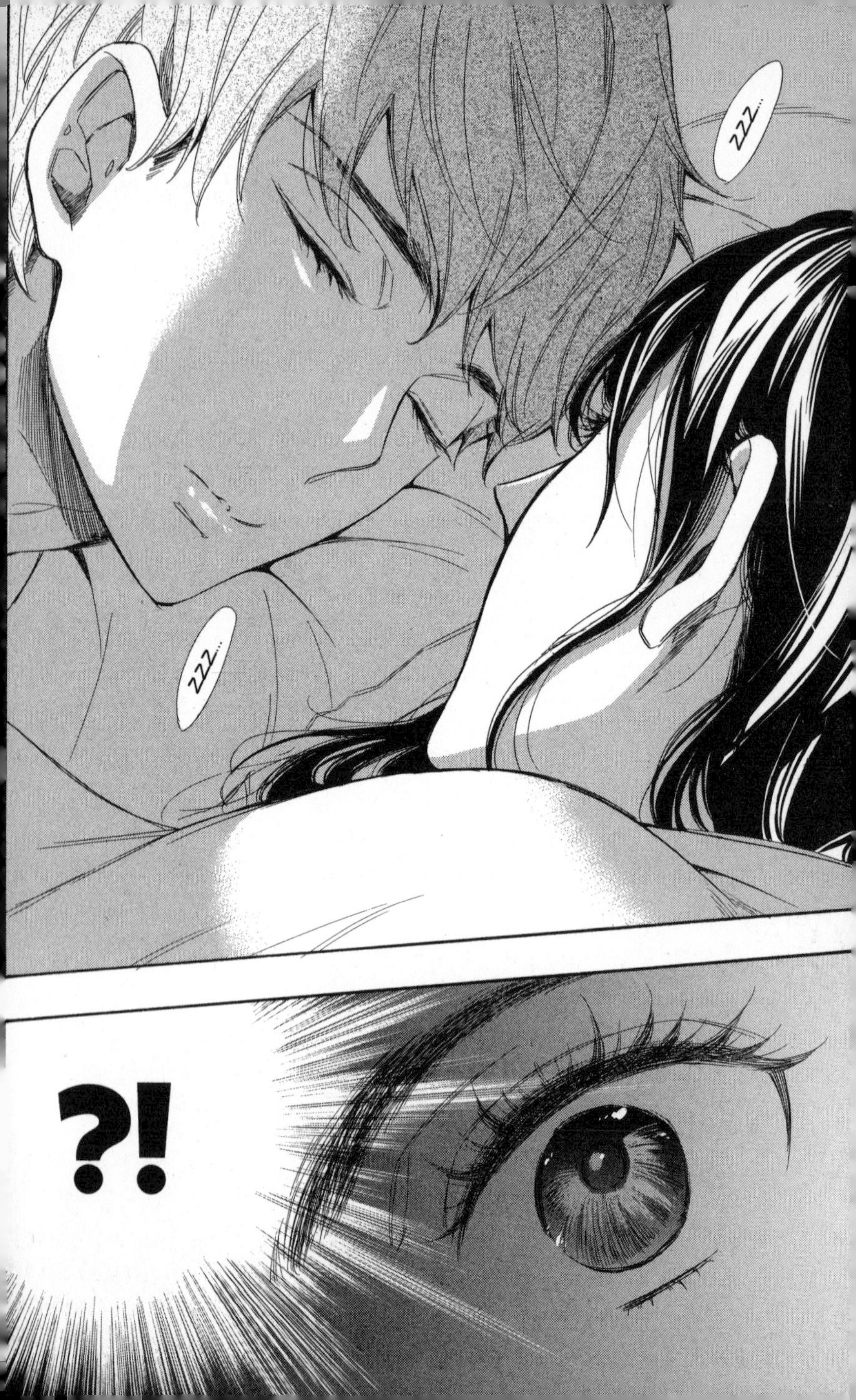
zzz...
zzz...
?!

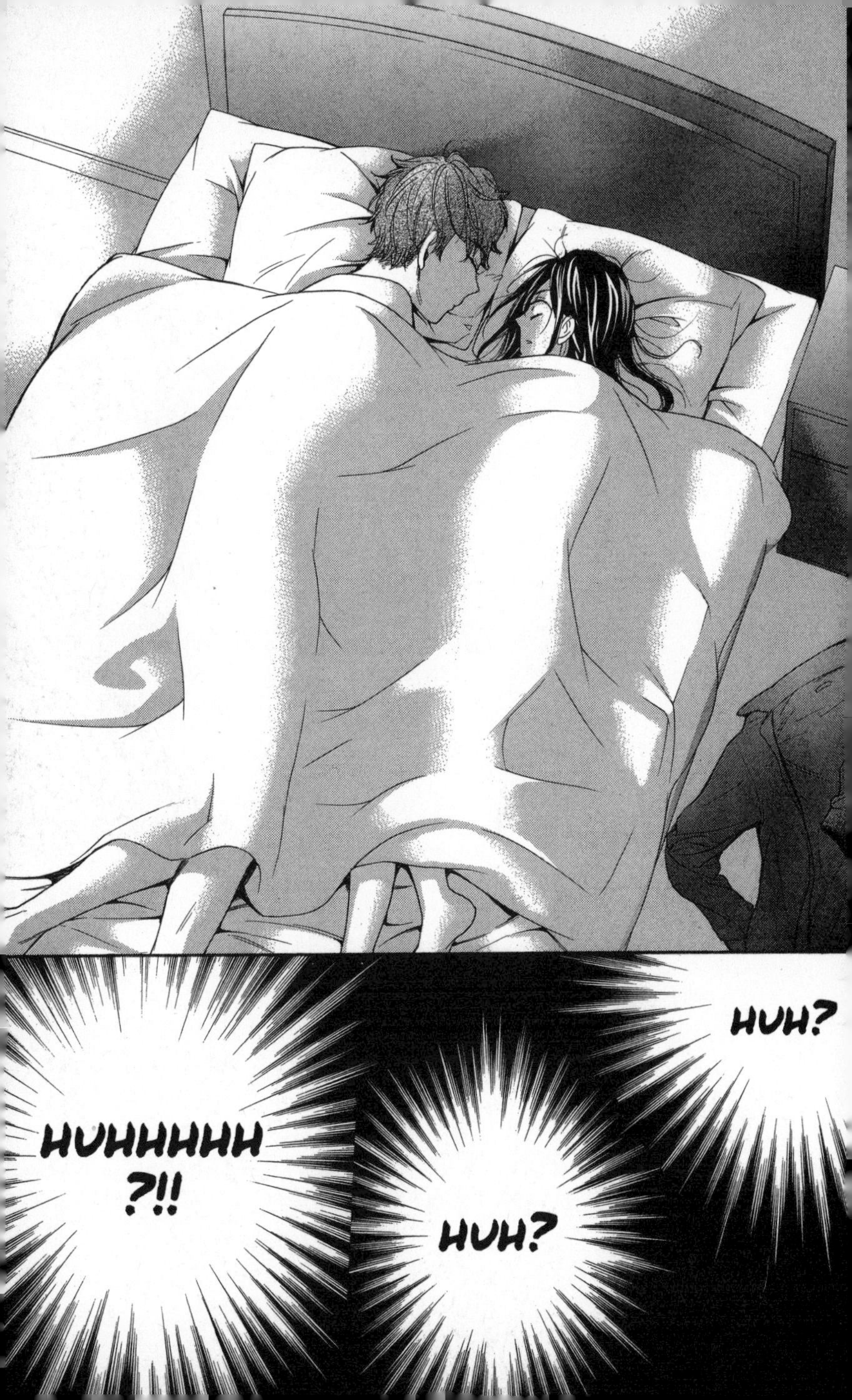
HUH?
HUH?
HUHHHHH ?!!

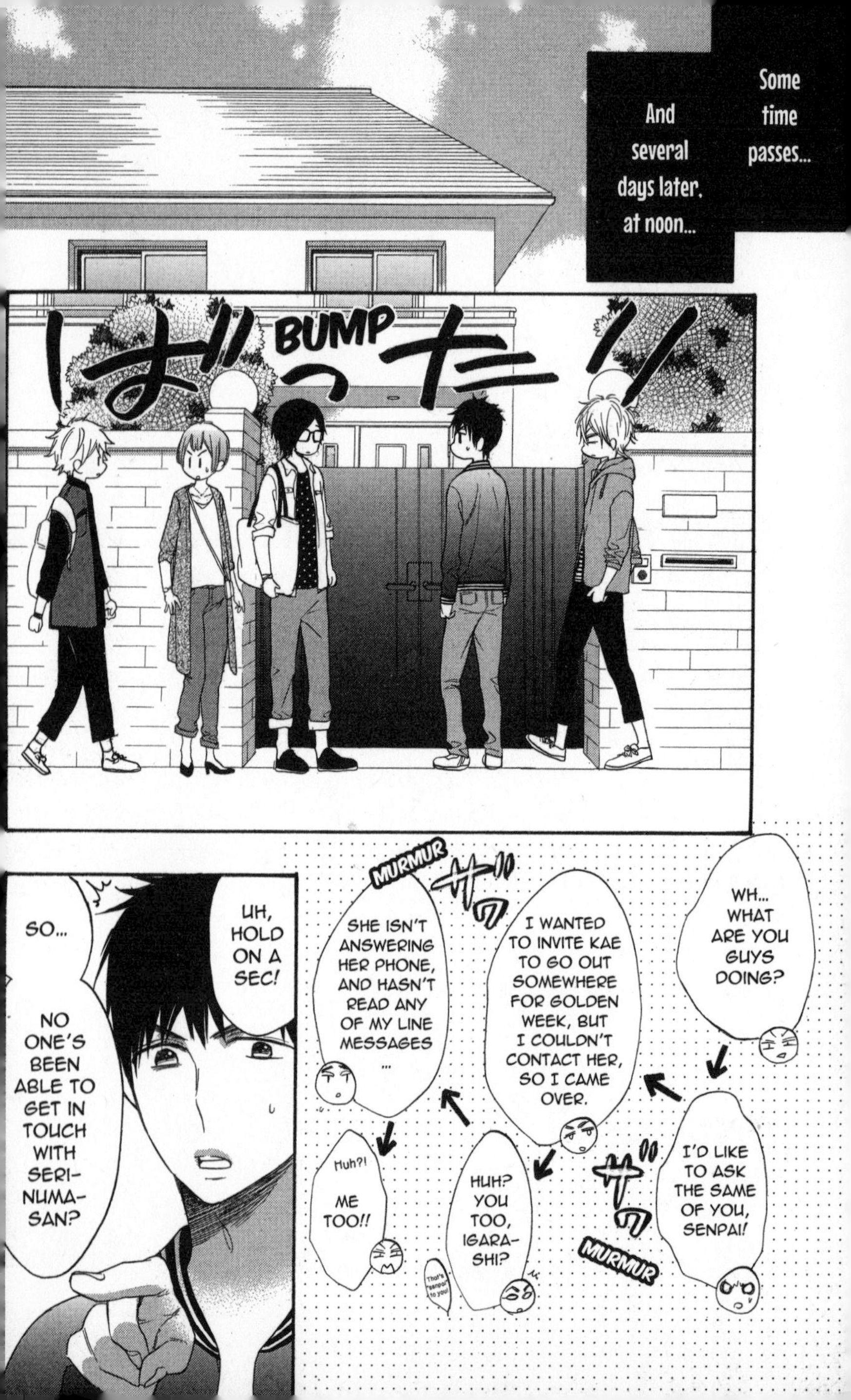
Some time passes...
And several days later, at noon...
BUMP
はっ たー!!
WH... WHAT ARE YOU GUYS DOING?
I'D LIKE TO ASK THE SAME OF YOU, SENPAI!
MURMUR
I WANTED TO INVITE KAE TO GO OUT SOMEWHERE FOR GOLDEN WEEK, BUT I COULDN'T CONTACT HER, SO I CAME OVER.
HUH? YOU TOO, IGARASHI?
That's "senpai" to you!
MURMUR
SHE ISN'T ANSWERING HER PHONE, AND HASN'T READ ANY OF MY LINE MESSAGES ...
Huh?!
ME TOO!!
UH, HOLD ON A SEC!
SO...
NO ONE'S BEEN ABLE TO GET IN TOUCH WITH SERI-NUMA-SAN?

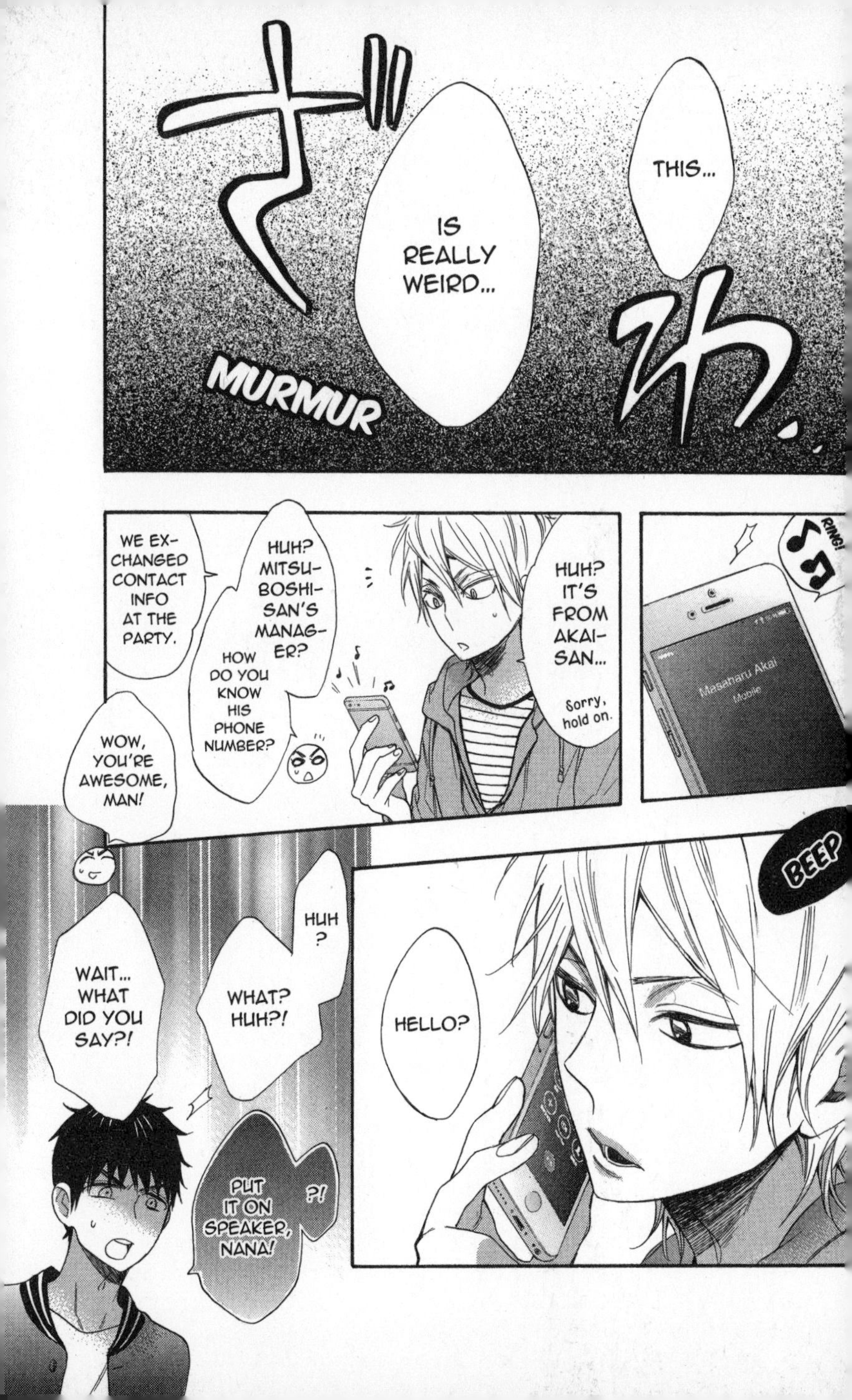
THIS...
ざわ
IS REALLY WEIRD...
MURMUR
RING!
Masaharu Akai
Mobile
HUH? IT'S FROM AKAI-SAN...
Sorry, hold on.
HUH? MITSUBOSHI-SAN'S MANAGER?
HOW DO YOU KNOW HIS PHONE NUMBER?
WE EXCHANGED CONTACT INFO AT THE PARTY.
WOW, YOU'RE AWESOME, MAN!
BEEP
HELLO?
HUH?
WHAT? HUH?!
WAIT... WHAT DID YOU SAY?!
?!
PUT IT ON SPEAKER, NANA!

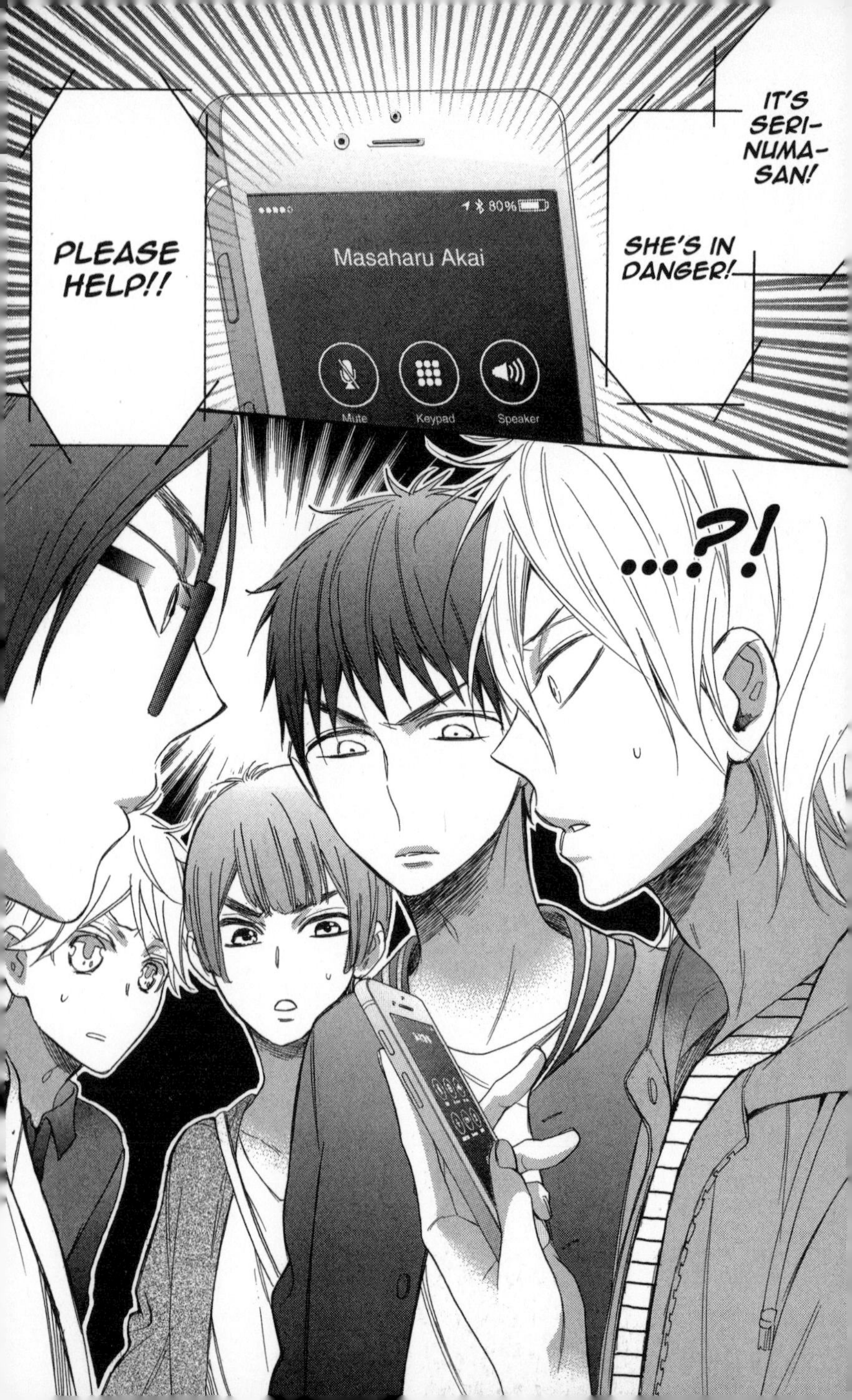
IT'S SERI-NUMA-SAN!
SHE'S IN DANGER!
80%
Masaharu Akai
Mute
Keypad
Speaker
PLEASE HELP!!
...?!

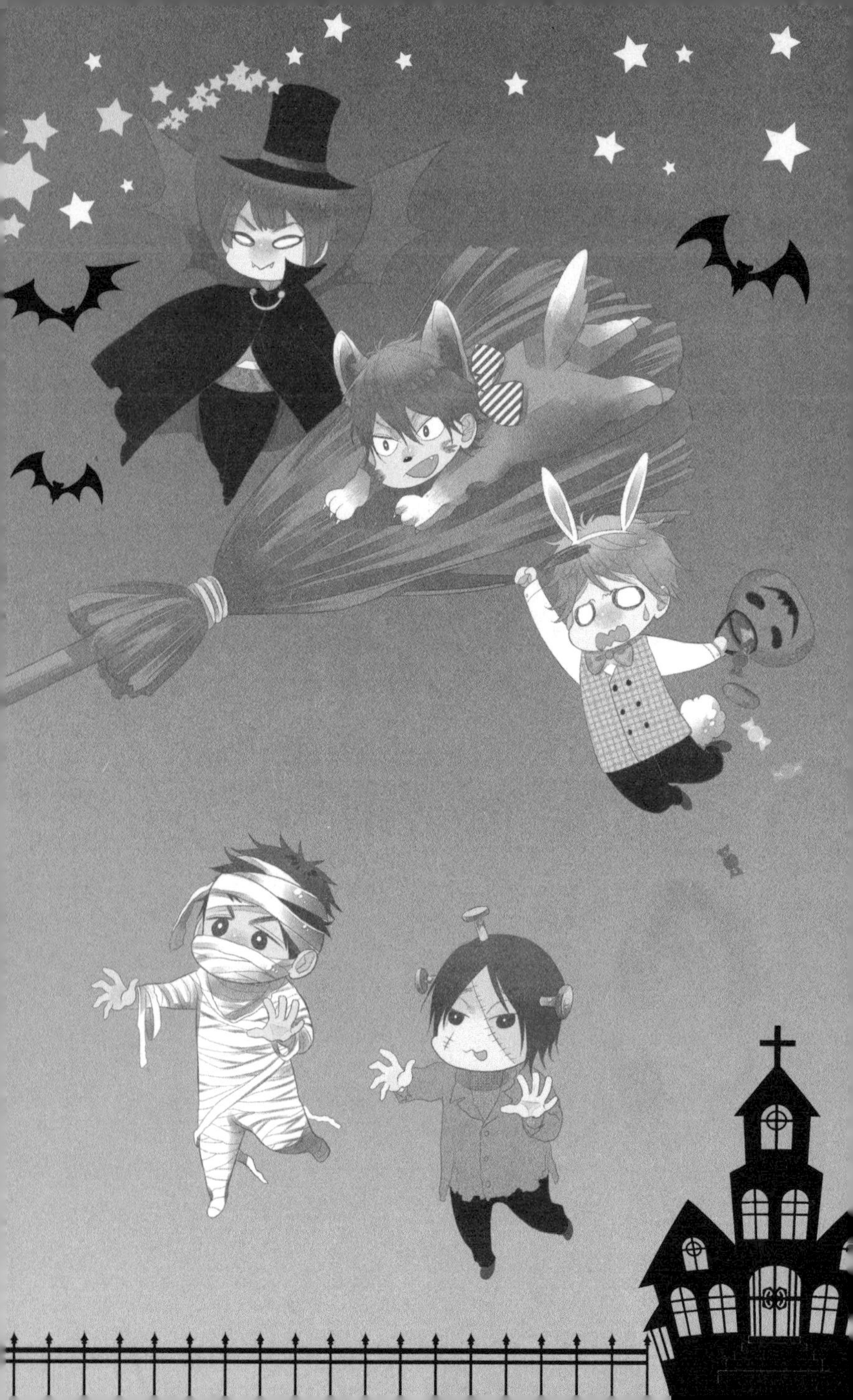

#40 SHE'S MINE

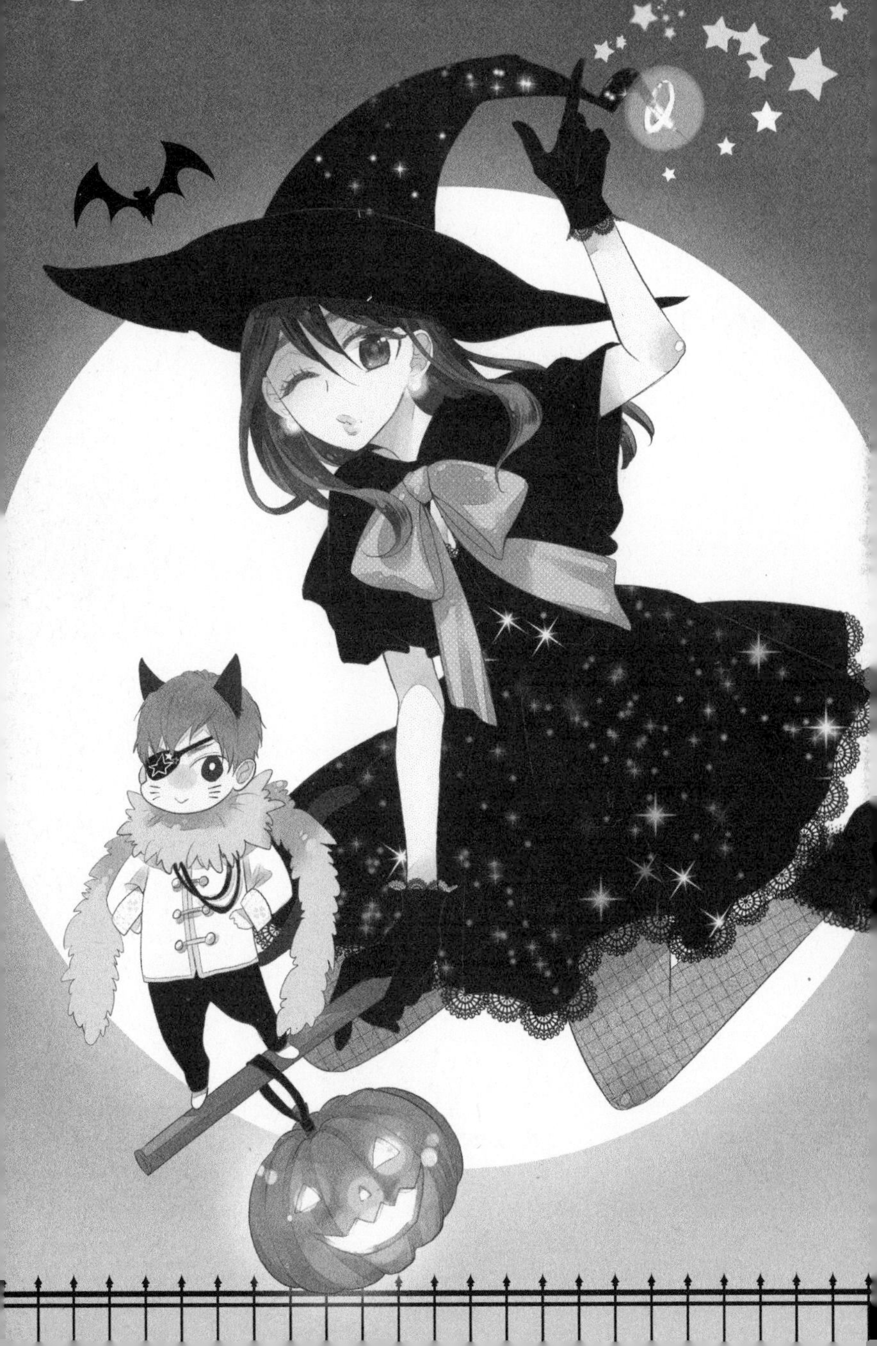

KiSS HiM, NOT ME!

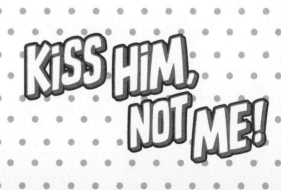

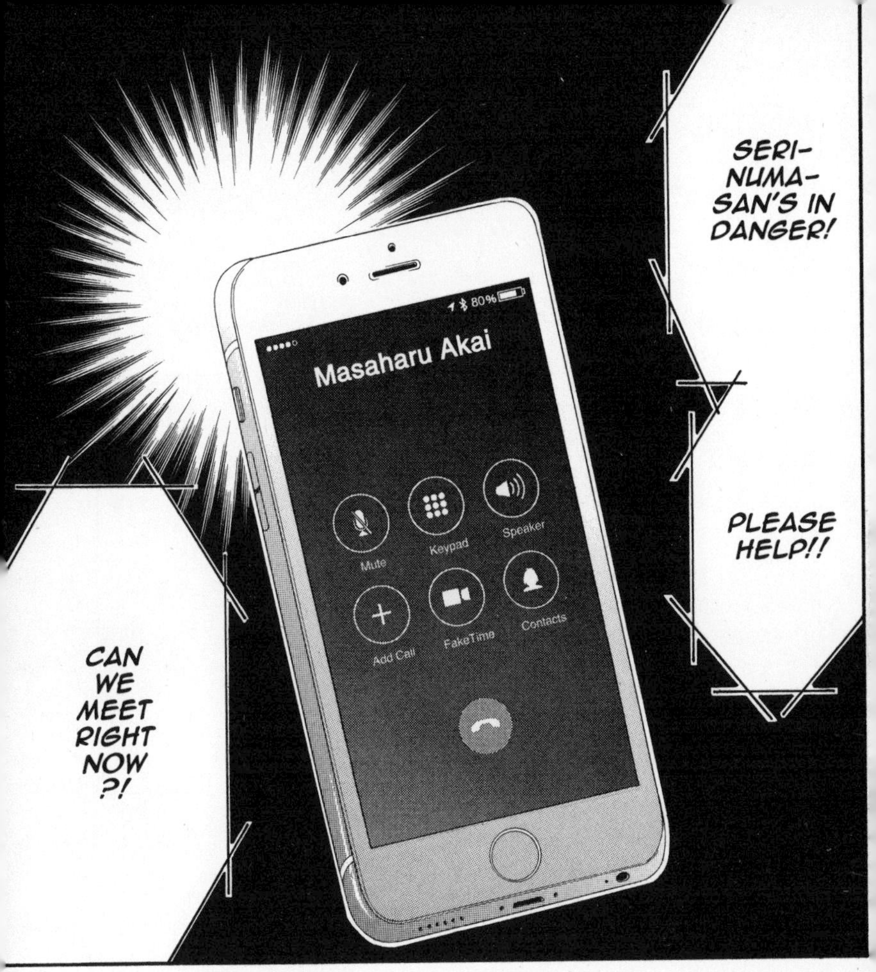
SERI-NUMA-SAN'S IN DANGER!
PLEASE HELP!!
80%
Masaharu Akai
Mute
Keypad
Speaker
Add Call
FakeTime
Contacts
CAN WE MEET RIGHT NOW?!

KiSS HiM, NOT ME!

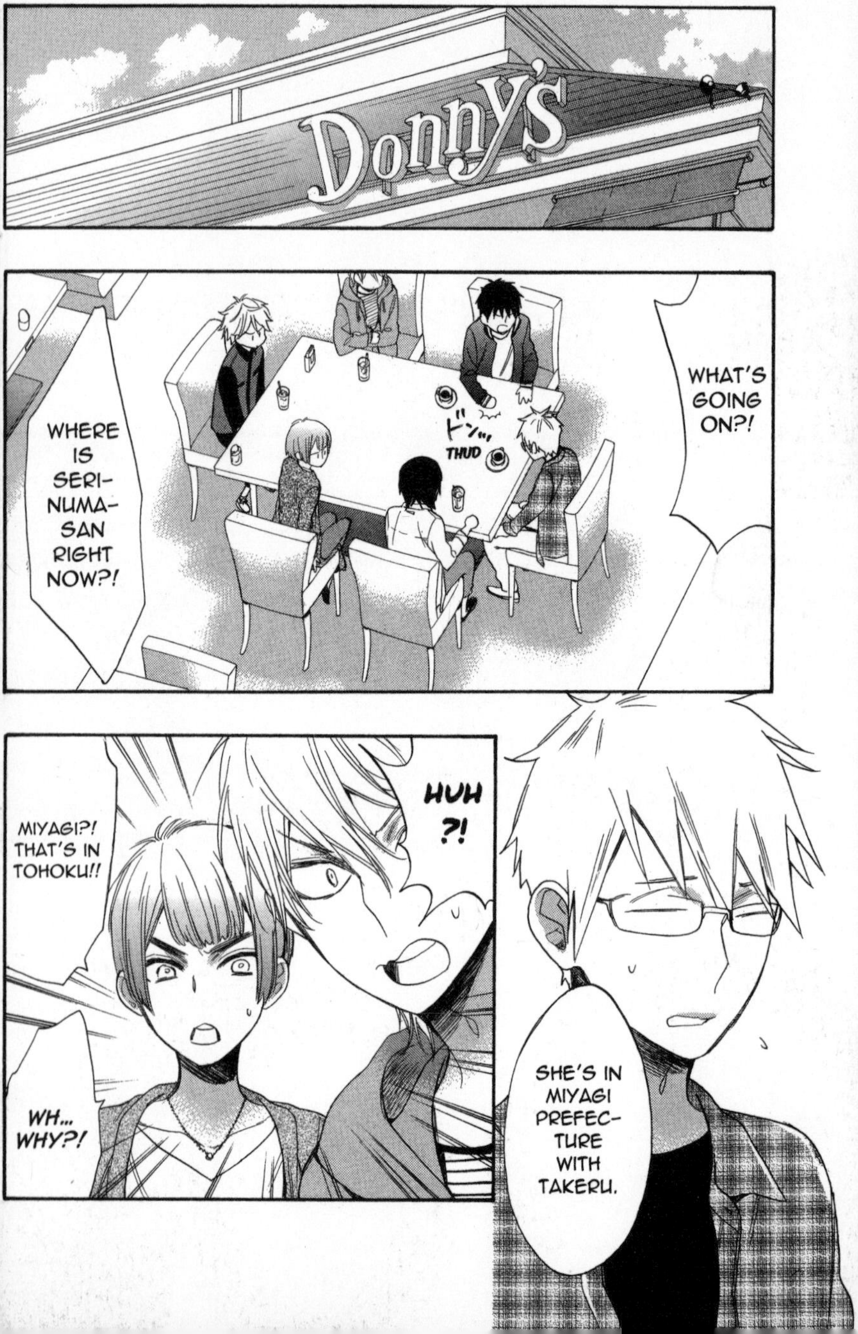
Donny's
WHAT'S GOING ON?!
THUD
WHERE IS SERI-NUMA-SAN RIGHT NOW?!
SHE'S IN MIYAGI PREFEC-TURE WITH TAKERU.
HUH ?!
MIYAGI?! THAT'S IN TOHOKU!!
WH... WHY?!

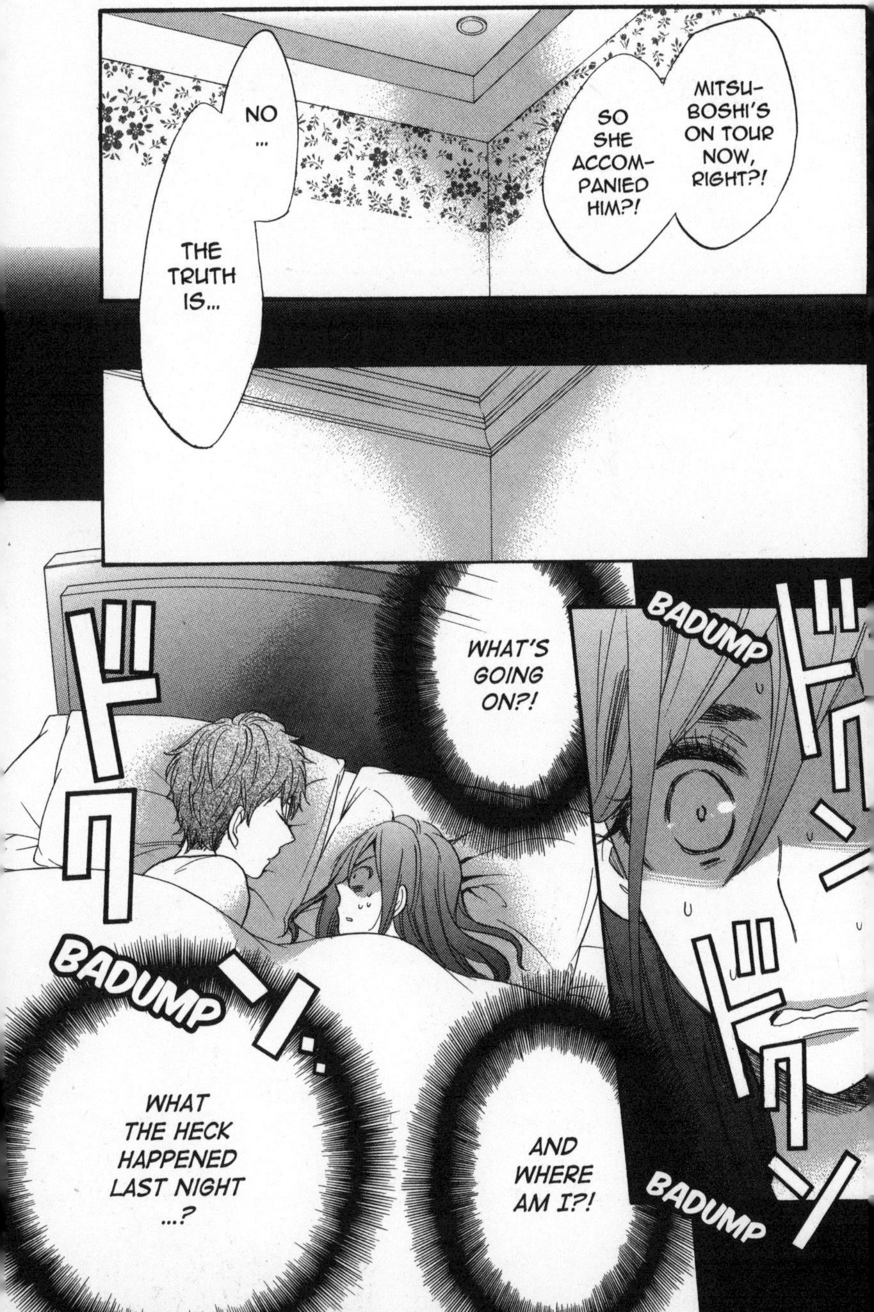
MITSU-BOSHI'S ON TOUR NOW, RIGHT?!
SO SHE ACCOM-PANIED HIM?!
NO ...
THE TRUTH IS...
BADUMP
WHAT'S GOING ON?!
BADUMP
AND WHERE AM I?!
WHAT THE HECK HAPPENED LAST NIGHT ...?
BADUMP

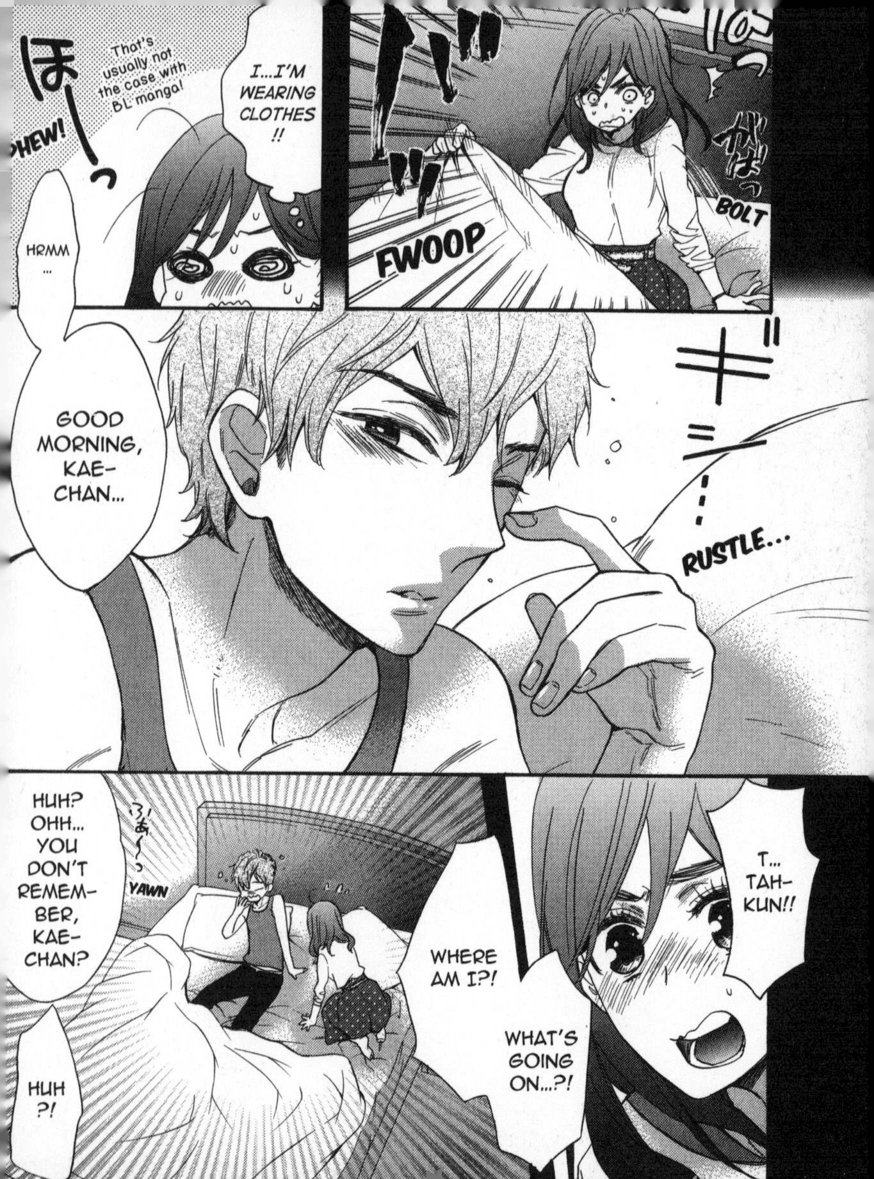
BOLT
FWOOP
I...I'M WEARING CLOTHES!!
That's usually not the case with BL manga!
PHEW!
HRMM...
RUSTLE...
GOOD MORNING, KAE-CHAN...
T... TAH-KUN!!
WHERE AM I?!
WHAT'S GOING ON...?!
HUH? OHH... YOU DON'T REMEMBER, KAE-CHAN?
YAWN
HUH?!

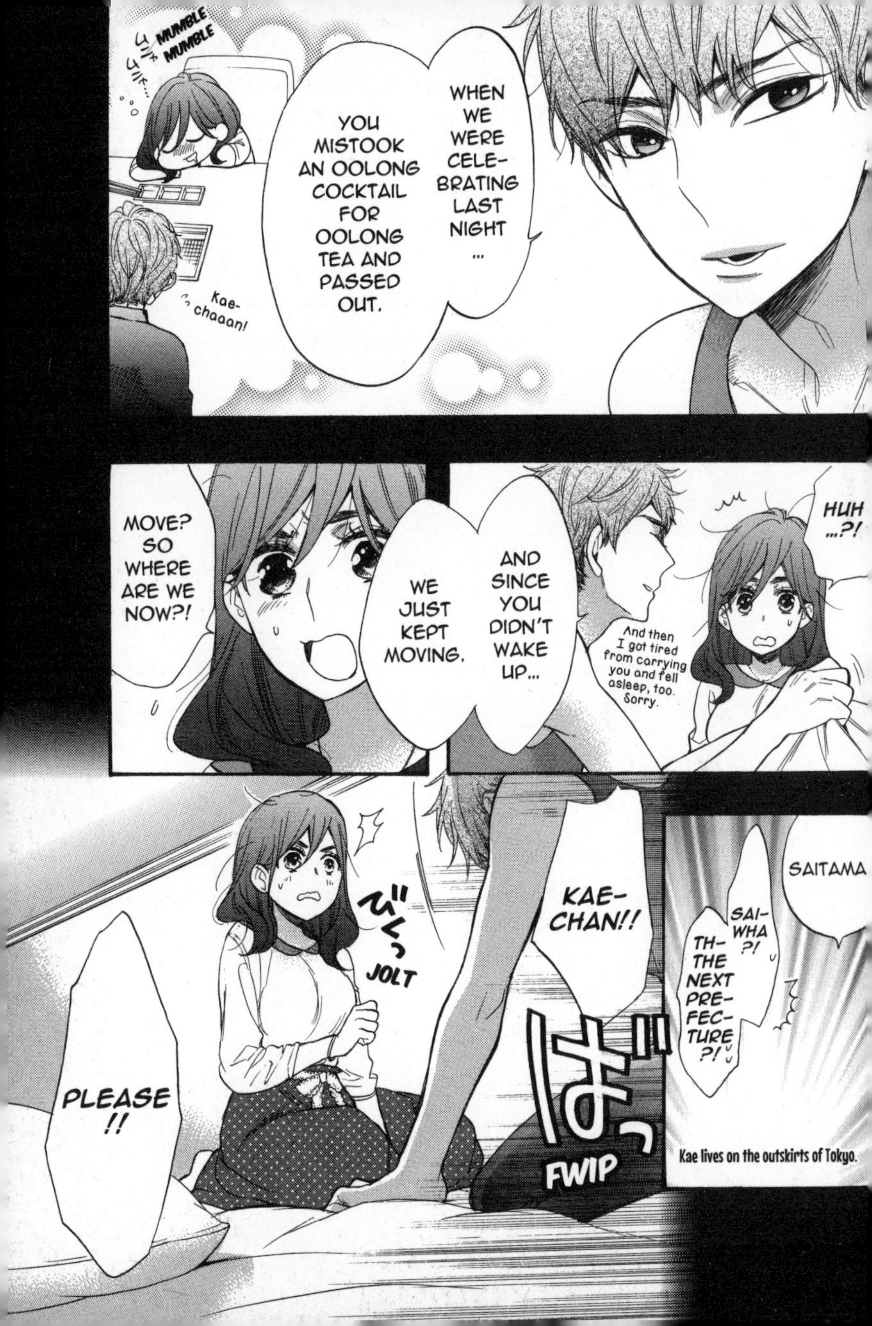
WHEN WE WERE CELEBRATING LAST NIGHT...
YOU MISTOOK AN OOLONG COCKTAIL FOR OOLONG TEA AND PASSED OUT.
MUMBLE MUMBLE
Kae-chaaan!
HUH ...?!
And then I got tired from carrying you and fell asleep, too. Sorry.
AND SINCE YOU DIDN'T WAKE UP...
WE JUST KEPT MOVING.
MOVE? SO WHERE ARE WE NOW?!
SAITAMA
SAI-WHA?!
TH-THE NEXT PREFECTURE?!
Kae lives on the outskirts of Tokyo.
KAE-CHAN!!
ばっ
FWIP
びくっ
JOLT
PLEASE!!

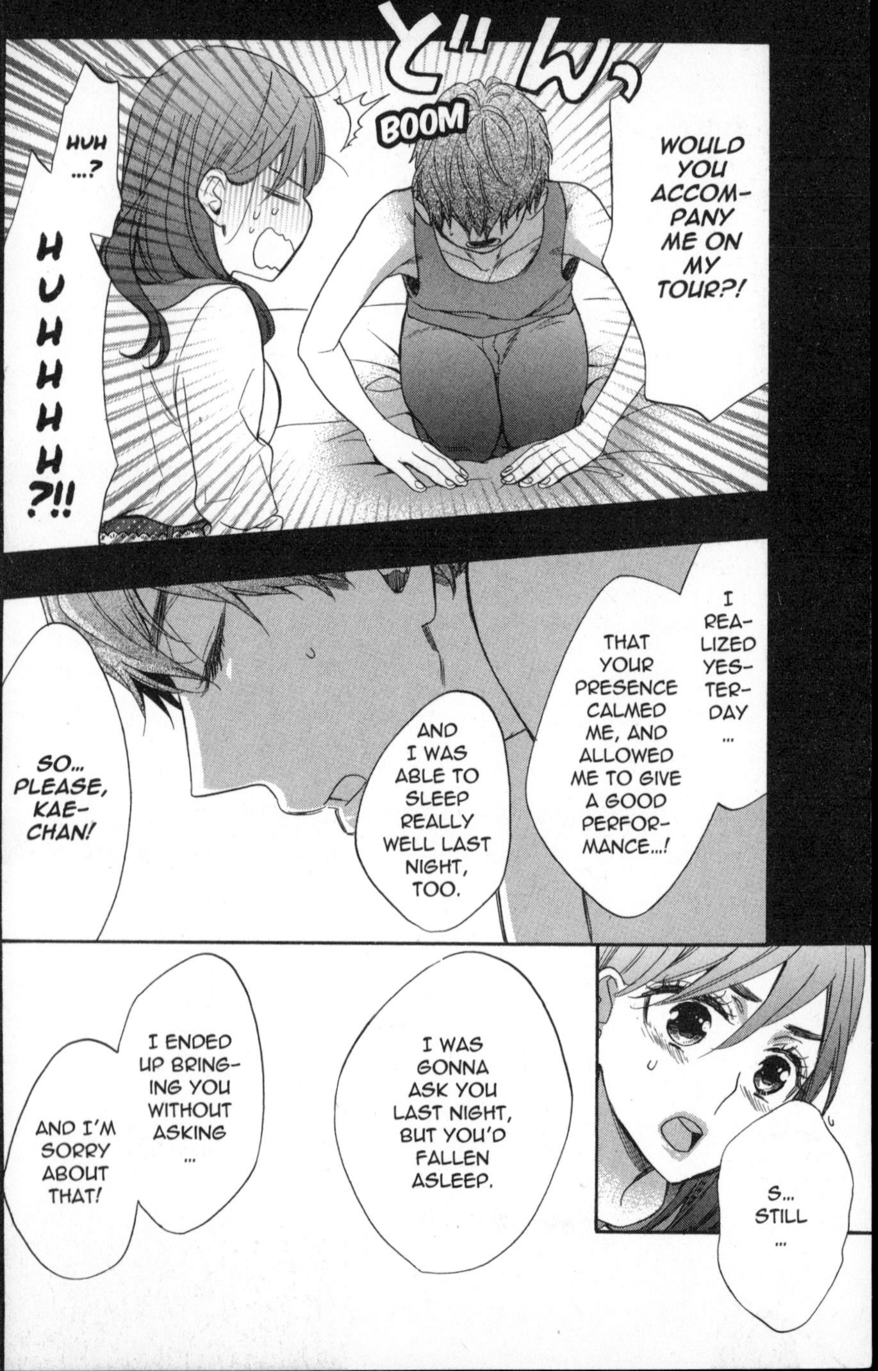
どん
BOOM
WOULD YOU ACCOMPANY ME ON MY TOUR?!
HUH ...?
HUHHHHHH?!!
I REALIZED YESTERDAY ...
THAT YOUR PRESENCE CALMED ME, AND ALLOWED ME TO GIVE A GOOD PERFORMANCE...!
AND I WAS ABLE TO SLEEP REALLY WELL LAST NIGHT, TOO.
SO... PLEASE, KAE-CHAN!
S... STILL ...
I WAS GONNA ASK YOU LAST NIGHT, BUT YOU'D FALLEN ASLEEP.
I ENDED UP BRINGING YOU WITHOUT ASKING ...
AND I'M SORRY ABOUT THAT!

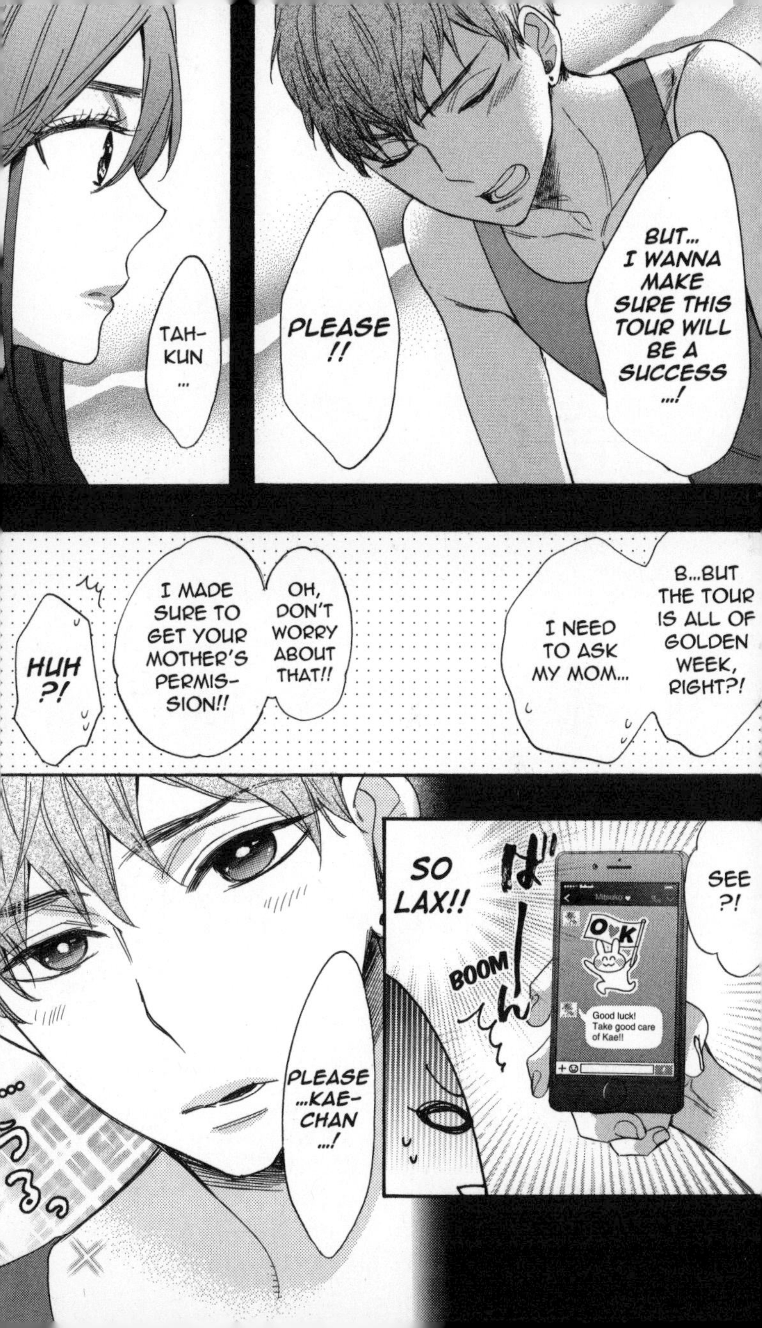
BUT... I WANNA MAKE SURE THIS TOUR WILL BE A SUCCESS ...!
PLEASE !!
TAH-KUN ...
B...BUT THE TOUR IS ALL OF GOLDEN WEEK, RIGHT?!
I NEED TO ASK MY MOM...
OH, DON'T WORRY ABOUT THAT!!
I MADE SURE TO GET YOUR MOTHER'S PERMISSION!!
HUH ?!
SEE ?!
OK
Good luck! Take good care of Kae!!
BOOM
SO LAX!!
PLEASE ...KAE-CHAN ...!

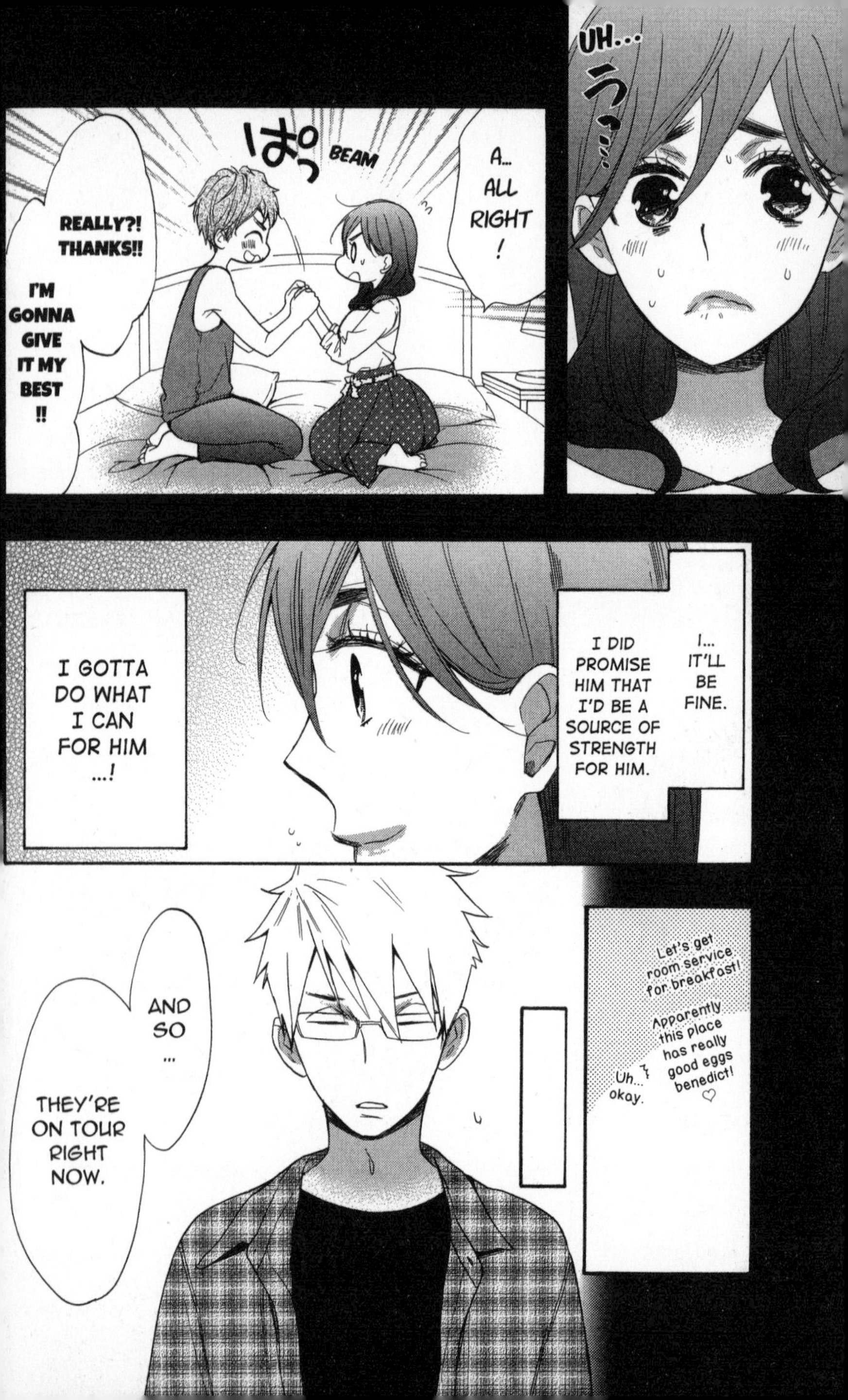
UH...
うっ…
A... ALL RIGHT!
ぱっ
BEAM
REALLY?! THANKS!!
I'M GONNA GIVE IT MY BEST!!
I... IT'LL BE FINE.
I DID PROMISE HIM THAT I'D BE A SOURCE OF STRENGTH FOR HIM.
I GOTTA DO WHAT I CAN FOR HIM ...!
Let's get room service for breakfast!
Apparently this place has really good eggs benedict! ♡
Uh... okay.
AND SO ... THEY'RE ON TOUR RIGHT NOW.

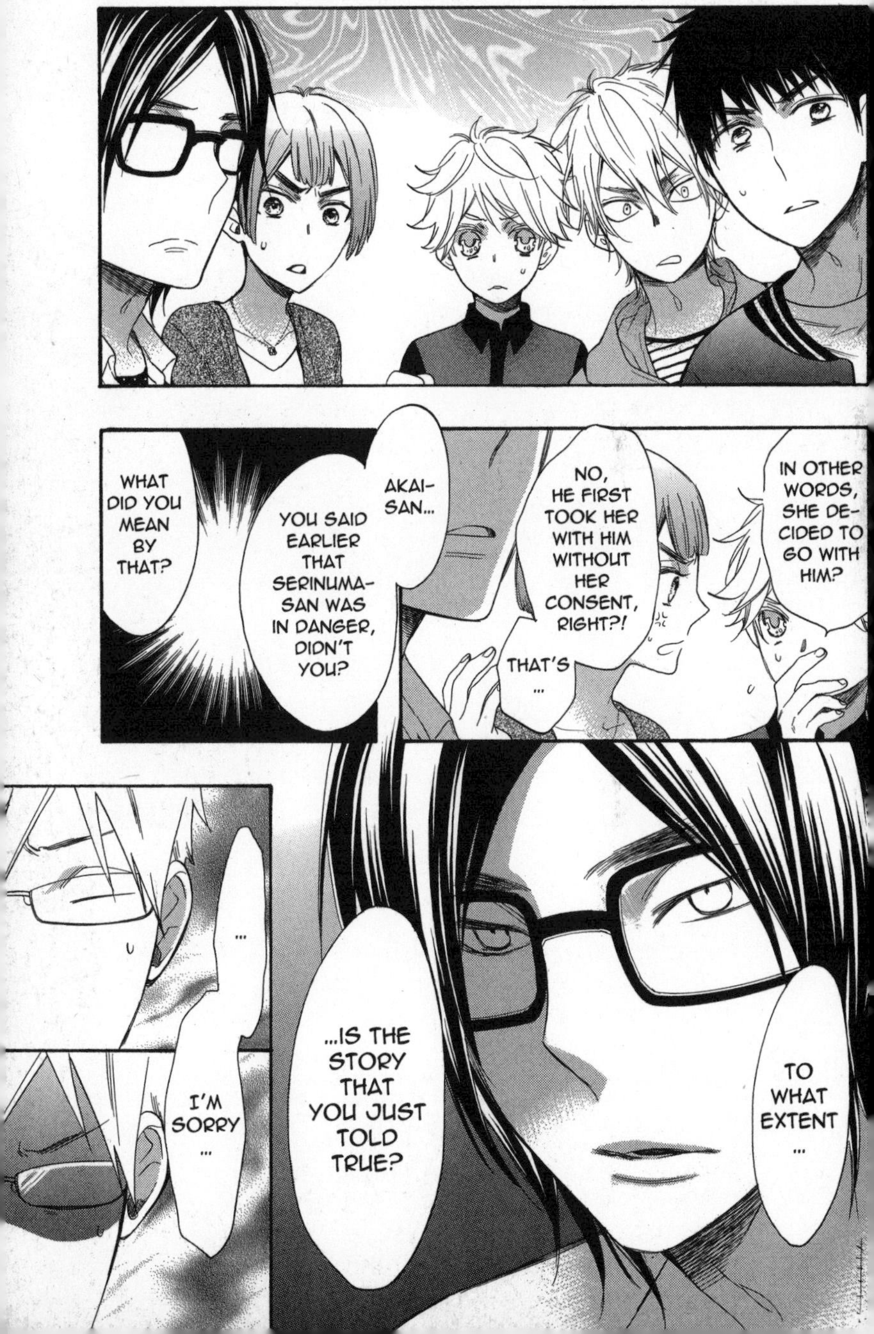
IN OTHER WORDS, SHE DECIDED TO GO WITH HIM?
NO, HE FIRST TOOK HER WITH HIM WITHOUT HER CONSENT, RIGHT?!
THAT'S ...
AKAI-SAN...
YOU SAID EARLIER THAT SERINUMA-SAN WAS IN DANGER, DIDN'T YOU?
WHAT DID YOU MEAN BY THAT?
TO WHAT EXTENT ...
...IS THE STORY THAT YOU JUST TOLD TRUE?
...
I'M SORRY ...

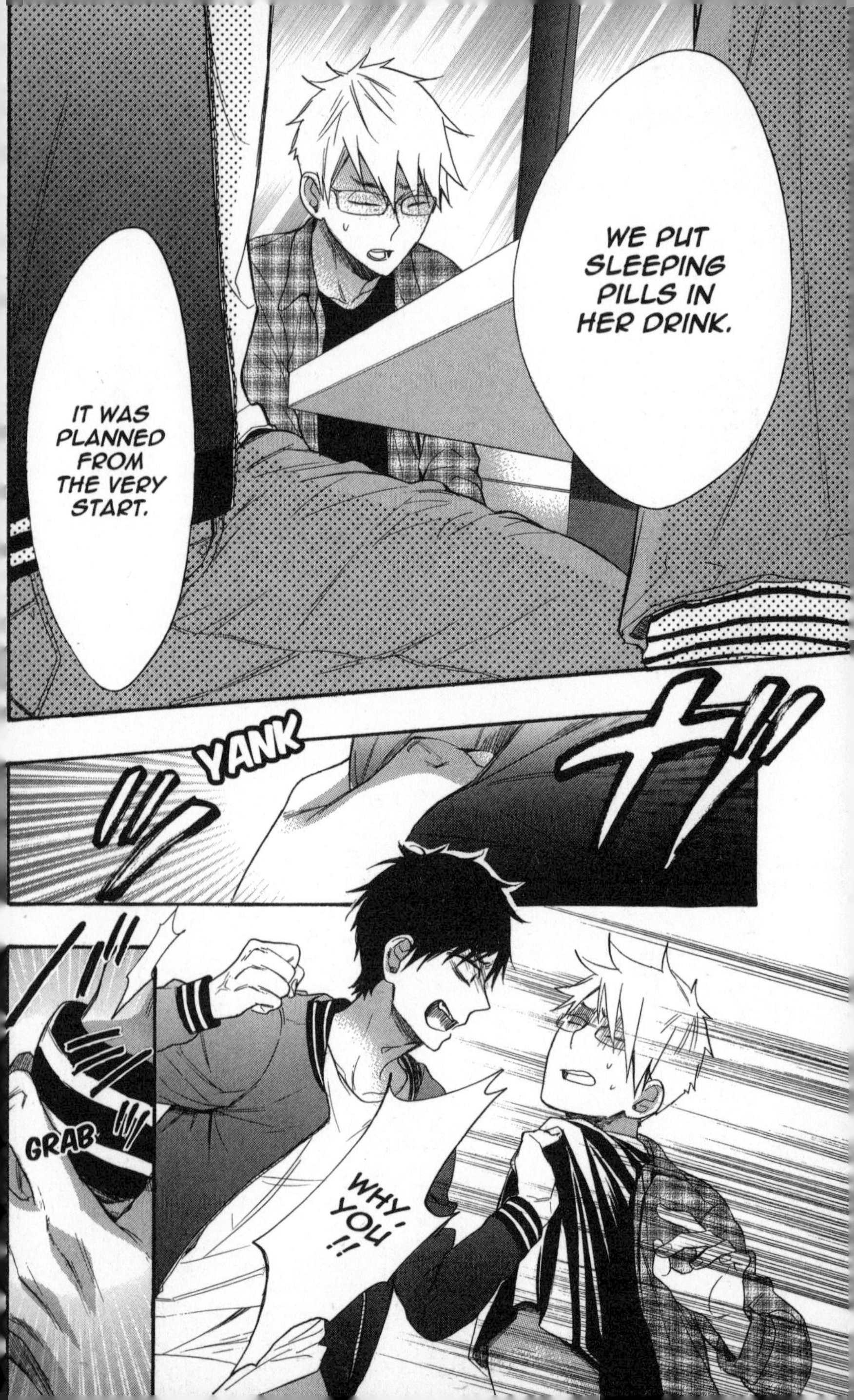
WE PUT SLEEPING PILLS IN HER DRINK.
IT WAS PLANNED FROM THE VERY START.
YANK
GRAB
WHY, YOU!!

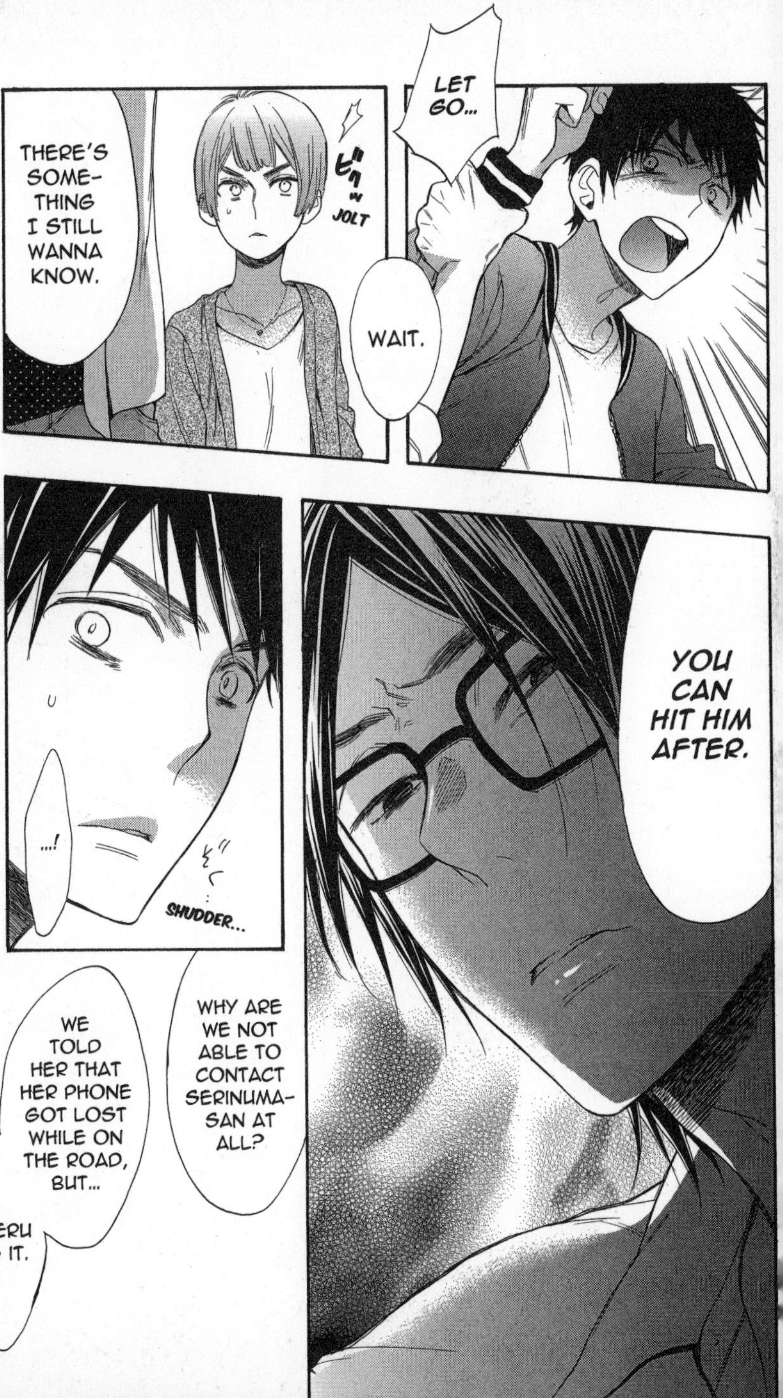
LET GO...
WAIT.
JOLT
THERE'S SOMETHING I STILL WANNA KNOW.
YOU CAN HIT HIM AFTER.
...!
SHUDDER...
WHY ARE WE NOT ABLE TO CONTACT SERINUMA-SAN AT ALL?
WE TOLD HER THAT HER PHONE GOT LOST WHILE ON THE ROAD, BUT...
TAKERU HAS IT.

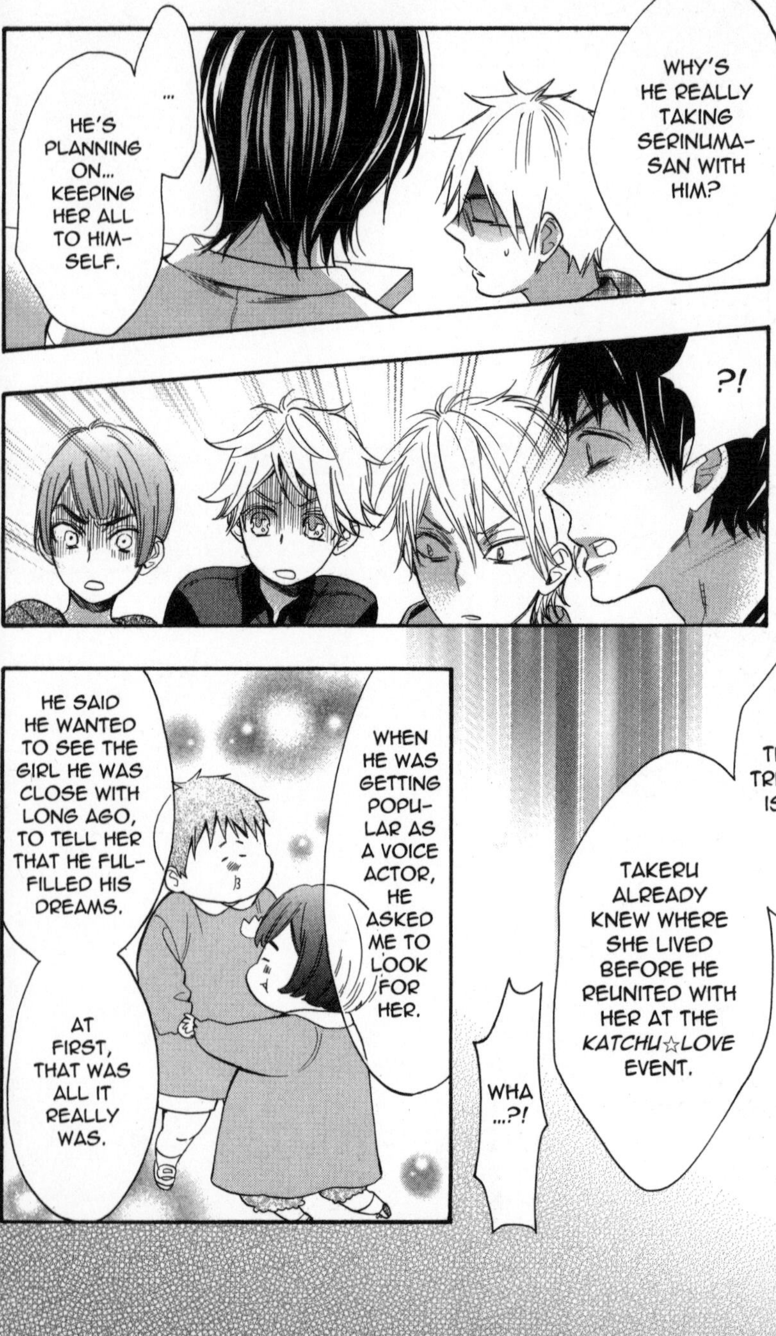
WHY'S HE REALLY TAKING SERINUMA-SAN WITH HIM?
...
HE'S PLANNING ON... KEEPING HER ALL TO HIM-SELF.
?!
THE TRUTH IS...
TAKERU ALREADY KNEW WHERE SHE LIVED BEFORE HE REUNITED WITH HER AT THE *KATCHU☆LOVE* EVENT.
WHA ...?!
WHEN HE WAS GETTING POPU-LAR AS A VOICE ACTOR, HE ASKED ME TO LOOK FOR HER.
HE SAID HE WANTED TO SEE THE GIRL HE WAS CLOSE WITH LONG AGO, TO TELL HER THAT HE FUL-FILLED HIS DREAMS.
AT FIRST, THAT WAS ALL IT REALLY WAS.

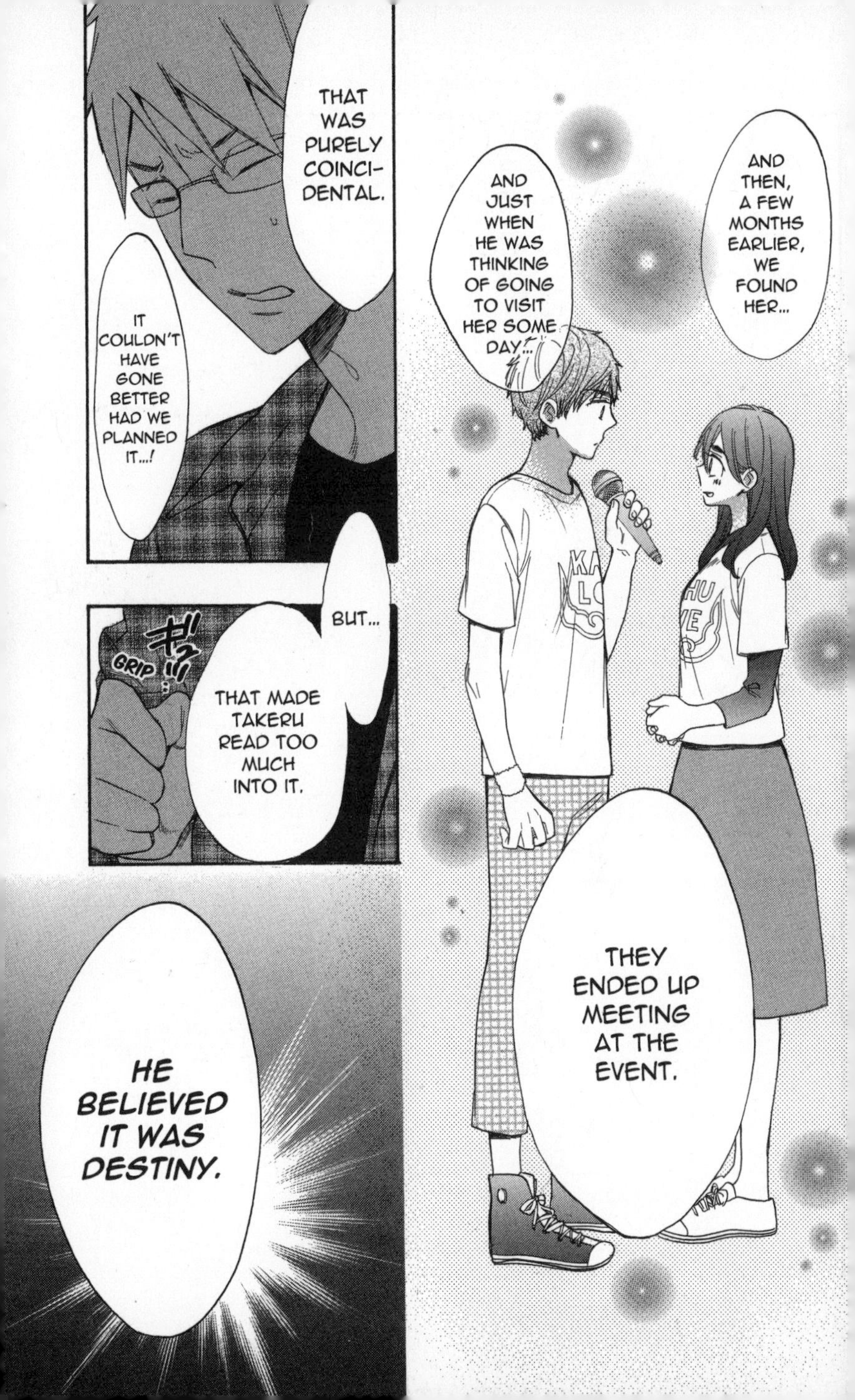
AND THEN, A FEW MONTHS EARLIER, WE FOUND HER...
AND JUST WHEN HE WAS THINKING OF GOING TO VISIT HER SOME DAY...
THEY ENDED UP MEETING AT THE EVENT.
THAT WAS PURELY COINCI-DENTAL.
IT COULDN'T HAVE GONE BETTER HAD WE PLANNED IT...!
BUT...
THAT MADE TAKERU READ TOO MUCH INTO IT.
GRIP
HE BELIEVED IT WAS DESTINY.

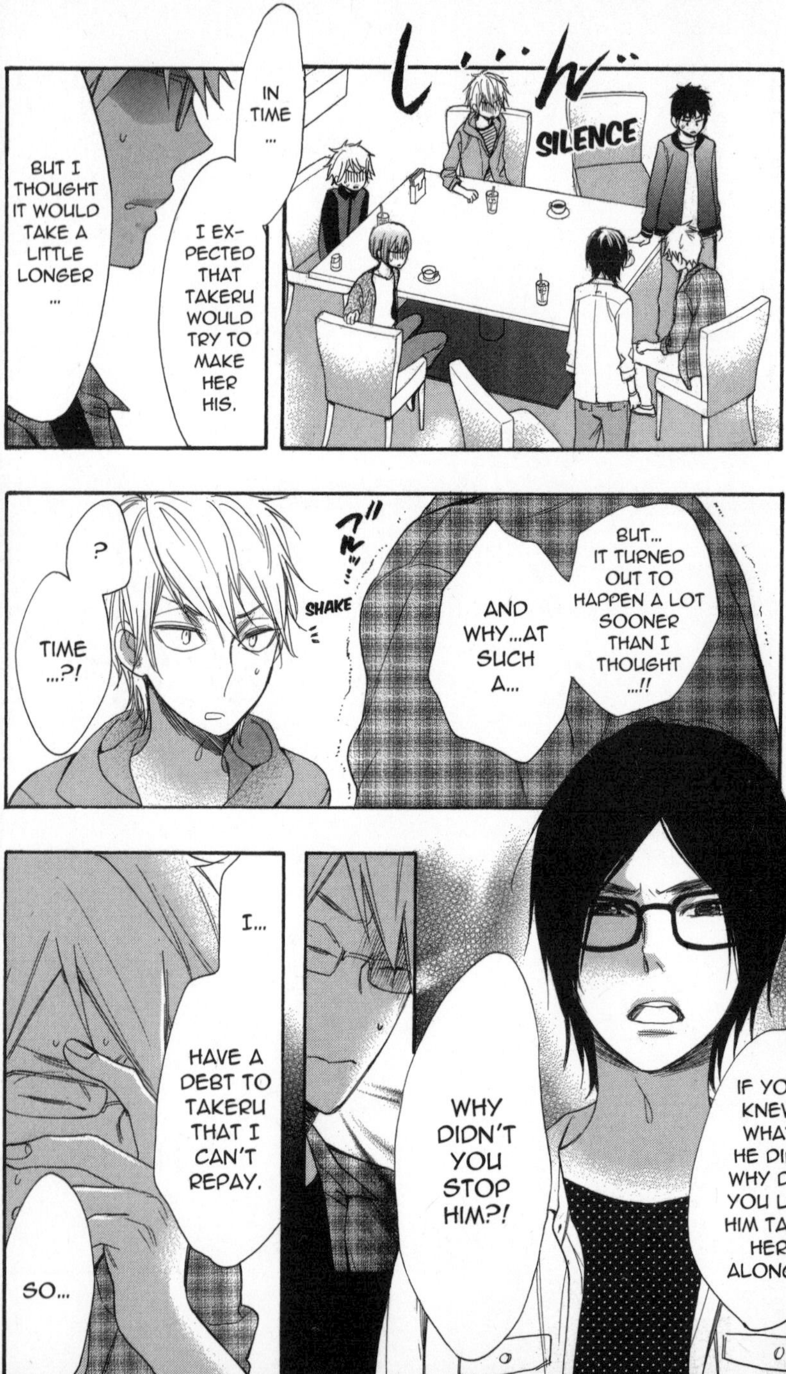
SILENCE
IN TIME...
I EXPECTED THAT TAKERU WOULD TRY TO MAKE HER HIS.
BUT I THOUGHT IT WOULD TAKE A LITTLE LONGER...
BUT... IT TURNED OUT TO HAPPEN A LOT SOONER THAN I THOUGHT...!!
AND WHY...AT SUCH A...
SHAKE
?
TIME...?!
IF YOU KNEW WHAT HE DID, WHY DID YOU LET HIM TAKE HER ALONG?
WHY DIDN'T YOU STOP HIM?!
I...
HAVE A DEBT TO TAKERU THAT I CAN'T REPAY.
SO...

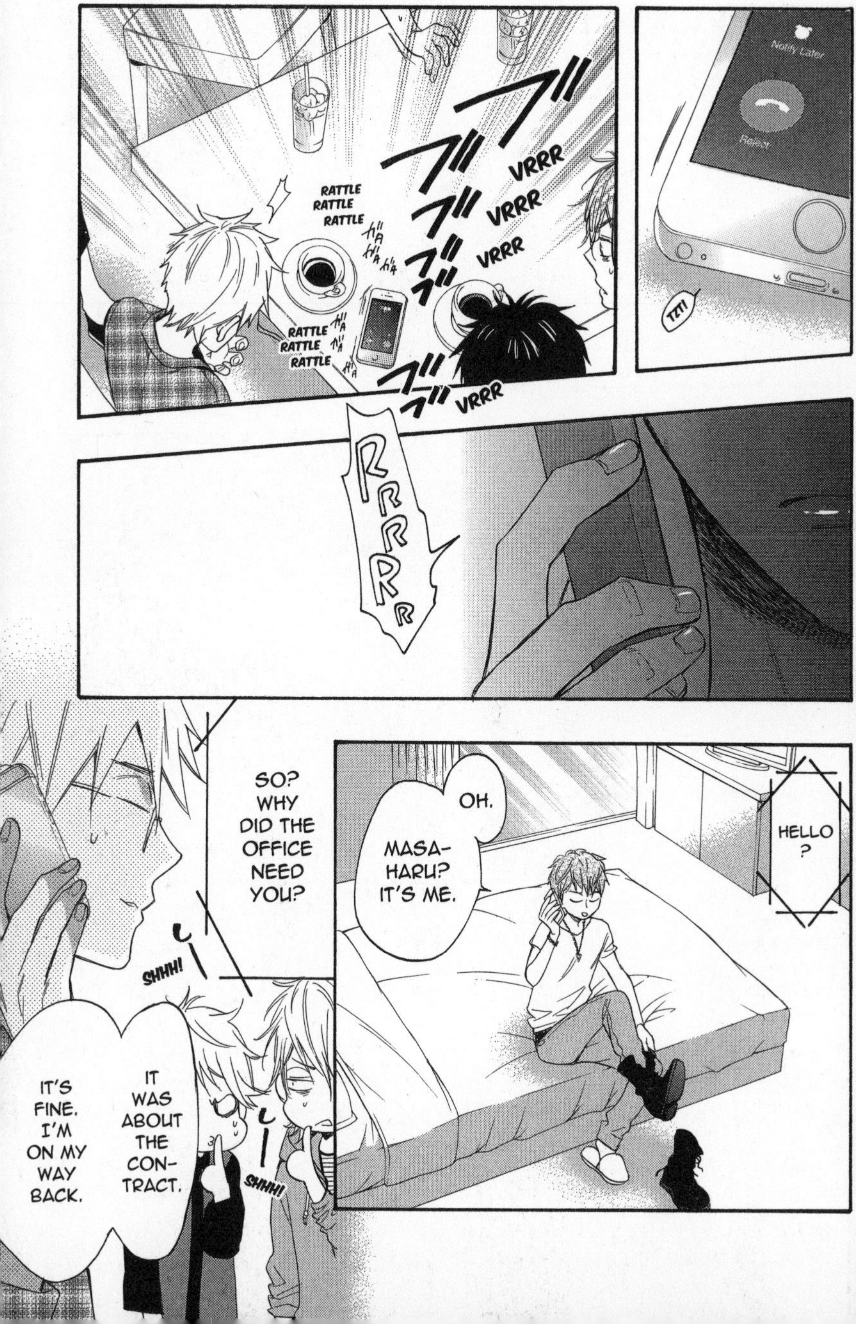
Notify Later
Reject
TZT!
VRRR
VRRR
VRRR
VRRR
RATTLE RATTLE RATTLE
RATTLE RATTLE RATTLE
RRRRRR
HELLO?
OH.
MASA-HARU? IT'S ME.
SO? WHY DID THE OFFICE NEED YOU?
SHHH!
SHHH!
IT WAS ABOUT THE CONTRACT.
IT'S FINE. I'M ON MY WAY BACK.

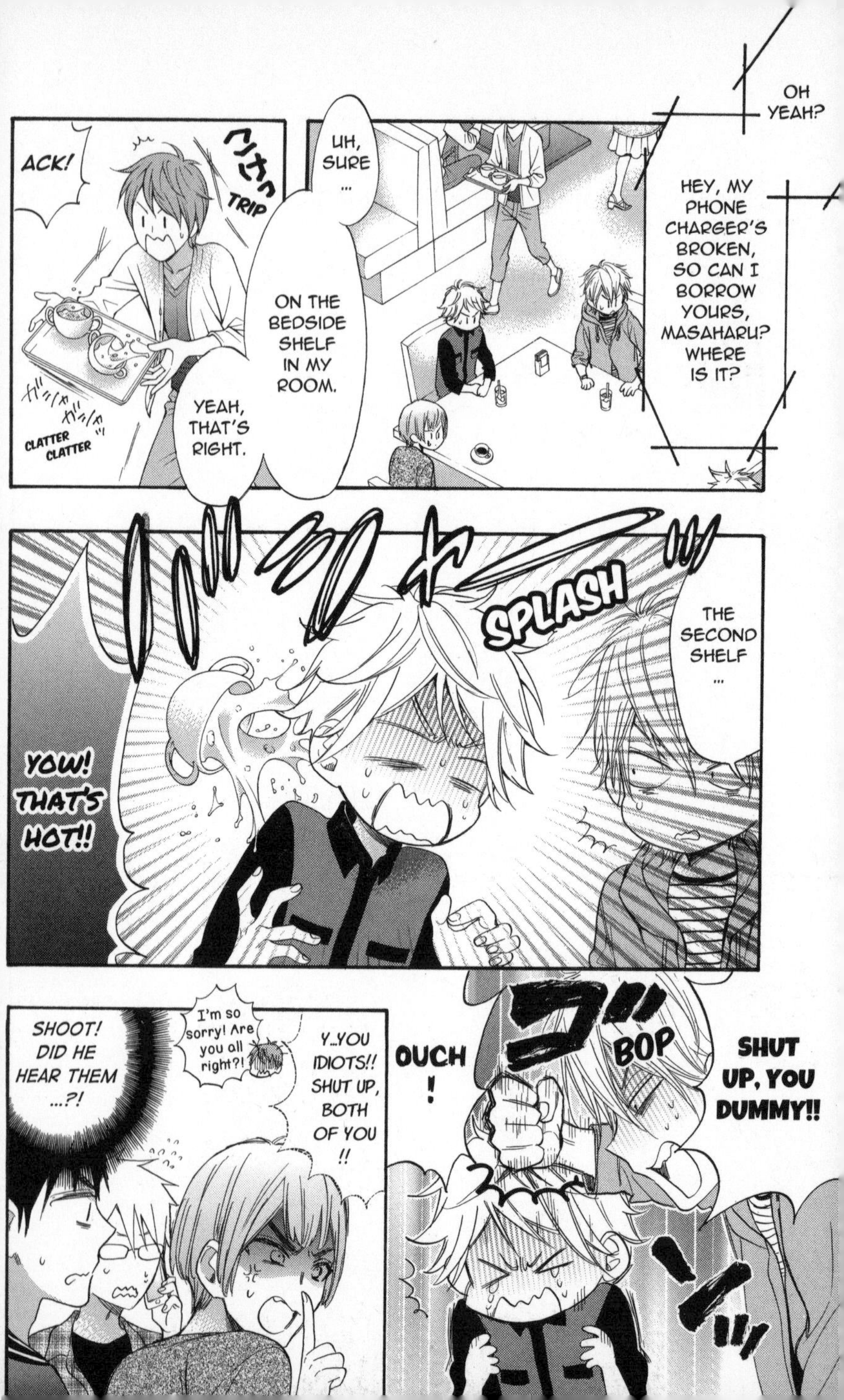
OH YEAH?
HEY, MY PHONE CHARGER'S BROKEN, SO CAN I BORROW YOURS, MASAHARU? WHERE IS IT?
UH, SURE ...
ON THE BEDSIDE SHELF IN MY ROOM.
YEAH, THAT'S RIGHT.
TRIP
ACK!
CLATTER CLATTER
THE SECOND SHELF ...
SPLASH
YOW! THAT'S HOT!!
SHUT UP, YOU DUMMY!!
BOP
OUCH!
Y...YOU IDIOTS!! SHUT UP, BOTH OF YOU!!
I'm so sorry! Are you all right?!
SHOOT! DID HE HEAR THEM ...?!

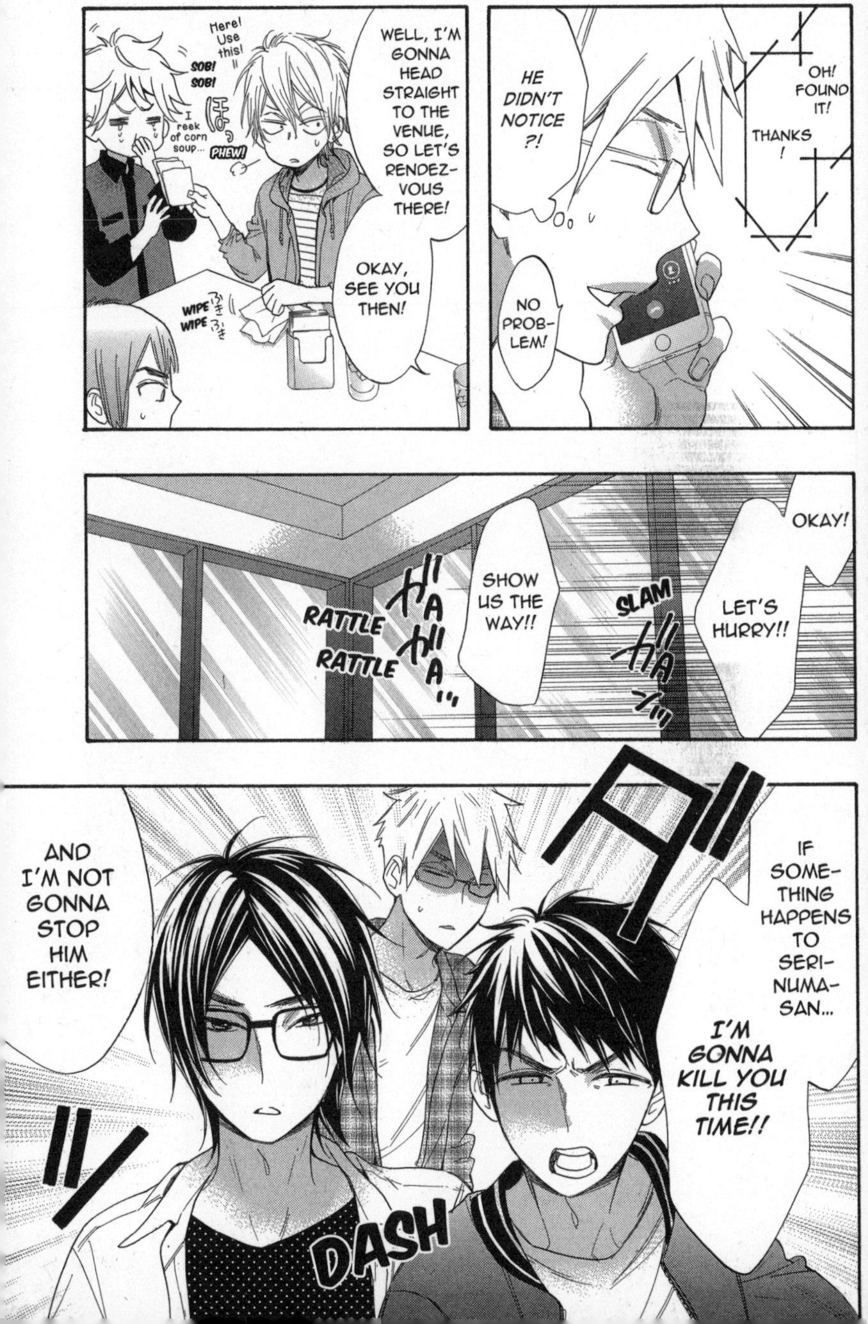
OH! FOUND IT!
THANKS!
HE DIDN'T NOTICE?!
NO PROBLEM!
WELL, I'M GONNA HEAD STRAIGHT TO THE VENUE, SO LET'S RENDEZVOUS THERE!
OKAY, SEE YOU THEN!
Here! Use this!!
SOB! SOB!
I reek of corn soup...
PHEW!
WIPE WIPE
OKAY!
LET'S HURRY!!
SLAM
SHOW US THE WAY!!
RATTLE RATTLE
IF SOMETHING HAPPENS TO SERINUMA-SAN...
I'M GONNA KILL YOU THIS TIME!!
AND I'M NOT GONNA STOP HIM EITHER!
DASH

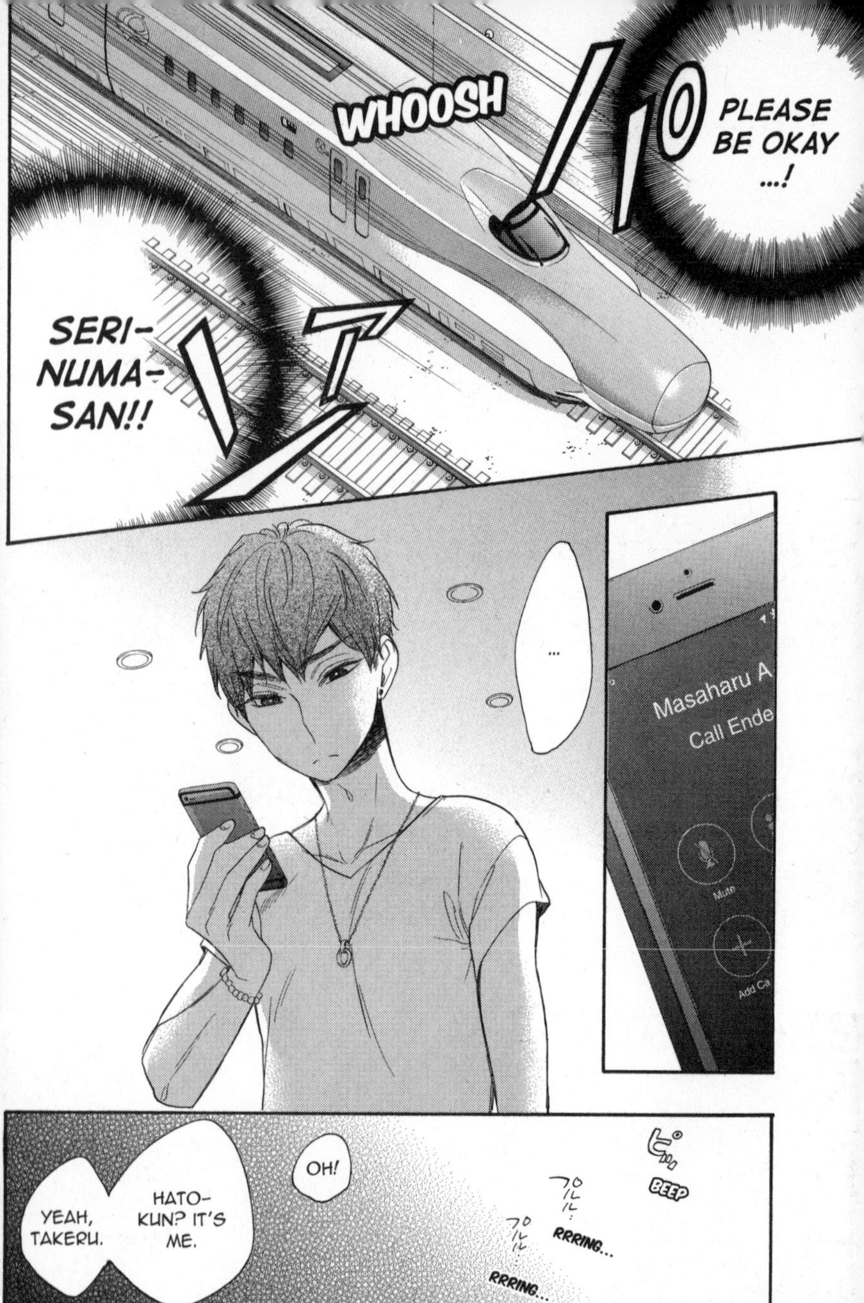
PLEASE BE OKAY ...!
WHOOSH
SERI-NUMA-SAN!!
Masaharu A
Call Ende
Mute
Add Ca
...
ピッ
BEEP
プルル
RRRING...
プルル
RRRING...
OH!
HATO-KUN? IT'S ME.
YEAH, TAKERU.

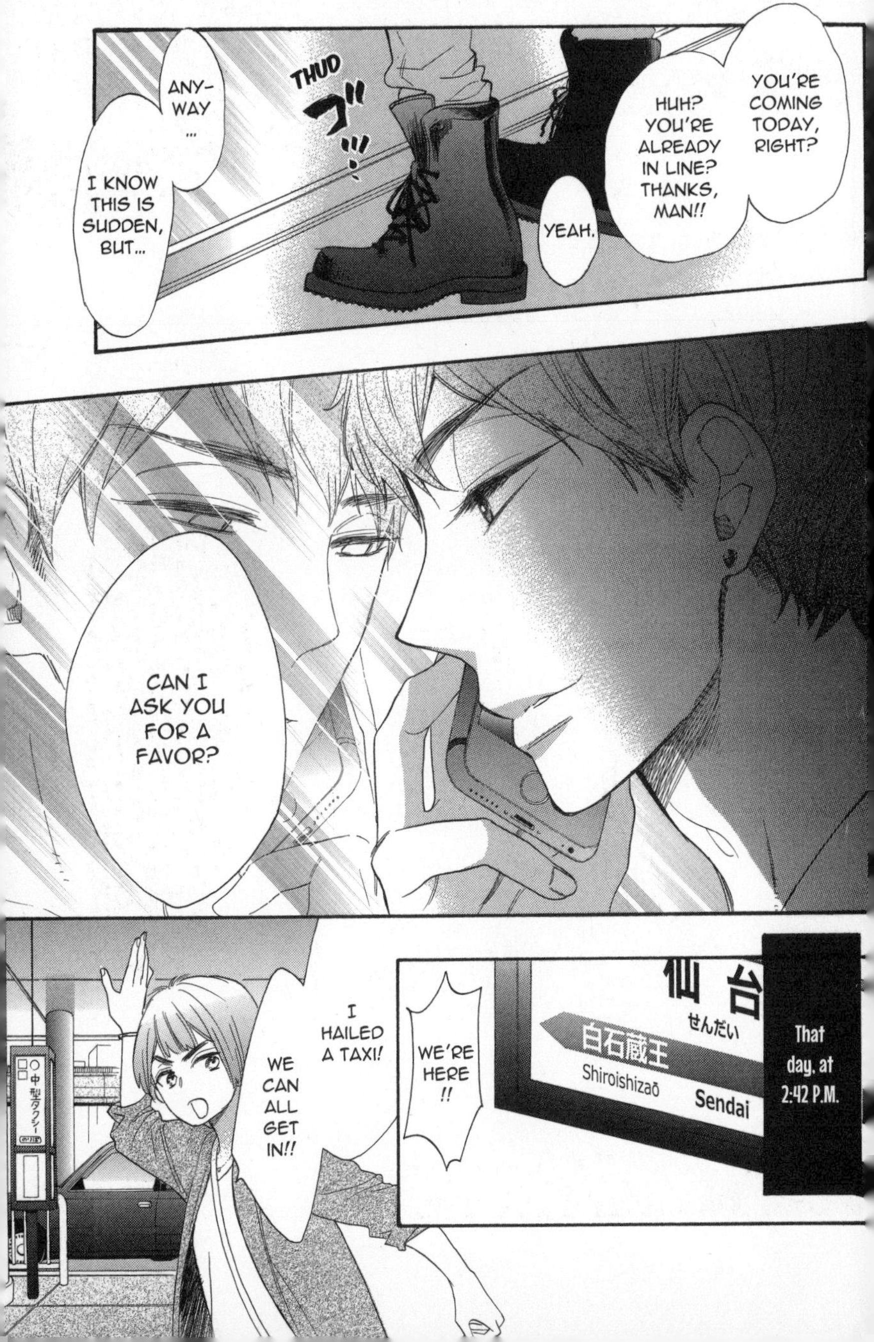
YOU'RE COMING TODAY, RIGHT?
HUH? YOU'RE ALREADY IN LINE? THANKS, MAN!!
YEAH.
THUD
ANY-WAY...
I KNOW THIS IS SUDDEN, BUT...
CAN I ASK YOU FOR A FAVOR?
That day, at 2:42 P.M.
仙台
せんだい
白石蔵王
Shiroishizaō
Sendai
WE'RE HERE!!
I HAILED A TAXI!
WE CAN ALL GET IN!!
中型タクシー

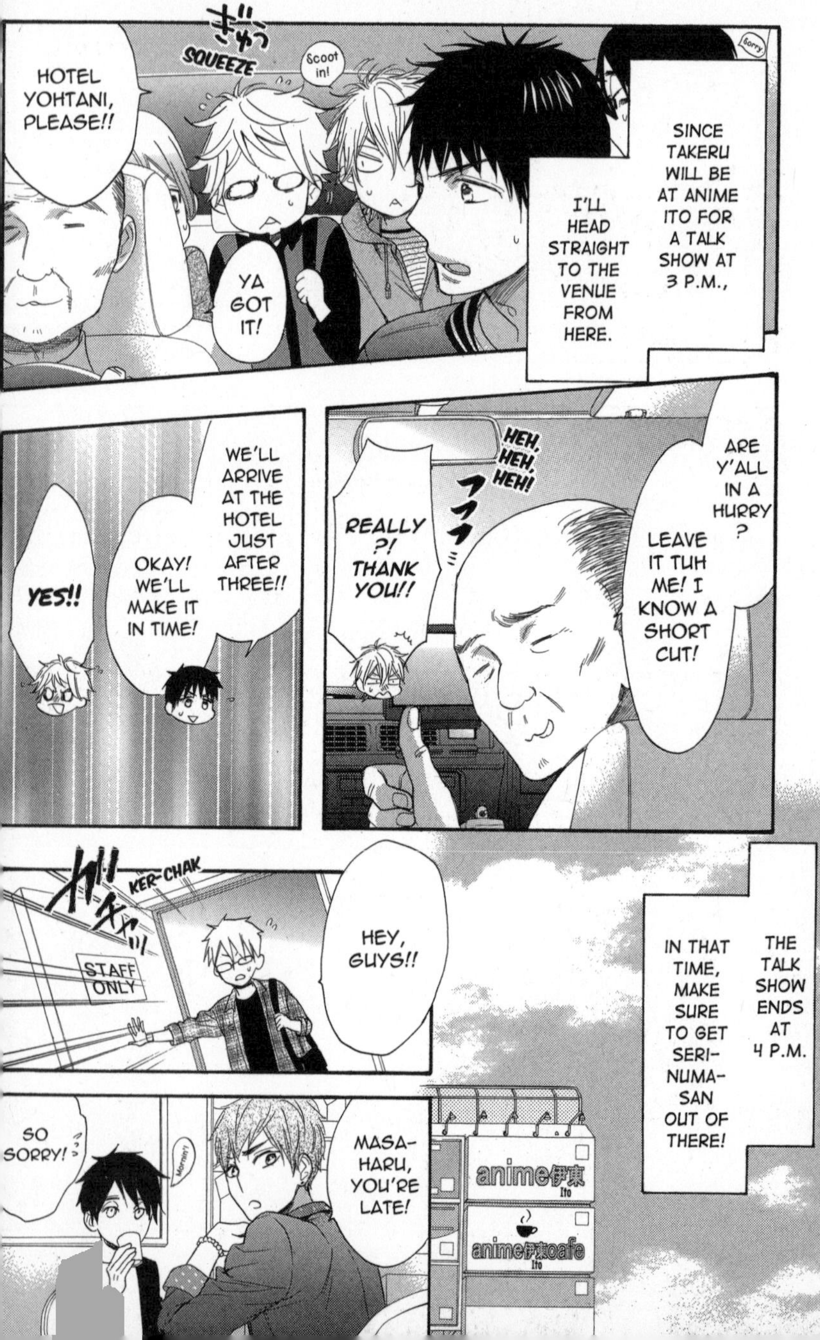
Sorry.
SINCE TAKERU WILL BE AT ANIME ITO FOR A TALK SHOW AT 3 P.M.,
I'LL HEAD STRAIGHT TO THE VENUE FROM HERE.
Scoot in!
SQUEEZE
YA GOT IT!
HOTEL YOHTANI, PLEASE!!
ARE Y'ALL IN A HURRY?
LEAVE IT TUH ME! I KNOW A SHORT CUT!
HEH, HEH, HEH!
REALLY?! THANK YOU!!
WE'LL ARRIVE AT THE HOTEL JUST AFTER THREE!!
OKAY! WE'LL MAKE IT IN TIME!
YES!!
THE TALK SHOW ENDS AT 4 P.M.
IN THAT TIME, MAKE SURE TO GET SERI-NUMA-SAN OUT OF THERE!
anime伊東 Ito
anime伊東cafe Ito
HEY, GUYS!!
KER-CHAK
STAFF ONLY
MASA-HARU, YOU'RE LATE!
Mornin'
SO SORRY!

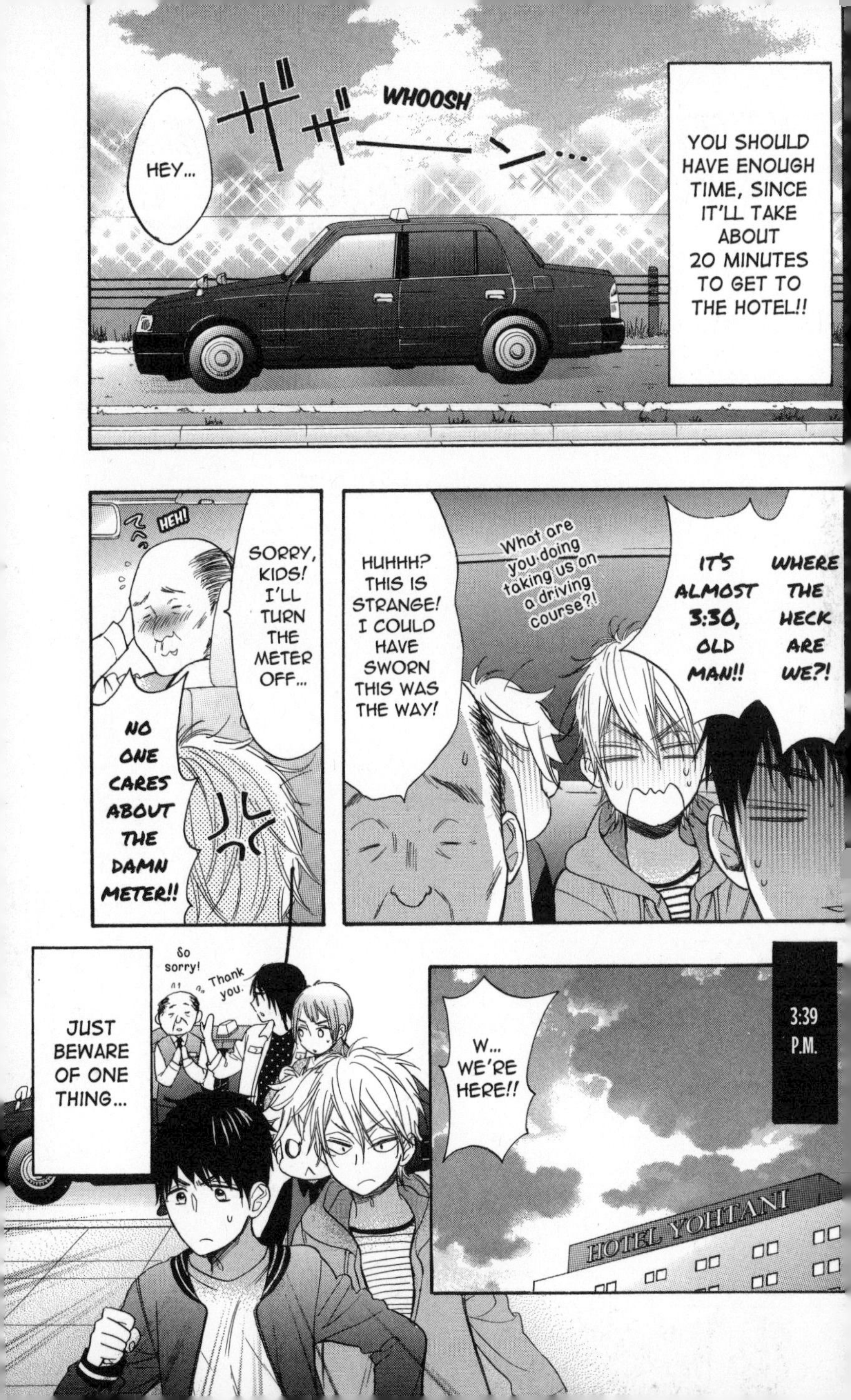
YOU SHOULD HAVE ENOUGH TIME, SINCE IT'LL TAKE ABOUT 20 MINUTES TO GET TO THE HOTEL!!
WHOOSH
HEY...
WHERE THE HECK ARE WE?!
IT'S ALMOST 3:30, OLD MAN!!
What are you doing taking us on a driving course?!
HUHHH? THIS IS STRANGE! I COULD HAVE SWORN THIS WAS THE WAY!
HEH!
SORRY, KIDS! I'LL TURN THE METER OFF...
NO ONE CARES ABOUT THE DAMN METER!!
3:39 P.M.
W... WE'RE HERE!!
HOTEL YOHTANI
Thank you.
So sorry!
JUST BEWARE OF ONE THING...

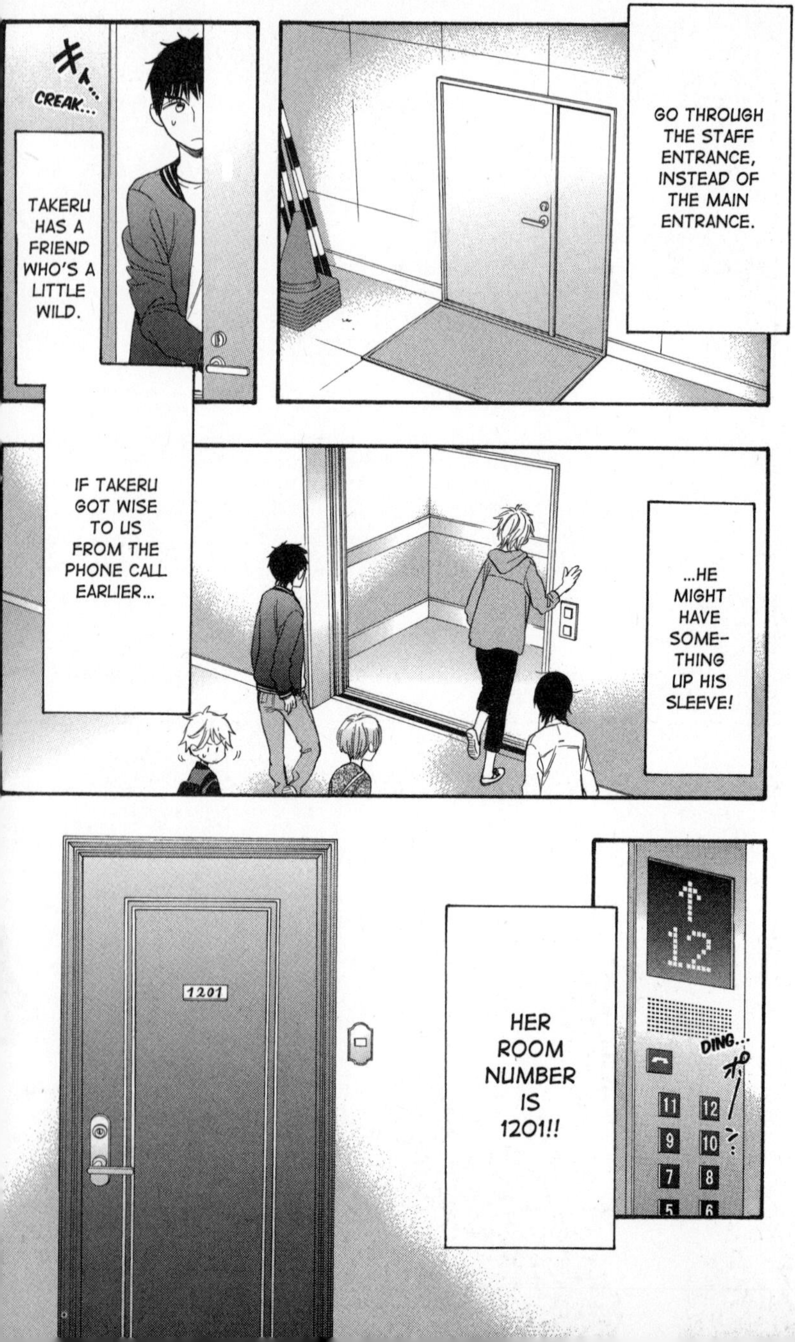

GO THROUGH THE STAFF ENTRANCE, INSTEAD OF THE MAIN ENTRANCE.
CREAK...
TAKERU HAS A FRIEND WHO'S A LITTLE WILD.
IF TAKERU GOT WISE TO US FROM THE PHONE CALL EARLIER...
...HE MIGHT HAVE SOME-THING UP HIS SLEEVE!
DING...
HER ROOM NUMBER IS 1201!!
1201

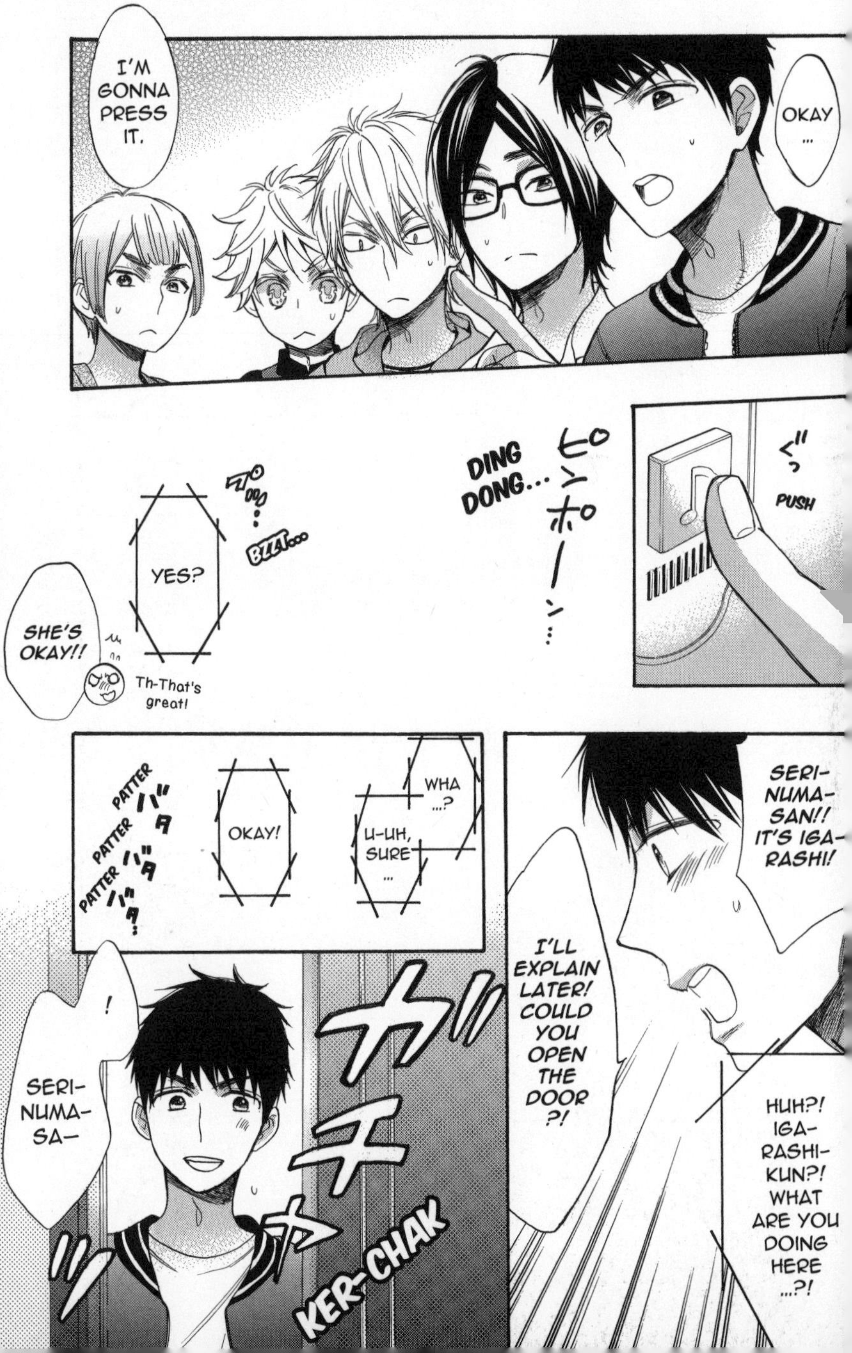
I'M GONNA PRESS IT.
OKAY ...
PUSH
DING DONG...
BZZT...
YES?
SHE'S OKAY!!
Th-That's great!
SERI-NUMA-SAN!! IT'S IGA-RASHI!
I'LL EXPLAIN LATER! COULD YOU OPEN THE DOOR?!
HUH?! IGA-RASHI-KUN?! WHAT ARE YOU DOING HERE ...?!
WHA ...?
U-UH, SURE ...
OKAY!
PATTER PATTER PATTER
KER-CHAK
!
SERI-NUMA-SA—

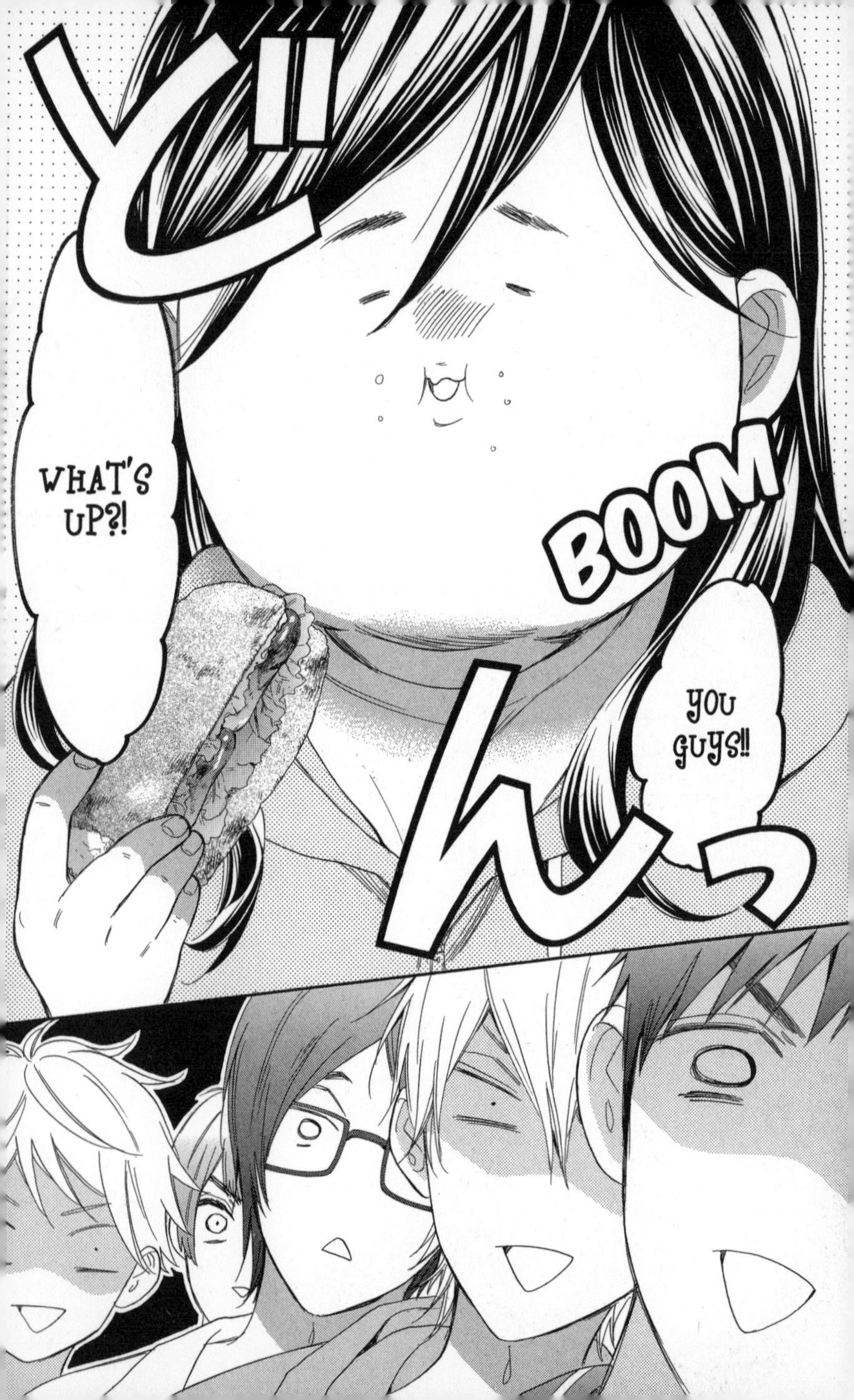
ソ!!
WHAT'S UP?!
BOOM
YOU GUYS!!
んっ

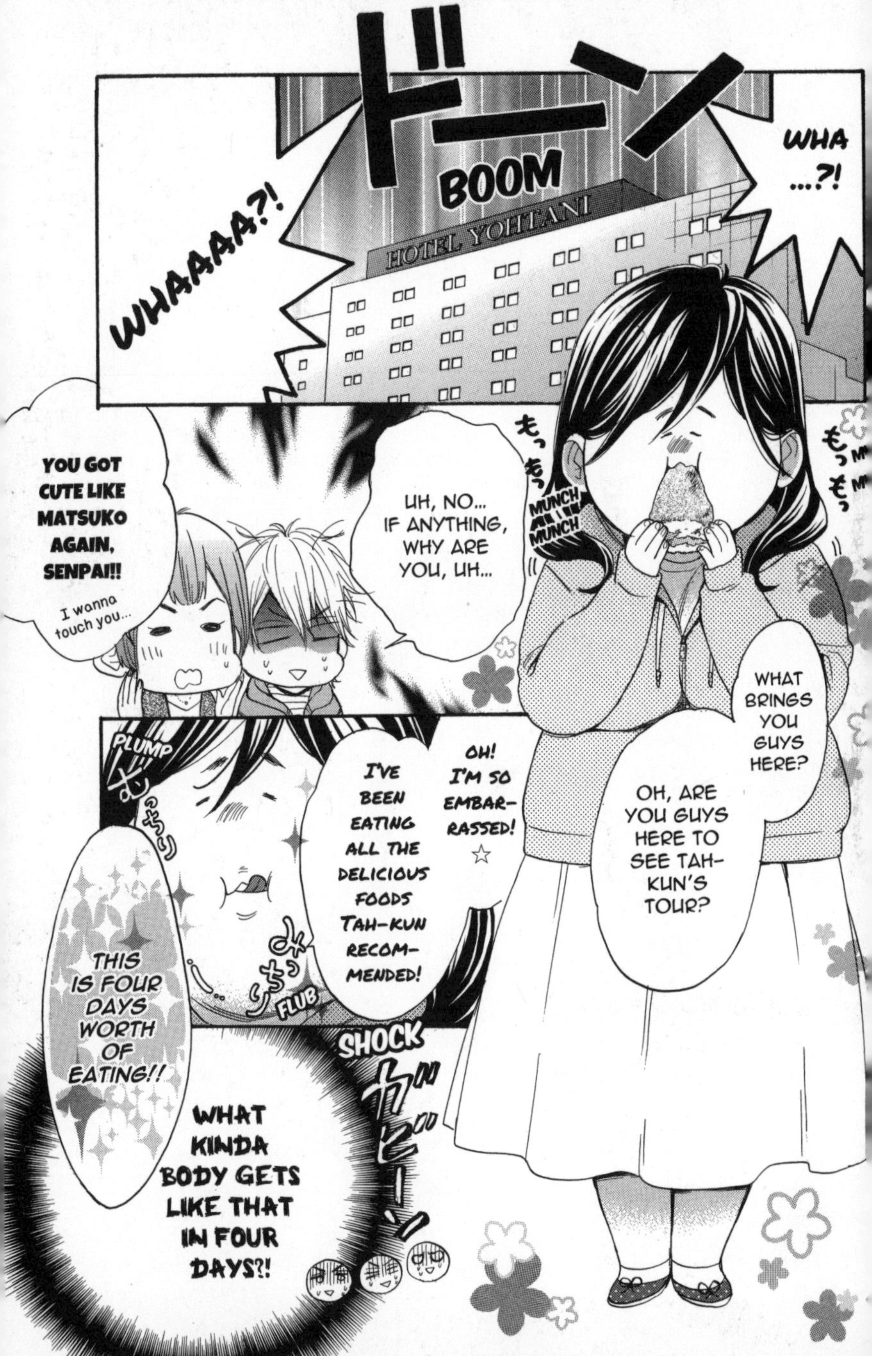
ドーン
BOOM
WHA ...?!
WHAAAA?!
HOTEL YOHTANI
もっもっ
MUNCH MUNCH
もっもっ
WHAT BRINGS YOU GUYS HERE?
OH, ARE YOU GUYS HERE TO SEE TAH-KUN'S TOUR?
UH, NO... IF ANYTHING, WHY ARE YOU, UH...
YOU GOT CUTE LIKE MATSUKO AGAIN, SENPAI!!
I wanna touch you...
OH! I'M SO EMBARRASSED! ☆
I'VE BEEN EATING ALL THE DELICIOUS FOODS TAH-KUN RECOMMENDED!
PLUMP
FLUB
THIS IS FOUR DAYS WORTH OF EATING!!
SHOCK
WHAT KINDA BODY GETS LIKE THAT IN FOUR DAYS?!

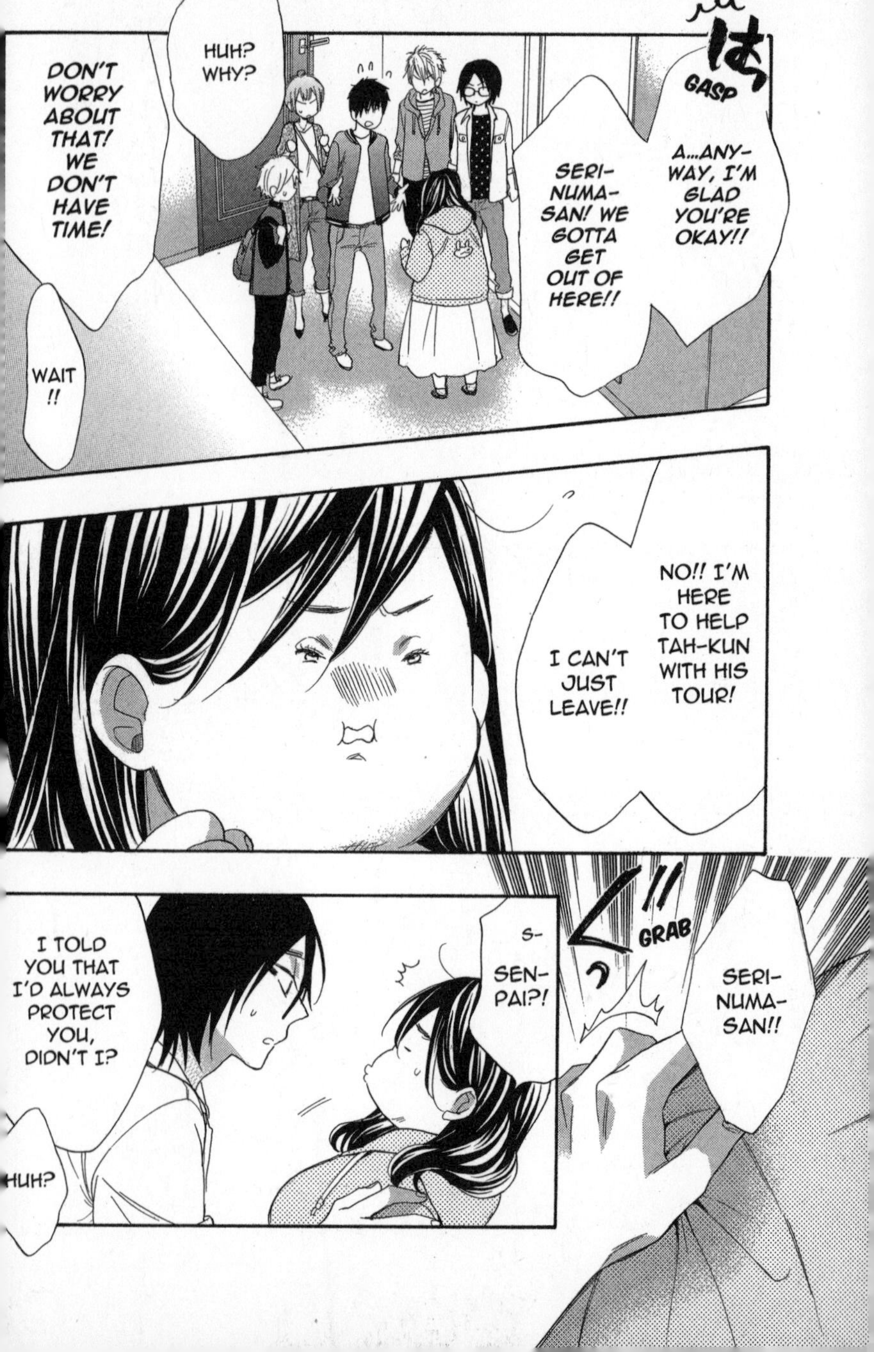
は
GASP
A...ANY-WAY, I'M GLAD YOU'RE OKAY!!
SERI-NUMA-SAN! WE GOTTA GET OUT OF HERE!!
HUH? WHY?
DON'T WORRY ABOUT THAT! WE DON'T HAVE TIME!
WAIT !!
NO!! I'M HERE TO HELP TAH-KUN WITH HIS TOUR!
I CAN'T JUST LEAVE!!
SERI-NUMA-SAN!!
GRAB
S- SEN-PAI?!
I TOLD YOU THAT I'D ALWAYS PROTECT YOU, DIDN'T I?
HUH?

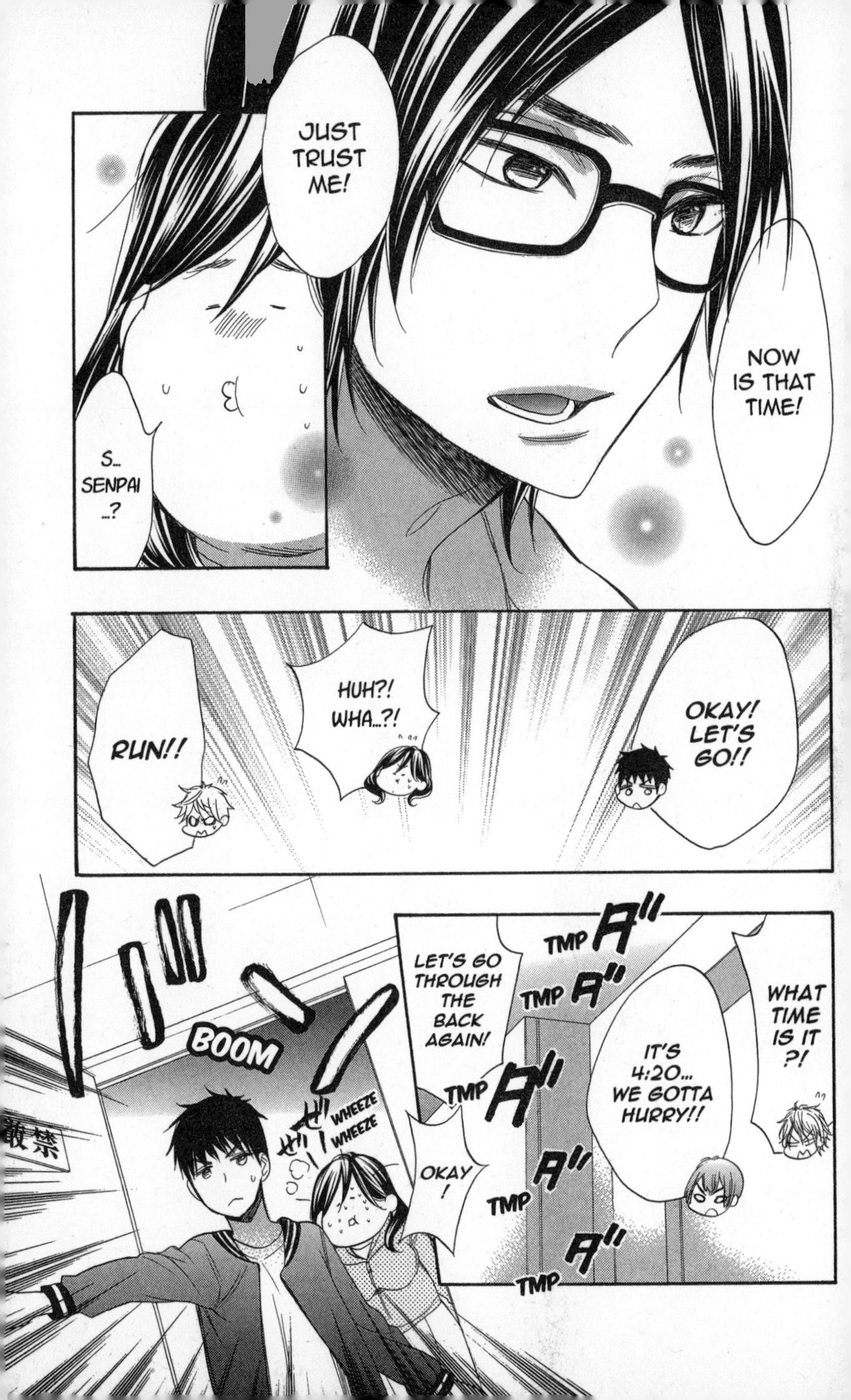
NOW IS THAT TIME!
JUST TRUST ME!
S... SENPAI ...?
OKAY! LET'S GO!!
HUH?! WHA...?!
RUN!!
WHAT TIME IS IT ?!
IT'S 4:20... WE GOTTA HURRY!!
LET'S GO THROUGH THE BACK AGAIN!
TMP
TMP
TMP
TMP
TMP
OKAY !
WHEEZE WHEEZE
BOOM

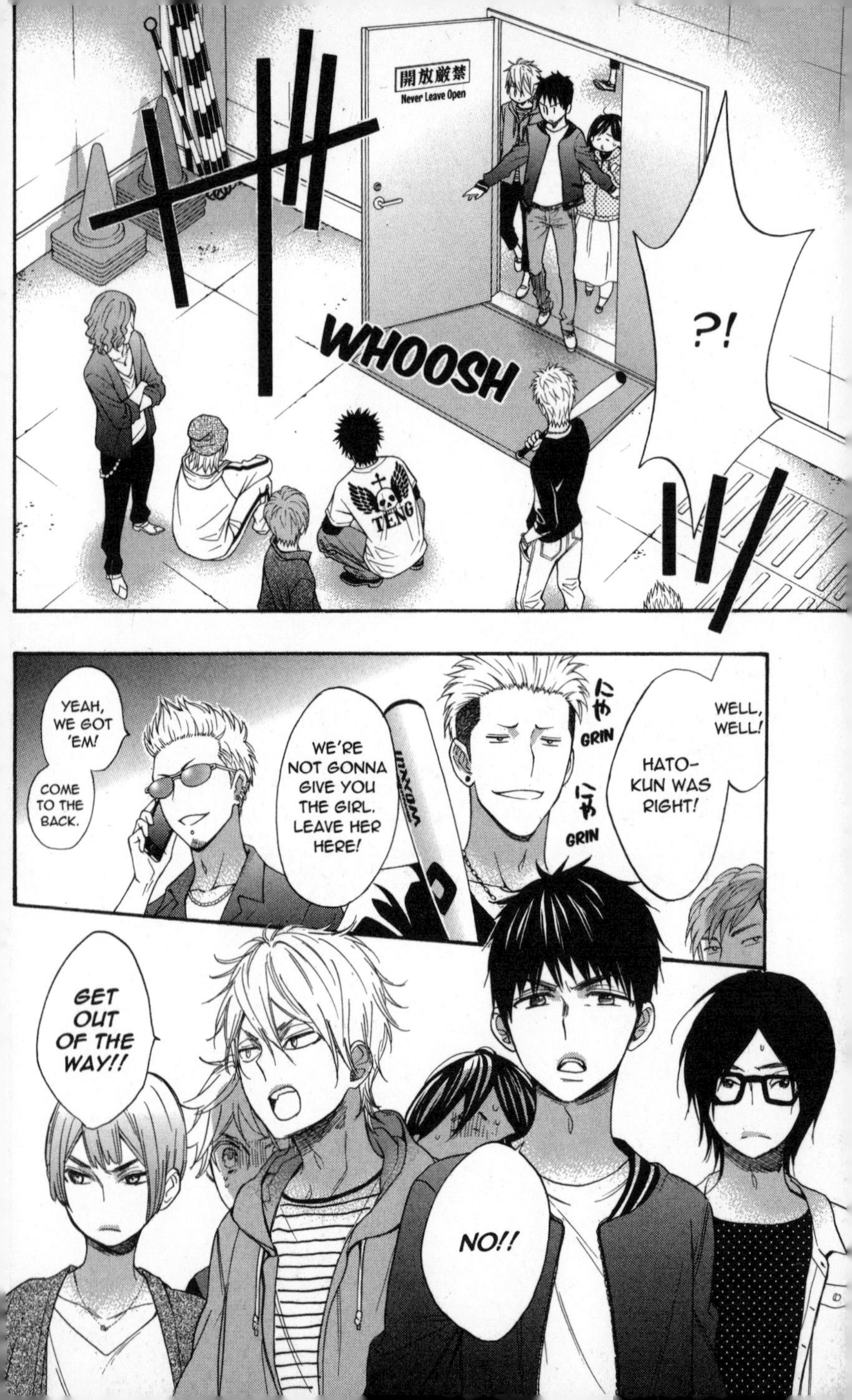
開放厳禁
Never Leave Open
?!
WHOOSH
WELL, WELL!
HATO-KUN WAS RIGHT!
にや GRIN
にや GRIN
WE'RE NOT GONNA GIVE YOU THE GIRL. LEAVE HER HERE!
YEAH, WE GOT 'EM!
COME TO THE BACK.
NO!!
GET OUT OF THE WAY!!

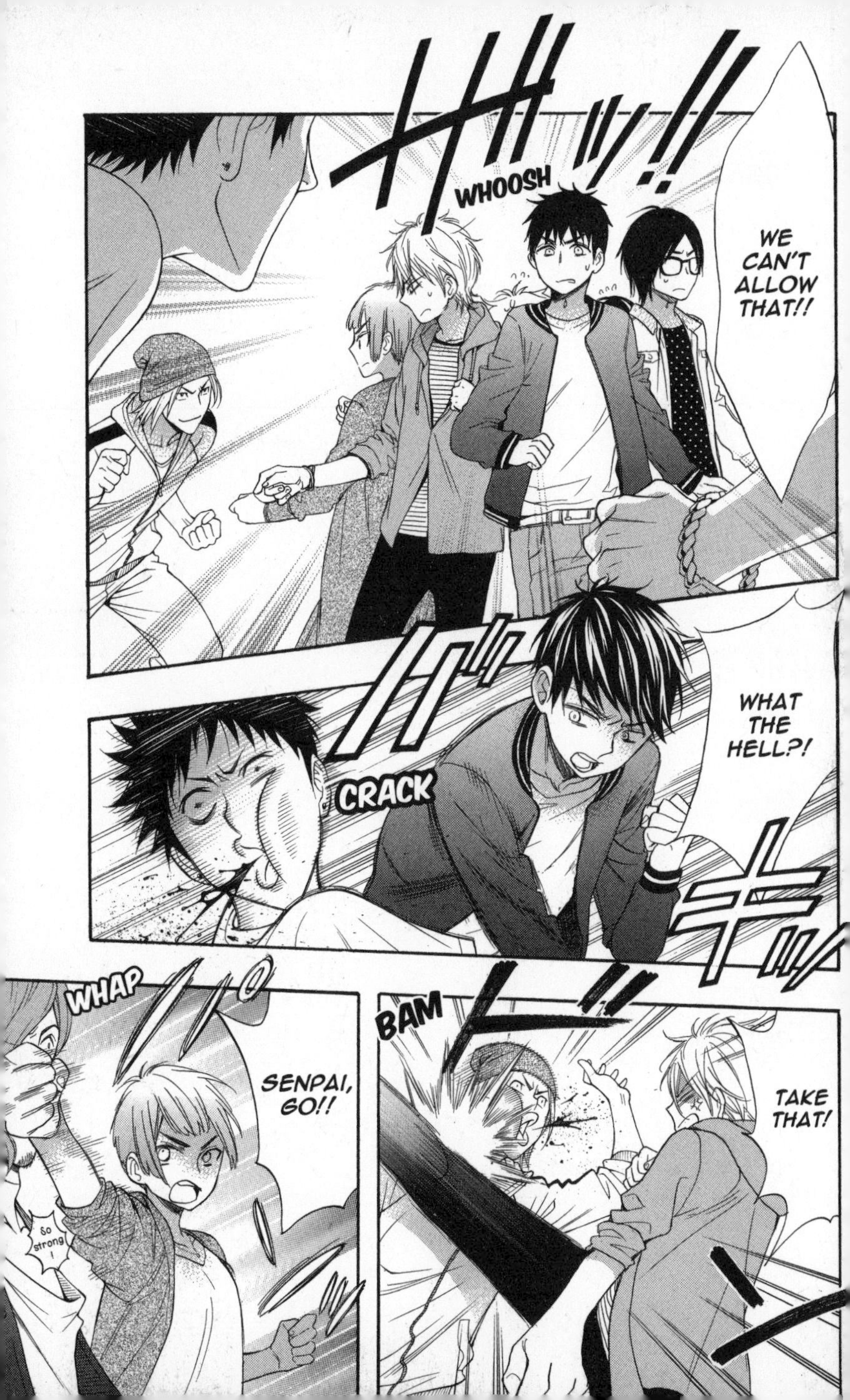
WE CAN'T ALLOW THAT!!
WHOOSH
WHAT THE HELL?!
CRACK
TAKE THAT!
BAM
SENPAI, GO!!
WHAP
So strong!

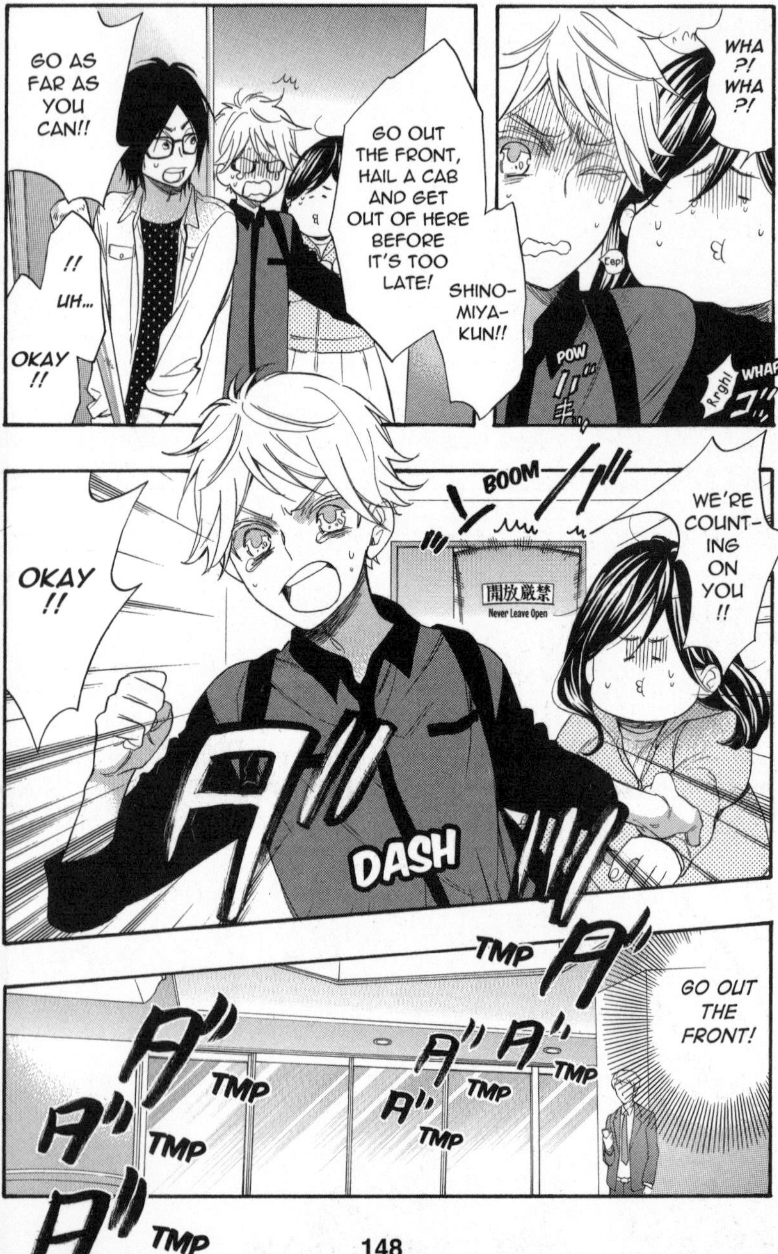

WHA?! WHA?!
Eep!
POW
Rrgh!
WHAP
SHINO-MIYA-KUN!!
GO OUT THE FRONT, HAIL A CAB AND GET OUT OF HERE BEFORE IT'S TOO LATE!
GO AS FAR AS YOU CAN!!
!! UH... OKAY!!
WE'RE COUNT-ING ON YOU!!
BOOM
開放厳禁
Never Leave Open
OKAY!!
DASH
TMP
GO OUT THE FRONT!
TMP
TMP
TMP
TMP
TMP
TMP

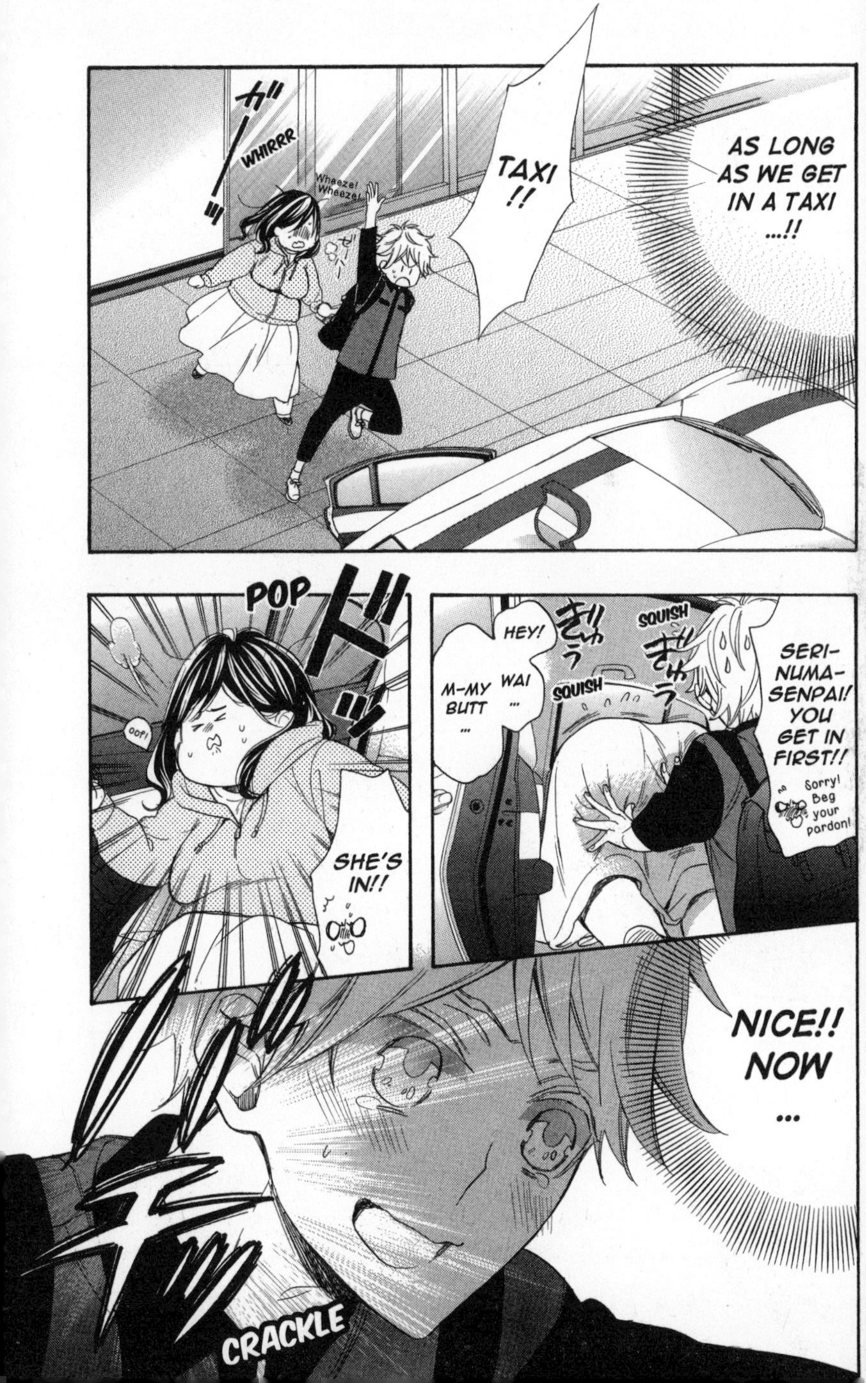
AS LONG AS WE GET IN A TAXI ...!!
TAXI !!
Wheeze! Wheeze!
WHIRRR
SERI-NUMA-SENPAI! YOU GET IN FIRST!!
Sorry! Beg your pardon!
SQUISH
HEY!
SQUISH
WAI ...
M-MY BUTT ...
POP
OOF!
SHE'S IN!!
NICE!! NOW ...
CRACKLE

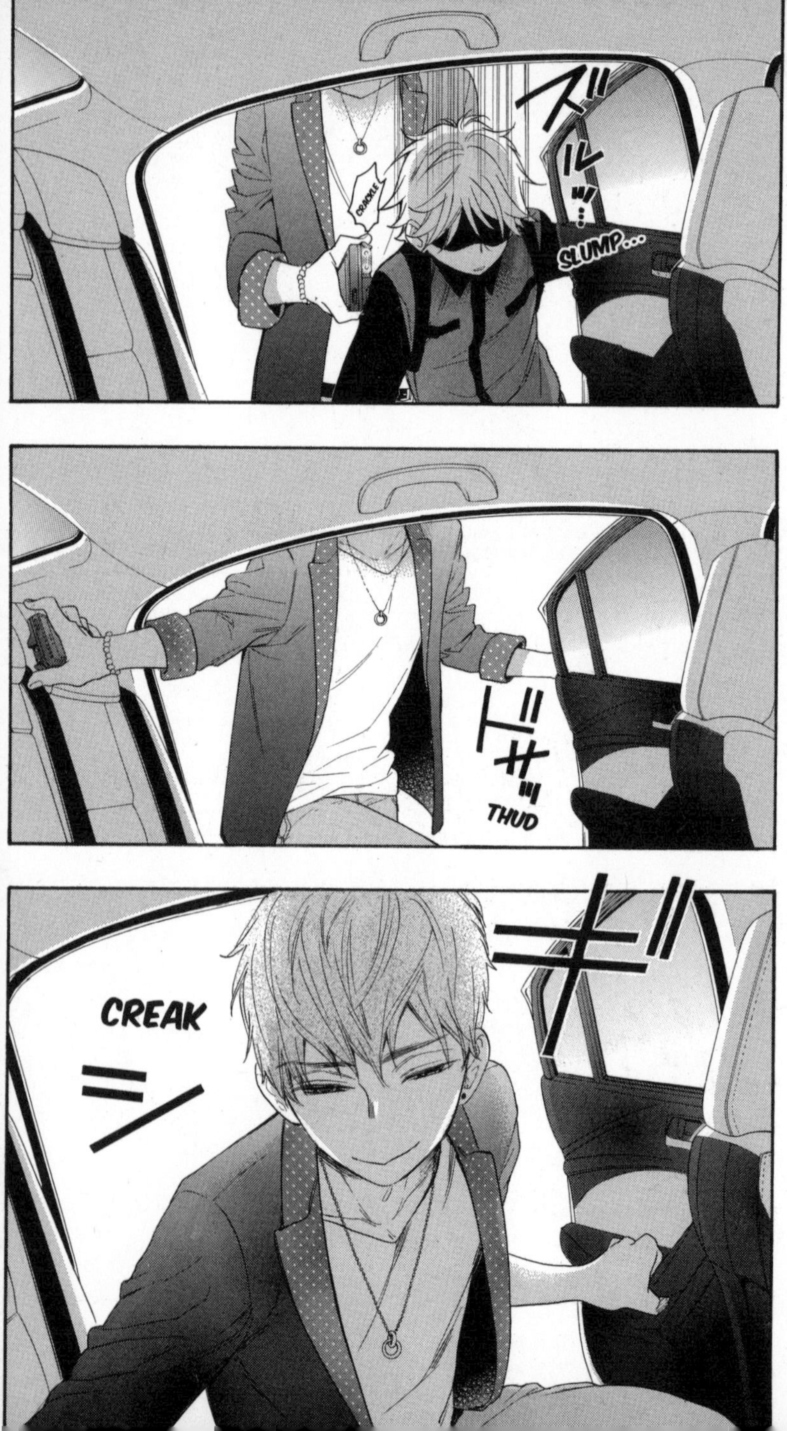
SLUMP...
CRACKLE
THUD
CREAK

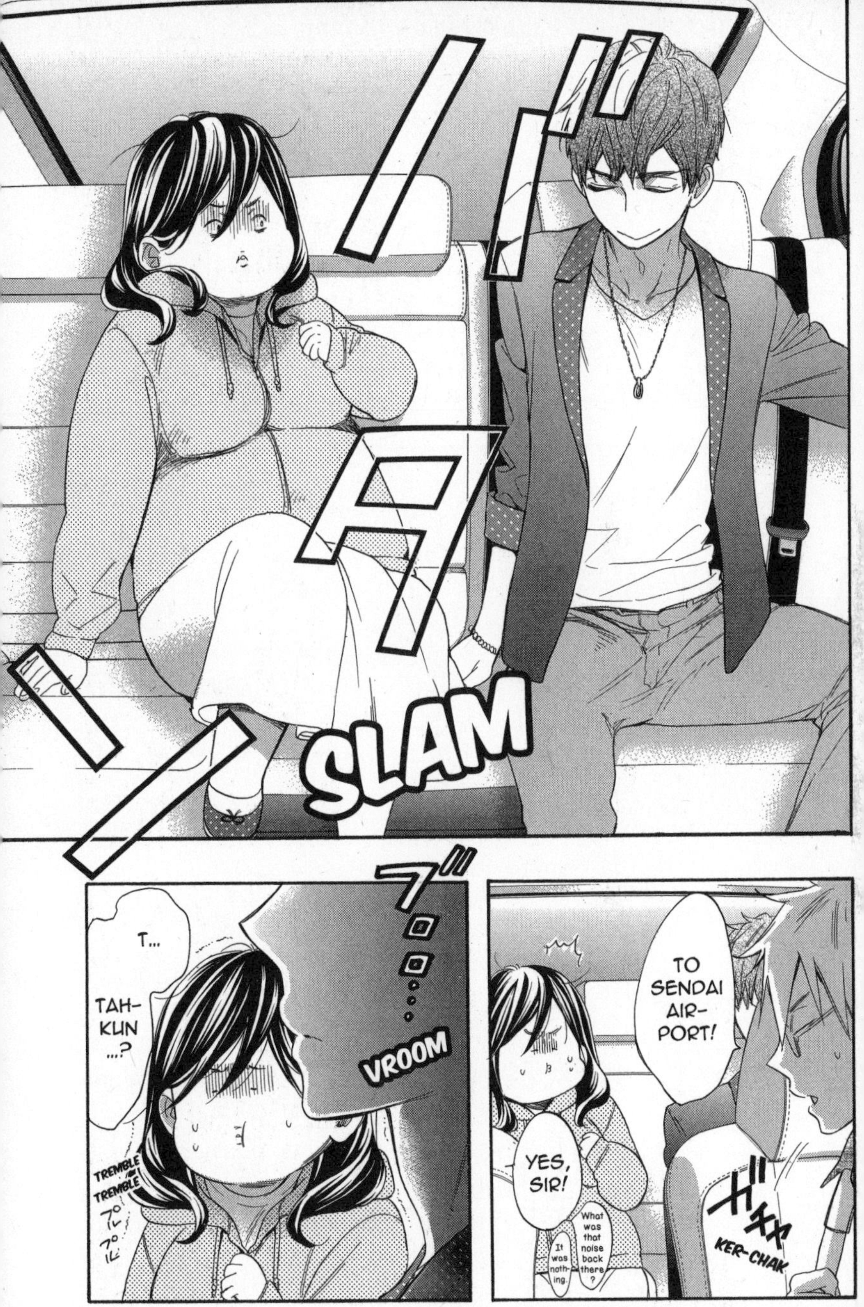
SLAM
TO SENDAI AIR-PORT!
YES, SIR!
What was that noise back there?
It was noth-ing.
KER-CHAK
T...
TAH-KUN ...?
VROOM
TREMBLE TREMBLE

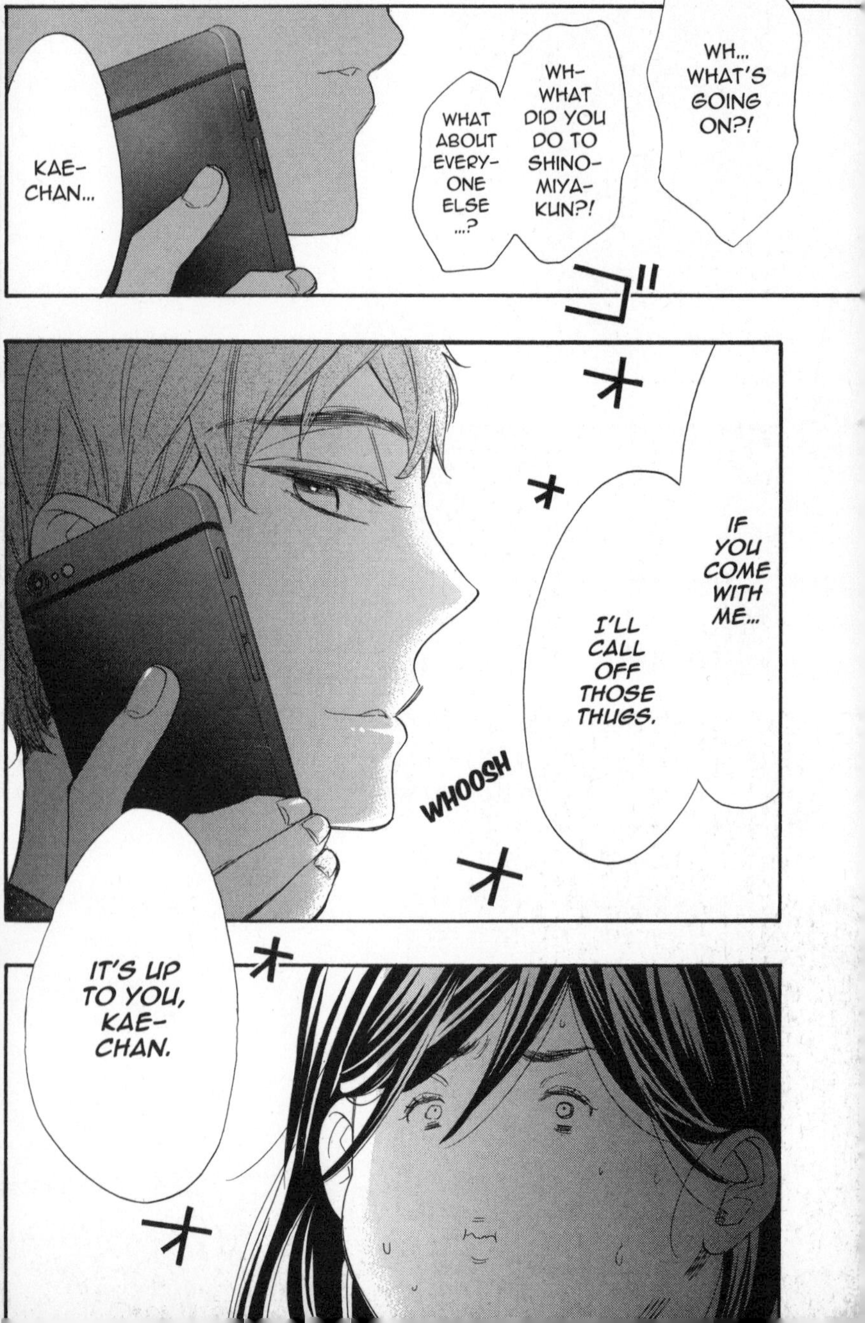
WH... WHAT'S GOING ON?!
WH- WHAT DID YOU DO TO SHINO-MIYA-KUN?!
WHAT ABOUT EVERY-ONE ELSE ...?
KAE-CHAN...
IF YOU COME WITH ME...
I'LL CALL OFF THOSE THUGS.
WHOOSH
IT'S UP TO YOU, KAE-CHAN.

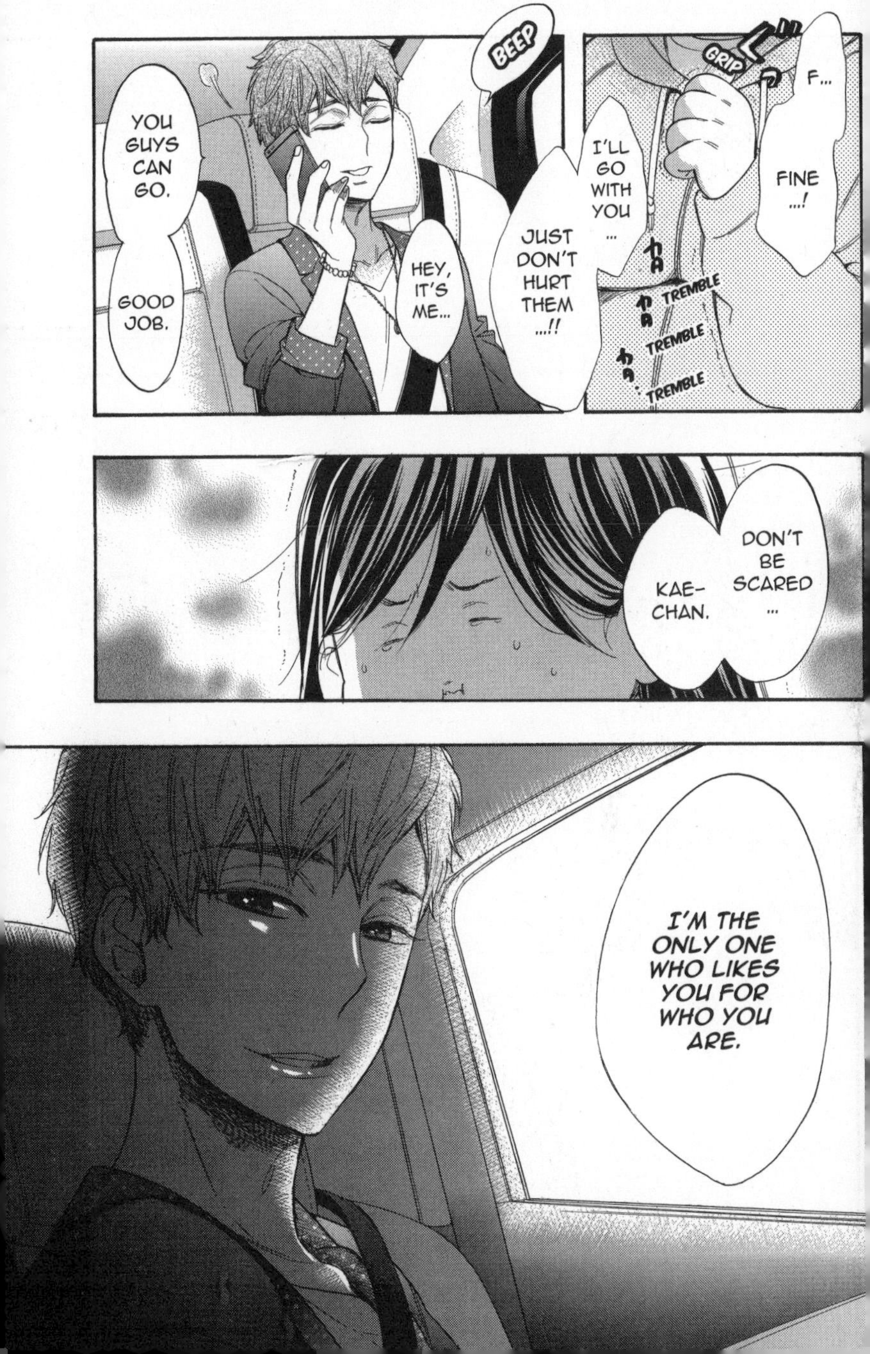
GRIP
F...
FINE ...!
I'LL GO WITH YOU ...
JUST DON'T HURT THEM ...!!
TREMBLE
TREMBLE
TREMBLE
BEEP
HEY, IT'S ME...
YOU GUYS CAN GO.
GOOD JOB.
DON'T BE SCARED ...
KAE-CHAN.
I'M THE ONLY ONE WHO LIKES YOU FOR WHO YOU ARE.

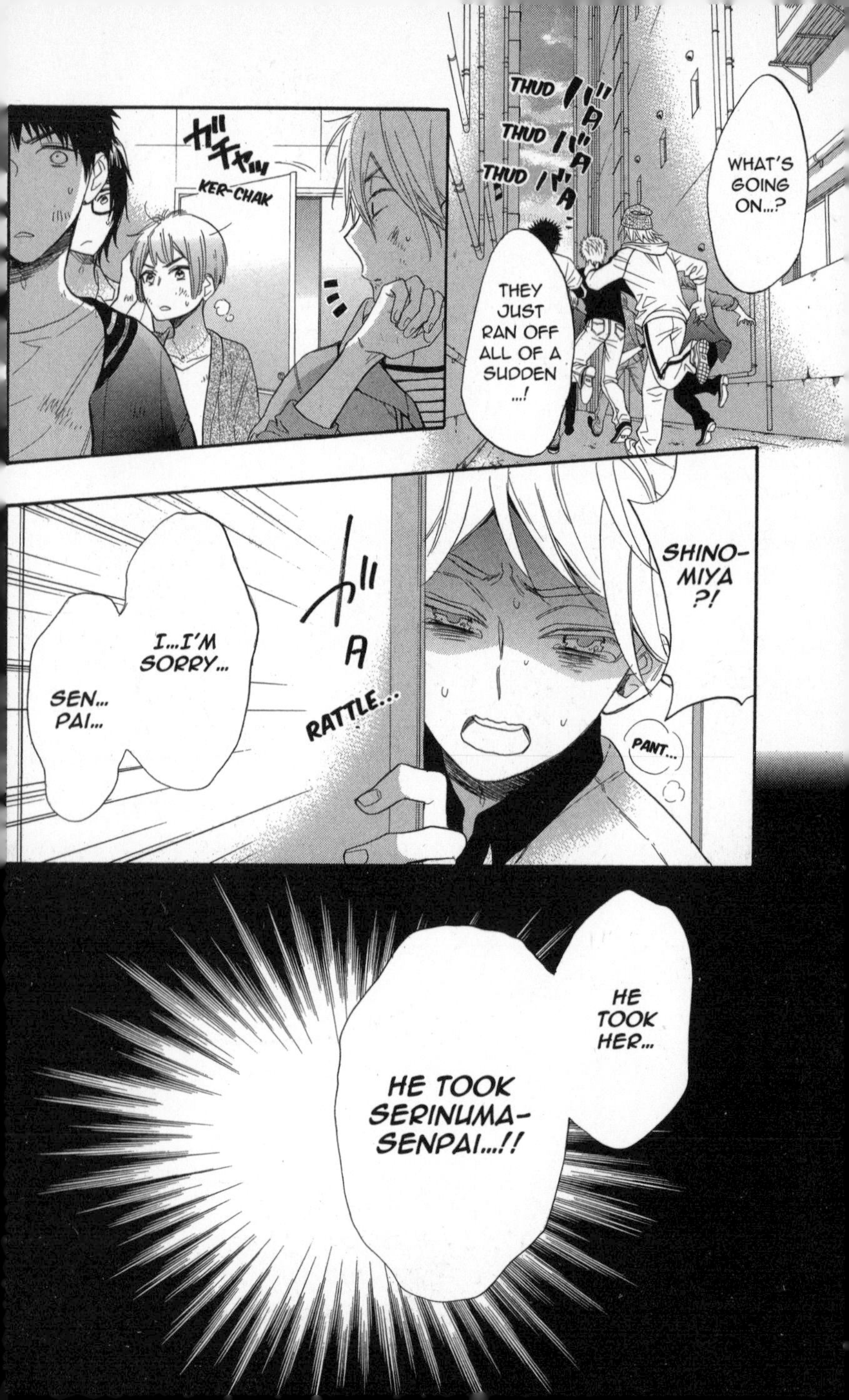
THUD
THUD
THUD
WHAT'S GOING ON...?
THEY JUST RAN OFF ALL OF A SUDDEN ...!
KER-CHAK
SHINO-MIYA ?!
PANT...
RATTLE...
I...I'M SORRY...
SEN... PAI...
HE TOOK HER...
HE TOOK SERINUMA-SENPAI...!!

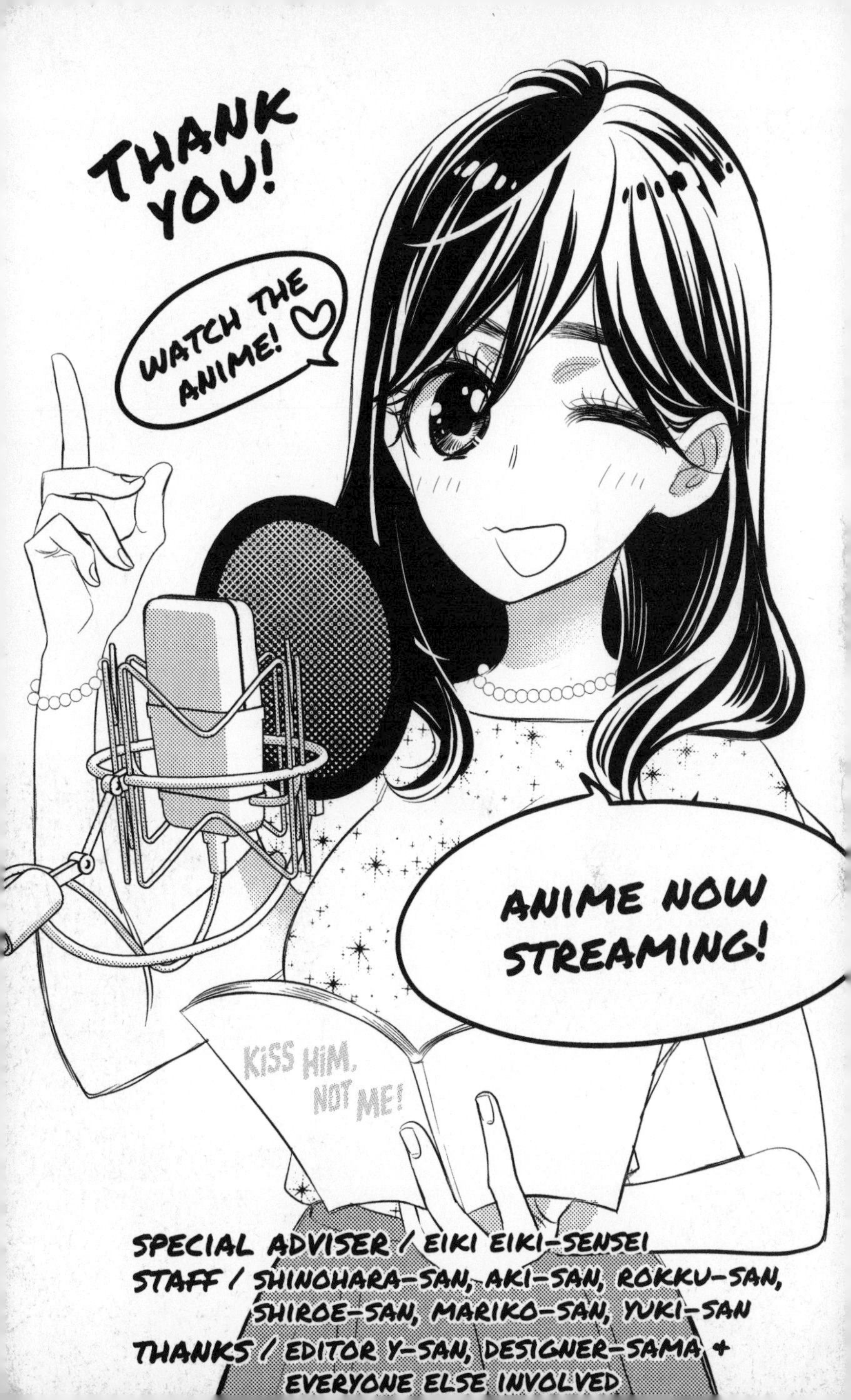
THANK YOU!
WATCH THE ANIME! ♡
ANIME NOW STREAMING!
KiSS HiM, NOT ME!
SPECIAL ADVISER / EIKI EIKI-SENSEI
STAFF / SHINOHARA-SAN, AKI-SAN, ROKKU-SAN, SHIROE-SAN, MARIKO-SAN, YUKI-SAN
THANKS / EDITOR Y-SAN, DESIGNER-SAMA + EVERYONE ELSE INVOLVED

AUTHOR'S NOTE

VOLUME 10! I NEVER IMAGINED THAT I'D MAKE IT TO VOLUMES IN THE DOUBLE DIGITS. I'M SO HAPPY! AND NOW WE HAVE THE APPEARANCE OF MITSUBOSHI—A NEW CHARACTER WITH DIFFERENT COLORED HAIR. I HOPE YOU CONTINUE READING!
-JUNKO

I ♥ BL

Translation Notes

An-punch, page 31

This is the signature move of the most popular and beloved children's character in Japan, Anpanman. Anpanman is a superhero whose head is a sweet, bean-filled pastry called *anpan*. The character started out in picture books that ran from 1973 until the death of Anpanman's author in 2013. Anpanman has also been a staple of children's anime, with a show (*Soreike! Anpanman*) that has been broadcasting since 1988.

WAAAHHH!
ワー
Why, you!
AGHHH!
ギャー
"An-punch"!
Eek!

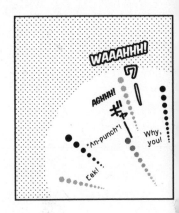

***Ina-Ele*, page 56**

In Japan, most popular anime/manga end up getting an abbreviated nickname. In this case, the popular game and anime series *Inazuma Eleven* has been shortened to *Ina-Ele*.

WOW! THE GUYS ARE REALLY FIRED UP!
They're like Ina-Ele! Heh, heh, heh!
They're taking it so seriously that...well, it's adorable.

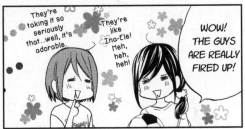

Karaage, page 64

Karaage is a Japanese style of cooking where food items are battered and fried. However, in most cases, it refers to Japanese-style fried chicken.

TIME TO EAT!!
I LOVE KARAAGE!!

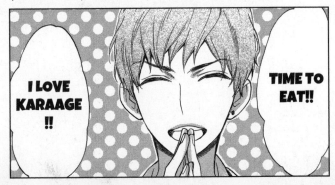

Golden Week, page 93

Golden Week (sometimes abbreviated to GW) is a series of Japanese holidays that start at the end of April and emcompass the first week of May. This is usually the longest holiday for workers in Japan.

Otome Road, page 101

Otome Road refers to a stretch of road in Ikebukuro, Tokyo in which there is a concentration of shops that sell merchandise aimed at fujoshi.

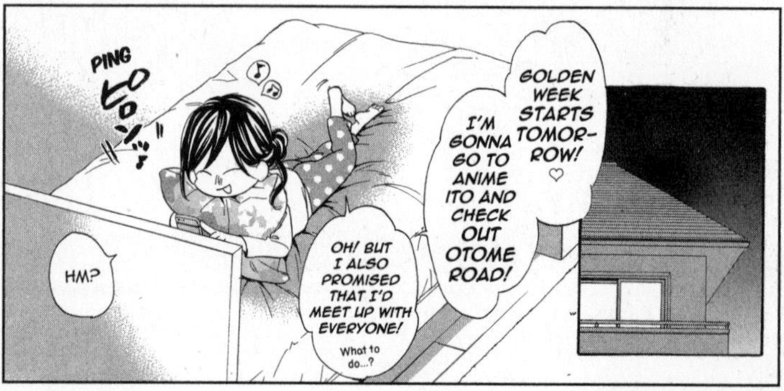
GOLDEN WEEK STARTS TOMORROW! ♡
I'M GONNA GO TO ANIME ITO AND CHECK OUT OTOME ROAD!
OH! BUT I ALSO PROMISED THAT I'D MEET UP WITH EVERYONE!
What to do...?
PING
HM?

Yaya-en, page 105

Yaya-en is a parody of Jojoen, a famous yakiniku (Korean BBQ) restaurant in Japan. The restaurant is typically known as a place to hold celebrations.

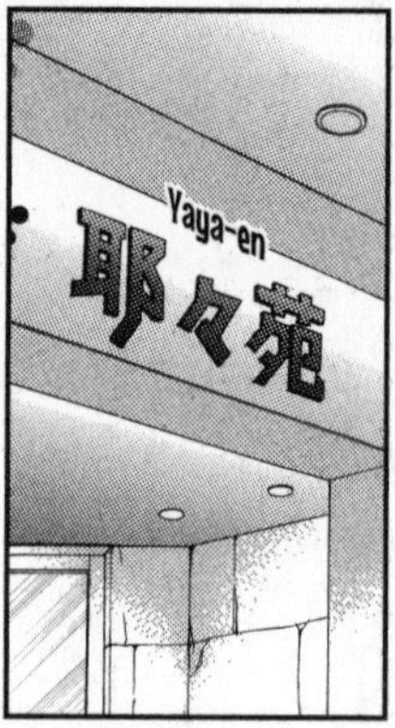
Yaya-en
耶々苑

Yukhoe and gukbap, page 106

These are the names of two dishes that are typically found at Korean BBQ restaurants in Japan. Yukhoe (*yukke* in Japanese) is a type of Korean beef tartare that has raw egg mixed in with it, and gukbap (*kuppa* in Japanese) is a Korean-style soup that has rice in it.

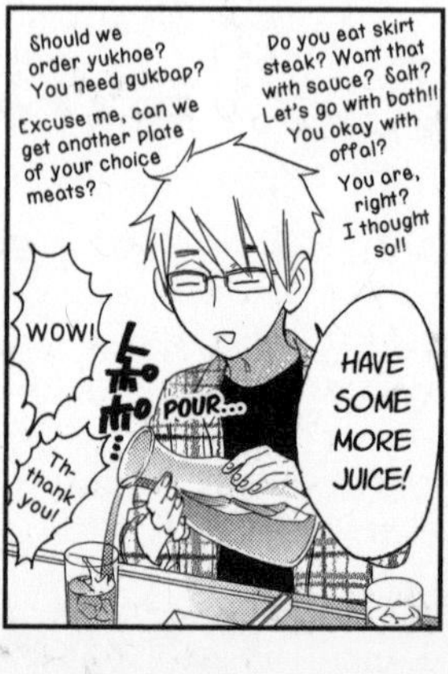
Do you eat skirt steak? Want that with sauce? Salt? Let's go with both!! You okay with offal? You are, right? I thought so!!
Should we order yukhoe? You need gukbap? Excuse me, can we get another plate of your choice meats?
HAVE SOME MORE JUICE!
POUR...
WOW!
Th-thank you!

SWAPPED WITH A KISS?!

Class troublemaker Ryu Yamada is already having a bad day when he stumbles down a staircase along with star student Urara Shiraishi. When he wakes up, he realizes they have switched bodies—and that Ryu has the power to trade places with anyone just by kissing them. Ryu and Urara take full advantage of the situation to improve their lives, but with such an oddly amazing power, just how long will they be able to keep their secret under wraps?

Available now in print and digitally!

A Kodansha Comics Trade Paperback Original.

Kiss Him, Not Me volume 10 copyright © 2016 Junko
English translation copyright © 2017 Junko

All rights reserved.

Published in the United States by Kodansha Comics,
an imprint of Kodansha USA Publishing, LLC, New York.

Publication rights for this English edition arranged through Kodansha Ltd.,
Tokyo.

First published in Japan in 2016 by Kodansha Ltd., Tokyo, as *Watashi Ga Motete Dousunda* volume 10.

ISBN 978-1-63236-344-2

Printed in the United States of America.

www.kodanshacomics.com

9 8 7 6 5 4 3 2 1

Translation: David Rhie
Lettering: Hiroko Mizuno
Editing: Ajani Oloye
Kodansha Comics edition cover design: Phil Balsman